The GOURMET ATLAS

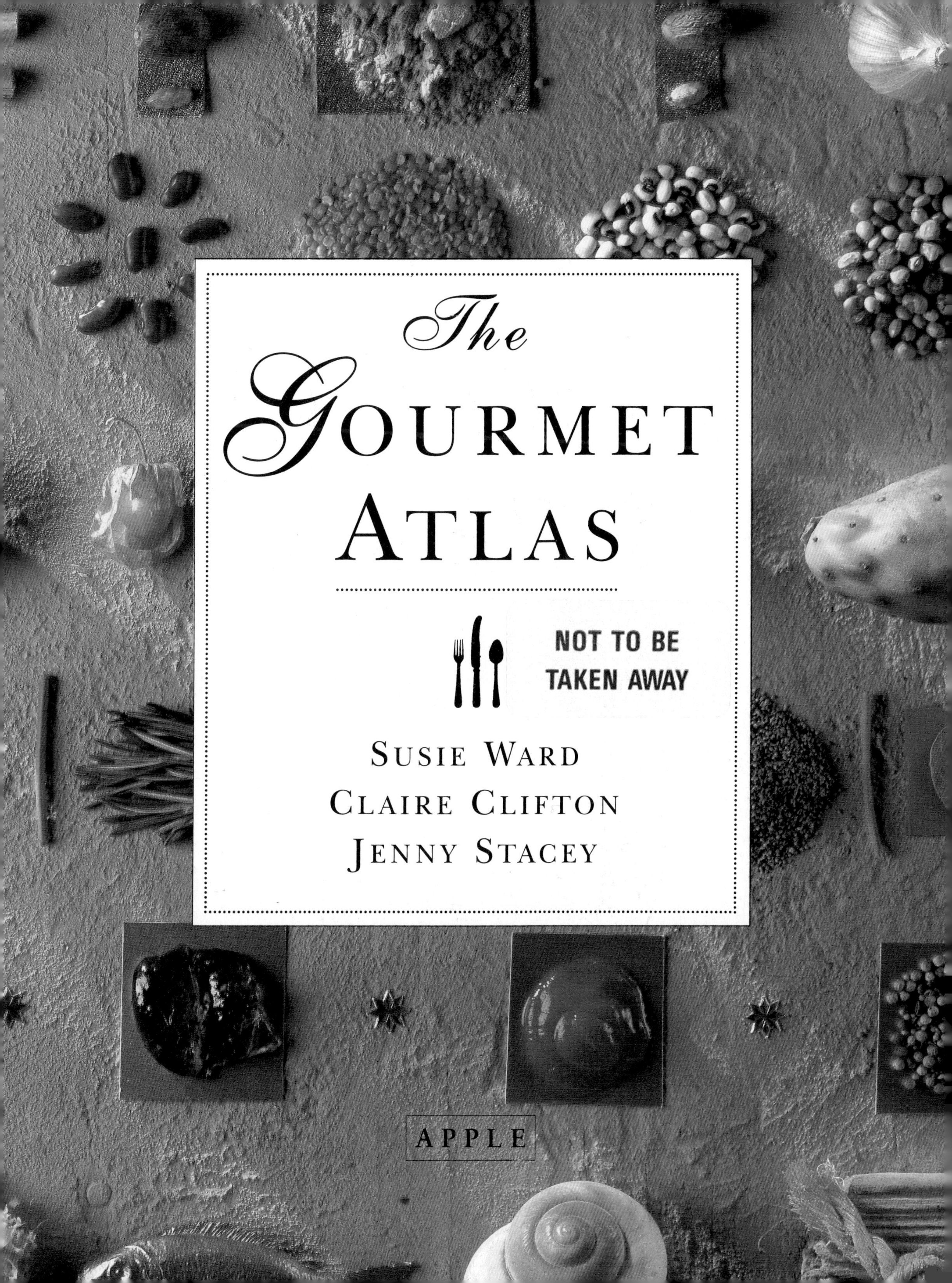

The GOURMET ATLAS

NOT TO BE TAKEN AWAY

SUSIE WARD

CLAIRE CLIFTON

JENNY STACEY

APPLE

A QUARTO BOOK

Published by the Apple Press
The Old Brewery
6 Blundell Street
London N7 9BH

ISBN 0-85076-918-4

This book was designed and
produced by

Quarto Publishing plc
The Old Brewery
6 Blundell Street
London N7 9BH

Senior editor *Kate Kirby*
Project editor *Elizabeth Wyse*
Editors *Jean Coppendale, Anne
Hildyard*
Senior art editor *Elizabeth Healey*
Assistant art director *Penny Cobb*
Designer *Sheila Volpe*
Cartography *Map Creation Limited*
Picture research *Miriam Hyman*
Photographer *Martin Norris*
Illustrator *Stuart Haygarth*
Art director *Moira Clinch*
Editorial director *Pippa Rubinstein*
Indexer *Dorothy Frame*

Typeset by Central Southern
Typesetters, Eastbourne

Manufactured in Singapore by Brigł
Arts (Singapore) Pte Ltd

Printed by Star Standard Industries
(Pte) Ltd, Singapore

CONTENTS

INTRODUCTION 6

INTRODUCTION

Love of good food is a gift to the spirit, one that is best shared with friends in a convivial atmosphere. Although it is an appreciation that does not seem to be given equally to all, there is no doubt that those blessed with it benefit from getting to know their subject better. Like other exercises in connoisseurship—an appreciation of art, music, drama, or wine—knowledge of the subject's history, a deeper understanding of what goes into the final product or work, makes for a much enhanced delight in it. We can enjoy the flavor of a delicious steak or lasagne without knowing about where the cattle were raised or the pasta dish originated, but if we have that insight, we are the richer. Preparing both will have made use of herbs, spices, and salt, all of which have marvelous anecdotal backgrounds, and the cheeses and vegetables in the pasta also have their own particular stories to tell. They are in this book.

The Gourmet Atlas is a compendium of geography, of social and cultural history, of fact, and of legend. It is *the* source book for both the avid student and the casual inquirer into the sometimes surprising, sometimes amusing, but always fascinating, past and present of the food on our planet.

SUSIE WARD

HOW TO READ THE MAPS

Look at the map to pinpoint a particular country, city or region, noting any reference number, symbol or trade route. Then consult the key for further information such as lists of food specialties, classic dishes or ingredients.

Land Layering

Many of the maps are designed in a traditional way so that areas of different heights are depicted by color. Most of these maps have symbols or numbers that correspond to a particular ingredient that will be shown on the key.

Tints

Some of the maps have limited cartographic shading so that colored tints can show where certain ingredients can be found.

Landlayering with hill shading

A combination of landlayering and hill shading is shown on these maps. Maps of this type show only numbers to refer to the location of ingredients.

HERBS & SPICES

If we ate only to survive, herbs and spices would have little use in our kitchens. Only salt has a verifiable prehistoric use—as a preservative. 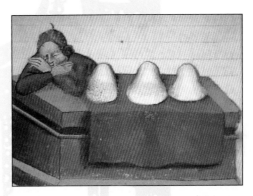 *But early nomadic tribes would surely have added savory grasses and twigs of fragrant shrubs to their cooking pots and, once settled as farmers, to their gardens. Spices have always had a more affluent slant given to their historical public relations, with*

many a reference to royalty. Men sailed unknown seas for spices; nations made treaties and went to war for them. Herbs never commanded that high a price—whether in money, in national pride, or in lives.

GREEN GROW THE HERBS

H erbs enrich both our gardens and national cuisines with their subtle, and sometimes assertive, flavors. Their aromatic leaves, stems, or flowers draw the hungry to the table, stimulate a jaded palate, and, in many cases, aid the digestion.

ABOVE

In Provence, garlic is called "the poor man's spice." Street vendors (here also selling bay leaves) were a common sight for generations.

Although there are references to herbs in earlier Chinese manuscripts, the first detailed description of the use of aromatic plants is found in Egyptian papyri and Sumerian tablets of 2800 to 2000 BC. Herbs such as marjoram and mint, and spices such as cinnamon and juniper berries, were all known, but they were reserved for the exclusive ritualistic and culinary use of kings, pharaohs, and priests. Over the centuries, the use of herbs filtered down; by the time of the diaspora of the Jewish people from Egypt in about 1450 BC, even the slaves and the conquered had access to some of the commoner flavorings. The Biblical account of the Passover and its annual commemoration commands the Jews to eat "bitter herbs" in remembrance of their flight and salvation. This symbolic gesture recalls their unhappy existence before divine intervention, while the uncultivated nature of the chosen herbs, thought to include sorrel, chicory, and the leaf vegetable, watercress, emphasize the haste of their departure.

It fell to the Greeks and Romans, however, to truly widen herbal horizons. They attached religious and superstitious associations to particular herbs, among them basil and bay, as well as valuing herbs for their flavor and restorative effects. Parsley, thyme, chives, lovage, cilantro, dill, and sage were all stalwarts of the Roman kitchen, and were transported to the farthest corners of the empire by Roman legions.

LEFT

The Benedictine distillery, Fecamp, where monks once made the amber elixir from over 20 different herbs.

THE MONASTIC REVIVAL

Although the Gauls seem to have consumed a diet strong in native herbs, the successive invasions of Saxons, Danes, and warlike Teutons in Britain and the Germanic provinces did little for herbal conservation. The triumph of Christianity over the barbarian hordes was herbiculture's salvation. Herbs came under the protection of the monks of the great abbeys, a group who had the wit to appreciate them, the knowledge to assess and catalog them, and the patience to cultivate them. During the 800 years that stretched from the beginning of the Dark Ages to the Renaissance, they became highly informed about the properties and uses of all manner of herbs, fruits, and vegetables. The records of a thirteenth-century English monk, Alexander Necker, show that in addition to parsley, fennel, cilantro, sage, savory, hyssop, and rue, he was also growing spices from abroad which would tolerate the British climate— aniseed, mustard seed, and white pepper. By the next century, medieval gardeners had added licorice, caraway, and cumin to the list.

The fifteenth and sixteenth centuries witnessed the apogee of herbal expertise. Salads made with a wide variety of herbs were the height of fashion. A typical salad might be composed of parsley, sage, green garlic, leeks, mint, fennel, cress, lovage, arugula, baby sorrel, purslane, and the bitter herbs rue and hyssop, all dressed with "raw oil" (imported olive oil), wine vinegar, and colorful blossoms. Such extravagant compositions were thought to have exceptional restorative properties, especially in the spring, after the salt meat and fish diet of winter and the ecclesiastically imposed rigors of Lent.

HERBS FOR THE NEW WORLD

Increasingly, however, transplanted Mediterranean herbs came to be regarded as more fitting for the tables of *haute monde* seventeenth- and eighteenth-century London and Paris. Most fashionable of all were the sweet herbs of Provence—rosemary, basil, bay, and savory—said to have been sown there by Balthazar of the three Magi. But as old-fashioned herbs lost their admirers in the Old World, they became well-rooted in the New. Lovage and sorrel were stewed as vegetables, while parsley, thyme, rue, and mint figured largely in early New World "receipts." By the mid-1800s, America had become the trustee of much of the world's herbal lore.

By the late nineteenth century, Britain had suffered a cataclysmic reversal of taste. Mediterranean flavors (led by the much-maligned garlic) were considered almost unholy, foreign, and Papist. Culinary invention stultified to such an extent that only sage, thyme, and mint were commonly used (the first two in stuffing and the last in mint sauce), and parsley became nothing more than a frilly green afterthought on the margins of a serving platter.

But the culinary heritage of the United States was already welcoming Poles, Russians, Scandinavians, and Germans with their dill and caraway; Italians with their basil, rosemary, and sage; and Greeks and Lebanese bringing oregano, cilantro, and adventurous uses of old standbys such as mint and parsley. Today, while we look farther and farther afield for herbal inspiration, it is salutary to remember the journeys our "common garden herbs" have already made.

ABOVE

An illumination of summer savory from the Hours of Anne of Burgundy. *Savory was grown to attract bees rather than dragonflies, and was respected both as a digestive and a flavoring.*

WORLD OF HERBS

Herbs are seen as an essential enhancement to flavor all over the world, and today are cultivated very widely. This map, and the geographical keybox (below), show where the world's major herbs originated. The individual herbs are described in more detail in the numbered A-Z listing on the following pages.

Herb areas

- **CAUCASIAN REPUBLICS** *oregano* (**14**)
- **CENTRAL ASIA** *dill* (**7**); *tarragon* (**21**)
- **CHINA** *chives* (**5**); *cilantro* (**6**)
- **EASTERN MEDITERRANEAN** *chervil* (**4**); *marjoram* (**12**); *mint* (**13**)
- **GREECE** *chives* (**5**); *lemon balm* (**10**)
- **INDIA** *basil* (**2**)
- **MEDITERRANEAN BASIN** *bay* (**3**); *dill* (**7**); *sorrel* (**20**); *thyme* (**22**)
- **MIDDLE EAST** *lemon balm* (**10**)
- **NEPAL** *oregano* (**14**)
- **NORTH AFRICA** *mint* (**13**)
- **NORTHERN EUROPE** *angelica* (**1**)
- **NORTHERN MEDITERRANEAN** *rosemary* (**16**); *sage* (**17**)
- **RUSSIA** *chervil* (**4**)
- **SARDINIA** *parsley* (**15**)
- **SOUTHEAST ASIA** *kaffir lime* (**9**); *lemongrass* (**11**)
- **SOUTHERN EUROPE** *fennel* (**8**); *oregano* (**14**)
- **SYRIA** *angelica* (**1**)

A Classic Bouquet Garni

4 sprigs fresh thyme
1 bay leaf
3 sprigs fresh parsley
2–3 sprigs fresh chervil (optional)

Bind the herbs together with strong thread or kitchen string and hang into the cooking broth from the side of the pot; tie the ends to the handle.

Remove the bundle when directed by the recipe or when it has finished infusing the liquid. The chervil adds a delicate nuance and accentuates the other herbs, but it is not essential. In Provence a strip of orange or lemon peel is often added to the bundle to flavor meat *daubes* and fish respectively.

AN A - Z OF HERBS

ANGELICA (1)
(Angelica archangelica officinalis)

Native to northern Europe and Syria, and brought to England in the sixteenth century, this is now grown throughout Europe and Asia. Angelica's roots were chewed as an antidote to the plague and later as a cure against hydrophobia. Among the tallest of the herbs, angelica reaches 8 feet/2.4 m in height. Its stems can be braised like celery, its roots stewed with fruit to sweeten puddings and fools, and its leaves used to flavor fish. But it is most often encountered candied, its stems crystalized for use in cakes and as decoration.

BASIL (2)
(Sweet basil – Ocimum basilicum; bush basil – O. minimum)

A low-growing plant, native to India, which came to be cultivated in the Middle East; the former is the more valued of the two. In Greece, basil was a holy herb, gathered under the supervision of priests. Though available dried, it is appreciably better fresh. In the West, Italy and France make the most use of this herb and its particular affinity for tomatoes, fish, and pasta. It is the basis of the famous pesto of Genoa and the *soupe au pistou* of Provence. The Thai variety (called "holy basil") is even more pungent than the European, and is a common ingredient in stir-fries and curries.

BAY (3)
(Laurus nobilis)

A large tree found throughout the Mediterranean, whose glossy, scented leaves were used to crown Greek and Roman victors in wars, games, and literary contests. A traditional strewing herb in medieval times, bay was thought to ward off the devil. Its strong smell is detectable in many liniments and toilet waters. Much valued today as a culinary herb—a requisite of bouquet garni—bay is also one of the four essential spices of the Mogul kitchen. Available as leaves, both fresh and dried, and in powdered form, bay is an important addition to marinades, courts bouillons, and stews. It is also a common ingredient in sauces and pickles, and has a particular affinity with fish, meats, and game.

CHERVIL (4)
(Anthriscus cerefolium)

A native of Russia and the eastern Mediterranean, this sweet-flavored herb —like a delicate parsley—was brought to Britain by the Romans, reaching the height of its popularity in the Middle Ages, when it was eaten as a purgative during Lent. It was also recommended as an antispasmodic and blood purifier. Despite chervil's inherent delicacy, it has the power to enhance other herbs, and is therefore a constituent of the French *fines herbes*. Chervil's slightly aniseed flavor is also well-partnered with fish, chicken, eggs, and cheese dishes, and is excellent in cold consommés and salads.

CHIVES (5)
(Allium schoenoprasum)

Found all over Europe, the Americas, and southeast Asia, the spiky, hollow leaves of this member of the onion family were used in Chinese medicine as early as 3000 BC, were a gourmet delight of the Greeks, and were exploited by the French as a culinary herb Unlike most herbs, chives respond well to aggressive trimming: more grasslike leaves simply shoot up to take the place of those that were cut. Chives are best used fresh; even freeze-drying quickly dissipates the flavor. The light onion taste goes well with egg and cheese dishes and as a liberal garnish over soups and salads. It is one of the ingredients of *fines herbes*.

CILANTRO (6)
(Coriandrum sativum)

Also known as coriander, the feathery leaves of cilantro are a familiar ingredient to lovers of spicy Tex-Mex and Mexican cooking. The herb made its way to the New World from China (hence its sobriquet "Chinese parsley") and India via Moorish Spain, where it had been brought by Arab settlers. The acrid flavor of the leaves is still much appreciated by Levantine and North African cooks, who make liberal use of cilantro in cooked dishes and salads. India retains its use in "curried" dishes, but traditional European cooking outside Spain has never found the flavor of the leaves—as opposed to that of the seeds—generally appealing. (See also Coriander under Spices.)

DILL LEAVES (7)
(Anethum graveolens)

A relative of parsley and fennel, dill grew wild and wide across central Asia and the Mediterranean region, where it is still a staple herb of Lebanese cuisine. The Romans respected its strengthening properties, and included it in the diet of gladiators. It traveled in their camp kitchens to western, and thence to northern, Europe; it naturalized in the former but must be cultivated in the

Basil

Chervil

latter. The leaves and seeds now feature strongly in the cuisines of these areas—particularly Poland, Germany, and Scandinavia. Heavy immigration from those countries to the United States, has made dill a fixture of American cooking, the indispensable ingredient in the eponymous "dill pickles" which accompany pastrami on rye, hot dogs, potato salad, and most outdoor meals. Now available across Europe, dill is an exceptional partner to cucumbers, salmon, and new potatoes. (See also Dill seeds under Spices.)

FENNEL LEAVES (8)
(Foeniculum vulgare)
Light, feathery fennel leaves are easily confused with dill leaves, yet this native southern European plant was valued for its digestive properties long before dill. Fennel is now found both wild and cultivated everywhere, although it is still most appreciated in Italy and Provence, where it is seen as an accent to grilled or baked fish, and used in sauces, soups, and marinades. The stems are also thrown onto coals when barbecuing fish. (See also Fennel seeds under Spices.)

KAFFIR LIME (9)
(Citrus hystrix)
The leaves of this southeast Asian tree are sold in pairs in Thai, Indonesian, and Malaysian markets, and are used to flavor fish and shellfish soups and casseroles.

Dill

Oregano

LEMON BALM (10)
(Melissa officinalis)
Found on the hillsides of the Middle East, this herb's Latin name is a clue to its earliest use in apiculture by Greek monks (*melissa*—"of the bee"). Today, its aromatic leaves, which dry successfully, make refreshing infusions, teas, cordials, punches, and wines. It marries with any dish that benefits from a hint of citron—be it chicken, fish, soup, or a salad.

LEMONGRASS (11)
(Cymbopogon citratus; C. flexuosus)
There are several species of this aquatic grass, all native to southeast Asia. Only recently appreciated in Western kitchens, lemongrass is today grown in Australia, Africa, South America, and the United States. The citric oil in the stem has the zesty kick of lemon and is often combined with the leaves of the Kaffir lime and cilantro to produce the characteristic flavor of Thai, Malay, and Indonesian cooking. It can be dried but fresh lemongrass has a far finer flavor.

MARJORAM (12)
(sweet marjoram—Origanum majorana; pot marjoram—O. onites)
A native of the eastern Mediterranean, marjoram has been grown for its medicinal and culinary properties since medieval times. The preferred variety is sweet marjoram, an annual; perennial pot marjoram is more sprawling with a less intense flavor. Marjoram's pleasing aroma and healing power has continued to make it useful for herbal shampoos, and as a palliative for earache and toothache. Its spicy flavor complements tomato dishes and many Mediterranean recipes, often in tandem with, or replacing, thyme. (See also Oregano.)

Marjoram

MINT (13)
(spearmint—Mentha spicata; peppermint —M. piperata; apple mint—M. rotundifolia; pennyroyal—M. pulegium)
Of these, the most useful in the kitchen is spearmint; its tangy, refreshing taste lifts young vegetables (potatoes, carrots, peas, and so on) and lamb. Mint is cited as the chief herb of Mogul cuisine, and the cucumber, tomato, and bulgur salads of its place of origin—the Maghreb—also display its accents, as does the heady mint tea characteristic of the area. The other mints of the family can serve when spearmint is unavailable; peppermint is a well-known digestive and has been a traditional ingredient in lozenges for generations. Pennyroyal (its Latin name means "flea mint") is particularly strong-flavored, and is the customary seasoning for black pudding (blood sausage). If used in place of other mints, it should be with a light hand.

OREGANO (14)
(Origanum vulgare)
As its Latin name implies, this is the "common" cousin of marjoram, found growing wild across southern Europe, to the steppes of the Caucasus and Nepal. Known as "the joy of the mountains" to the Greeks, it is still much favored by Mediterranean cooks. In Italy it flavors pizzas, pastas, and many tomato dishes; in Greece, where the even more pungent variety *O. heracleoticum* (colloquially known as *rigani*) covers the dry slopes of the mainland and islands, the dried leaves and flowers distinguish lamb dishes, classic moussakas, and salads.

PARSLEY (15)
(Petroselinum crispum)
An ingredient in bouquet garni and *fines herbes*, parsley is probably the single most used herb in the European and North America repertoires, and is grown worldwide. Initially a staple of the

Mediterranean kitchen (Sardinia claims it as its own), parsley's use was spread throughout Europe by the Romans, who valued its appetite-enhancing qualities during their epicurean banquets. From early popularity as a tonic and elixir (to cleanse the blood and promote sexual prowess and fecundity), it has dwindled to more prosaic—if practically universal —culinary use. It is still valued for its high vitamin, calcium, and iron content, while eating a sprig or two after consuming garlic is said to freshen the breath. It is available in curly-leaved and flat-leaved varieties, the latter usually preferred by Mediterranean (and gourmet) cooks.

ROSEMARY (16)
(Rosmarinus officinalis)
"Rosemary for remembrance" said Shakespeare, recalling the herb's traditional role as a mental stimulant, and a symbolic plant in the language of love. Its Latin name, meaning "dew of the sea," is probably a reference to its wild northern Mediterranean origins, particularly dry coastal hills. Brought to Britain and France by the Romans, it was respected as a sedative and as an aid in increasing circulation and in digestion. Its camphoric scent and flavor were appreciated by medieval cooks, but though its potency remained constant in Italy and southern France (and through immigration, in the United States), by the nineteenth century it had all but disappeared from British recipes. Its revived reputation as seasoning for meat, particularly lamb, poultry, and pasta sauces in northern Europe is due largely to the widespread popularity of the "cuisine of the sun."

SAGE (17)
(Salvia officinalis)
This herb shares with elderflower a reputation as a cure-all, and was cultivated by the Arabs as a prescriptive for longevity. Native to the northern Mediterranean, the gray-green shrub has taken root in chalky soil across Europe and North America, where its warm, slightly bitter flavor improves stuffing for meat and poultry. Sage displays a natural affinity for pork, making its fatty flesh more digestible. It is one of the herbs that dries most successfully.

SALAD BURNET (18)
(Pimpinella sanguisorba)
Introduced by the Romans to France and Britain, burnet was one of the main herbs in the Tudor knot garden, taken fresh or in a winter tonic, or as a blood cleanser. It was also valued as a coagulant. Today, its nutty flavor is less in demand, and usually used as an addition to a mixed green salad.

SAVORY (19)
(Summer savory—Satureja hortensis; winter savory—S. montana)
The annual summer variety is the more delicate of the two varieties of savory, and can be substituted for thyme in recipes, usually those for meat and fish (especially freshwater fish). It also has a remarkable affinity for green and haricot beans. The more piquant winter variety, a perennial, was very common in Britain in the sixteenth century, accompanying the first settlers to America.

SORREL (20)
(French sorrel—Rumex scutatus; garden or wild sorrel—R. acetosa)
The French variety has a subtler flavor and is much appreciated in that country, where it is often encountered as a sauce for fish or eggs, or in soup. A relative of dock, sorrel was prized by the ancient Egyptians as a medical and culinary herb. It is sometimes classed as a leaf vegetable, since it is the dominating ingredient in many of the dishes in which it is used.

TARRAGON (21)
(French tarragon—Artemesia dracunculus; Russian tarragon—A. dracunculoides)
A relative to wormwood and native to central Asia, tarragon now grows wild in central and southern Europe, where it was first brought by Arab traders. Its lightly licorice flavor was exploited as a breath freshener in the sixteenth century, when it was first introduced into Britain. The French variety is preferred for its richer flavor; the Russian for its hardiness. French tarragon is an indispensable ingredient in Béarnaise and Hollandaise sauces, and it possesses a natural affinity for both poultry and egg dishes.

THYME (22)
(common thyme—Thymus vulgaris; wild thyme—T. serpyllum; lemon thyme—T. citriodorus; broad-leaved thyme—T. pulegoides)
There are numerous (more than 100!) varieties of thyme, of which the four listed are among the most frequently encountered. Introduced to the rest of Europe by the Romans, for whom it was a counter against depression and infection and a valued incense (its earlier Greek name means "burnt offering"), by medieval times it was one of the common strewing herbs. Lawns of creeping thyme were an extravagant whimsy of nineteenth-century country-house gardens; the herbs crushed underfoot perfumed the surrounding air. Today thyme is primarily a kitchen herb; an ingredient of bouquet garni.

The numbers on these pages key to the map on the previous page.

Sorrel

Thyme

SPICES & FLAVORINGS

I n popular imagination, spices hail from warmer climates, where palm trees sway or jungles swelter; not for them the prosaic civilization of a northern herb garden. Despite this idyllic provenance, spice-growing today is a large-scale, industrial enterprise.

ABOVE TOP

A fifteenth-century merchant, dwarfed by a giant nutmeg, used as a poison antidote and a calmative.

ABOVE

A Dutch East India fleet at dock in Mollucca, c. 1640, by H.C. Vroom.

The use of spices came from the East, where indigenous varieties such as ginger, ganagal, pepper, and nutmeg were first appreciated. Ancient caravan routes ran from those distant lands to the eastern Mediterranean, where the Phoenicians controlled the trade in spices to the West. By the second century BC, however, the mystery of the spice trade had passed to the Arabs. Roman middlemen met caravans at desert trading posts east of Palmyra in the steppes of the Pamir range. There they would barter Roman glass, itaglios, and wine in exchange for silk, ginger, pepper, and cassia bark.

The classical world's lust for spices reached its peak in the first century AD, when hosts at Roman dinner parties attempted to outdo one another with ever more extravagant and sumptuous meals. Pepper, brought up the Red Sea in Arab dhows, was king of the Roman table, and was so sought after it became the subject of an artificially imposed price rise. The frustrated Romans built and launched their own galleys from the Red Sea ports of their new conquest, Egypt, thus breaking the Arab monopoly. Until the fifth century AD, Roman merchant fleets sailed to India and the eastern isles; after the fall of the empire, the cosmopolitan Saracens took over as the spice vendors of western Europe. The spice route reverted to an overland trek from the Far East to the Arabian and Mediterranean shores, for the Moors were never sailors of the open seas.

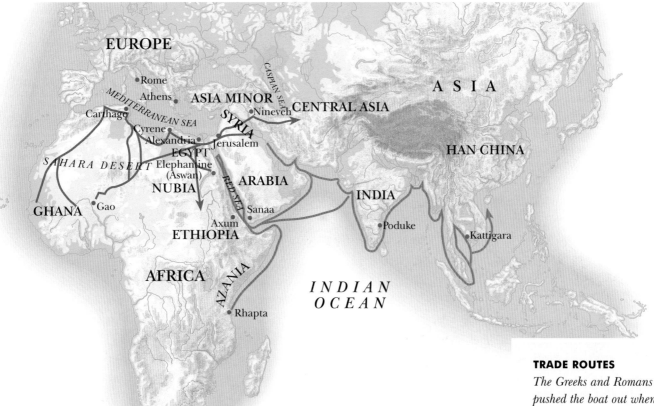

EUROPE
Rome
Athens
Carthage
MEDITERRANEAN SEA
Cyrene
Alexandria
EGYPT
Elephantine
(Aswan)
SAHARA DESERT
NUBIA
GHANA   Gao
ETHIOPIA
Axum
Sanaa
RED SEA
ARABIA
AFRICA
AZANIA
Rhapta
ASIA MINOR
SYRIA
Nineveh
CASPIAN SEA
CENTRAL ASIA
ASIA
HAN CHINA
INDIA
Poduke
Kattigara
INDIAN
OCEAN
Jerusalem

TRADE ROUTES

*The Greeks and Romans
pushed the boat out when
it came to spices.*

—————— Trade routes
—————— Principle caravan
routes

A VALUABLE COMMODITY

Medieval peoples treasured their spices. The rich left the contents of their
spice boxes to their nearest and dearest in their wills, and even the peasant
had his small cache of pepper to use as barter, as part of his daughter's dowry,
or even to enjoy sparingly on special occasions. In the homes of the wealthy,
conspicuous consumption of spices was as much an emblem of privilege as was
a silver plate or gold cloth. Spices concealed the onset of decay in fresh meat
and the overpowering taste of salt in preserved foodstuffs. Mead and wine
were also heavily doused, the latter with cinnamon, ginger, pepper, and
sunflower and pomegranate seeds. Spices generally, in particular ginger,
cardamom, and cinnamon, were valued for aiding circulation and hence
digestion; it was almost impossible to have too much of a good thing.

By the Renaissance, the merchants of Venice and of her rival, Genoa, were
making fortunes in trade with the Moors. Venetian ships unloaded
in ports from Rotterdam to Calais to Rochester, in England. But
the largest part of the journey still had to be made
overland. When the Ottoman Turks wrested control of
the eastern Mediterranean from the Saracen caliphate,
they increased the prices of spices. So the race was on
to bypass these obstacles. It was the Portuguese,
spurred on by their great sailor-king, Henry the
Navigator, who won—for a time—the prize.

BELOW

*A japanned black
spice cabinet from the
time of James I,
inlaid with silver
and mother-of-pearl.*

Hungarian Chicken Paprikash

SERVES 6

2 garlic cloves
Salt and pepper to taste
4 tablespoons (2 oz/60 g) butter
3 cups (1 lb/450 g) sliced onions
3 lb (1.3 kg) chicken, cut into pieces
1 tablespoon paprika
6 tablespoons (3 fl oz/90 ml) sour cream

Crush the garlic with a little salt with a mortar and pestle. Melt the butter gently in a large flameproof casserole and add the onions. Sauté them for about 15 minutes until they are golden and translucent. Add the garlic for the last 5 minutes. Add the chicken pieces and sauté until just colored.

Remove the casserole from the heat and stir in the paprika and pepper to taste, stirring until the paprika is well distributed. Add ⅔ cup (5 fl oz/150 ml) water and return the casserole to the heat. Bring to a boil, cover, and lower the heat. Simmer for one hour, checking the chicken remains in a little sauce. Add extra water, if necessary.

Transfer the chicken pieces to a warm platter. Increase the heat and reduce the liquid until thickened. Remove the casserole from the heat and, with a spoon, remove a little of the sauce; stir into the sour cream. Stir the sour cream into the casserole, a little at a time so the sauce does not separate. Pour the paprika sauce over the chicken pieces and serve with spätzle (*see also* page 58) or egg noodles.

THE SPICE ISLANDS TRADE

When Vasco da Gama, the Portuguese navigator, sailed into Calicut port on the west coast of India in 1498, his was the first Western ship to appear there since the Romans. Soon Portugal had gained control of the Spice Islands (the Moluccas) to the east, mounting an oppressive regime to force the natives into compliance, and ruthlessly eliminating all interlopers. Despite their rigorous precautions, however, the Portuguese had only 100 years in which to enjoy their good fortune. Ferdinand Magellan, a disgruntled Portuguese explorer, sold his services to the king of Spain, convinced there was a westward way to the islands of nutmegs and cloves. The Portuguese domination of the Indian Ocean made the western approach a necessity to the Spanish. In 1509, he vindicated his belief, although he did not live to bring back the edible proof. Spain used his triumph as a bargaining tool, allowing Portugal to keep the islands in return for other spoils.

But the new route had exposed the vulnerability of all the outposts of the far-away empire, and by the 1580s,

RIGHT
Red paprika chilies dry outside houses in Spain's Basque region, where they are ground for use in chorizo and sauces. In Hungary paprika is used to flavor pork and chicken dishes.

LEFT
Pepper-gathering in the kingdom of Quillon (on the Malabar coast, Kerala, India), from Le Livre de Merveilles, an early French account of the travels of Marco Polo. On the right, a Portuguese trader is seen inspecting the quality of the harvest.

Chilies—a Hot Handful

There is evidence that native peoples of the New World were using the fruits of the *Capsicum annuum* and *C. frutescens* as seasoning as long ago as 3300 BC.

Some of the most common are selected below:

Ancho Dark red-brown, dried poblano from Mexico. Used in *moles*, and in salsas.

Cayenne Very hot, bright-red chili from Louisiana, Mexico, Asia, and Africa. Used in ground seasoning and in commercial sauces.

Chipotle A dried brown, very hot smoked jalapeno. From the Rio Grande (U.S.A.) and Mexico. Used in seasoning and sauces.

Guajillo Green, medium-hot chili from northern and central Mexico. Used in enchiladas and salsas.

Habanero (or "Scotch bonnet") Extremely hot, Caribbean chili, for sauces and jerk chicken.

Jalapeño Green chili, available fresh and pickled. Grown in Texas and southwestern U.S.A. Used in sauces, salsas, and stews.

Mulato Medium-hot, dried, ripe poblano; central Mexico. Used in *moles* and sauces.

Mora rojo A jalepeño from central and northern Mexico. Used in *moles* and sauces

New Mexico chilies Warm flavored, green, orange, and red varieties, from Rio Grande Valley (U.S.A.). Used fresh roasted in stews and sauces; dried in cooked sauces and salsas.

Pastilla "Little raisin." A dried, brown, and mildish flavored *chilaca* from central Mexico. Usually ground and used in sauces and *moles*.

Serrano Long, thin, green chili, grown in Texas and southwestern U.S.A. Hot, most often used fresh in salsas.

Elizabeth I's English seahawks, Drake and Hawkins, were "tweaking the nose" of Philip II in the Spanish colonies of the West Indies and California, and of the Portuguese in the Moluccas. Closer to home, Philip's Dutch subjects were in revolt; their main attacks were against all Spanish and, for good measure, Portuguese assets in the Indian Ocean. The result was the establishment of the first of the great joint stock companies, the Dutch East India Company, which ruled the Spice Islands trade. Its eventual rival, England's East India Company, would eventually rule the fortunes of India and Sri Lanka.

These monopolies were not challenged until the end of the eighteenth century when the United States took to the seas in her streamlined tea and spice clippers. These ships represented a trading power no longer based on imperial conquest, but on Yankee opportunism. The concept of free trade dominated the nineteenth century—"to the fastest and sharpest go the spoils"— buttressing the establishment of specialist companies, such as McCormack and Schwartz, which still dominate the spice trade at the end of the twentieth century.

SPICE MIXES AND CONDIMENTS

This map shows where the world's favorite spices originally came from and where they are currently cultivated. The geographical regions are listed below and a numbered A-Z listing of spices can be found on the following pages.

![grinder icon] Place of origin   Place of cultivation

![grinder icon] Places of origin

AFGHANISTAN *asafoetida* (**5**); *garlic* (**20**) **ANTILLES** *vanilla* (**38**) **BALEARICS** *capers* (**7**) **BALKANS** *horseradish* (**22**) **BANGLADESH** *turmeric* (**37**) **BRITISH ISLES** *juniper berries* (**23** **CENTRAL AMERICA** *vanilla* (**38**) **CENTRAL EUROPE** *poppy seeds* (**30**) **CHINA** *anise pepper* (**4**); *capers* (**7**); *star anise* (**34**); *turmeric* (**37**) **DOMINICAN REPUBLIC** *paprika* (**28**)**EGYPT** *aniseed* (**3**); *cumin* (**16**); *mustard seeds* (**25**) **FRANCE** *capers* (**7**); *dill seeds* (**17**); *fennel seeds* (**18**); *juniper berries* (**23**) **GERMANY** *juniper berries* (**23**) **GREECE** *dill seeds* (**17**); *fennel seeds* (**18**); *sesame seeds* (**33**) **INDIA** *ajowan* (**1**); *aniseed* (**3**); *asafoetida* (**5**); *coriander seeds* (**15**); *fenugreek* (**19**); *garlic* (**20**); *ginger* (**21**); *pepper* (**29**); *tamarind* (**36**); *turmeric* (**37**) **INDONESIA** *pepper* (**29**); *star anise* (**34**) **IRAN** *black cherry kernel* (**6**); *asafoetida* (**5**); *licorice* (**24**); *saffron* (**32**); *sumac* (**35**) **ISRAEL** *mustard seeds* (**25**) **ITALY** *capers* (**7**); *dill seeds* (**17**); *fennel seeds* (**18**) **JAMAICA** *allspice* (**2**) **JAVA** *pepper* (**29**)**KASHMIR** *saffron* (**32**) **KOREA** *sesame seeds* (**33**) **LEBANON** *mustard seeds* (**25**) **LEVANT** *fenugreek* (**19**) **MALAYSIA** *star anise* (**34**) **MEXICO** *vanilla* (**38**) **MIDDLE EAST** *carob* (**10**) **MOLUCCAS** *cloves* (**14**); *nutmeg* (**26**) **SCANDINAVIA** *juniper berries* (**23**) **SOUTHEAST ASIA** *cardamom* (**9**); *cayenne* (**11**); *tamarind* (**36**) **SPAIN** *dill seeds* (**17**); *fennel seeds* (**18**) **SYRIA** *black cherry kernel* (**6**); *licorice* (**24**); *sumac* (**35**) **SRI LANKA** *cinnamon* (**13**); *tamarind* (**36**) **TEXAS** *chili powder* (**12**) **TURKEY** *fenugreek* (**19**); *licorice* (**24**); *onion seeds* (**27**); *poppy seeds* (**30**); *saffron* (**32**); *sumac* (**35**)

![grinder icon] Places of cultivation (where different)

BANGLADESH *nutmeg* (**26**) **BRAZIL** *pepper* (**29**) **BRITISH ISLES** *caraway seeds* (**8**); *fennel seeds* (**18**); *mustard seeds* (**25**) **CALIFORNIA** *ginger* (**21**) **CANADA** (Alberta) *mustard seeds* (**25**) **CENTRAL AMERICA** *cumin* (**16**) **EAST AFRICA** *cayenne* (**11**) **FRANCE** *aniseed* (**3**); *capers* (**7**); *caraway seeds* (**8**); *fennel seeds* (**18**); *licorice* (**24**); *mustard seeds* (**25**); *paprika* (**28**) **GERMANY** *caraway seeds* (**8**); *coriander seeds* (**15**) **GREECE** *aniseed* (**3**); *coriander seeds* (**15**) **HONDURAS** *allspice* (**2**) **HUNGARY** *paprika* (**28**) **INDIA** *cardamom* (**9**); *cinnamon* (**13**); *coriander seeds* (**15**); *cumin* (**16**); *fennel seeds* (**18**); *onion seeds* (**27**); *poppy seeds* (**30**) **ITALY** *aniseed* (**3**) **JAVA** *cinnamon* (**13**); *nutmeg* (**26**) **MADAGASCAR** *cinnamon* (**13**); *ginger* (**21**); *vanilla* (**38**) **MALAYSIA** *cinnamon* (**13**); *pepper* (**29**) **MAURITIUS** *cinnamon* (**13**); *turmeric* (**37**) **MEXICO** *allspice* (**2**); *chili powder* (**12**) **MIDDLE EAST** *onion seeds* (**27**); *sesame seeds* (**33**) **MOLUCCAS** *cloves* (**14**) **NETHERLANDS** *mustard seeds* (**25**) **NORTH AFRICA** *aniseed* (**3**); *cumin* (**16** **NORTH AMERICA** *licorice* (**24**) **RÉUNION** *turmeric* (**13**); *vanilla* (**38**) **SCANDINAVIA** *caraway seeds* (**8**); *dill seeds* (**17**) **SEYCHELLES** *cinnamon* (**13**) **SOUTHEAST ASIA** *anise pepper* (**4**); *fennel seeds* (**18**) **SPAIN** *aniseed* (**3**); *fennel seeds* (**18**); *licorice* (**24**); *mustard seeds* (**25**); *paprika* (**28**); *saffron* (**32**) **SRI LANKA** *cardamom* (**9**) **SUMATRA** *nutmeg* (**26**) **TURKEY** *aniseed* (**3**) **WEST AFRICA** *ginger* (**21**) **WEST INDIES** *cinnamon* (**13**) **WORLDWIDE** *garlic* (**20**) **ZANZIBAR** *cloves* (**14**)

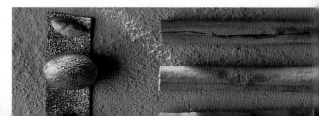

SCANDINAVIA
23 8 17 20

RUSSIAN FEDERATION

BRITISH ISLES
23
8 18 20 25

NETHERLANDS
20 25

HUNGARY
20 28

20

FRANCE
7 17 18 23
3 8 20 24 25

GERMANY
23 8 15 20

30

TURKEY
19 24 27
30 32 35
3 20

AFGHANISTAN
5 20 20

20

ASIA

CHINA
4 7 34 37
20

KOREA
33 20

ITALY
7 17 18 3

BALKANS
22 20

SPAIN
17 18
3 20 24
25 28 32

7

GREECE
17 18 33
3 15 20

LEBANON
25 20

19

SYRIA
6 24 35
20

3 16

3 16

ISRAEL
25 20

MIDDLE
EAST

IRAN
5 6 24
32 35 20

BANGLADESH
37 20 26

32

20

NORTH AFRICA

EGYPT
3 16 25
20

INDIA
1 3 5 15
19 20 21
29 36 37
9 13 15 16
18 20 27 30

20

9 11 36 4 18 20

20

SOUTHEAST
ASIA

21

20

10 20 27 33

AFRICA

20

MALAYSIA
34
13 20 29

INDONESIA
29 34
20

21

SRI LANKA
13 36
9 20

21

11

26

SEYCHELLES
13 20

INDIAN
OCEAN

JAVA
29 13 20 26

MOLUCCAS
14 26 20

11

20

MAURITIUS
13 20 37

11

REUNION
20 37 38

MADAGASCAR
13 20 21 38

AUSTRALIA

NEW
ZEALAND

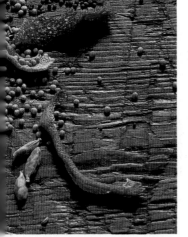

LEFT

*Scattered spices like these would have spelled
riches for a medieval household. Pictured are
quill cinnamon, ripe and dried pepper, chile,
garlic, tumeric, cardamon, nutmeg and cayenne.*

AN A - Z OF SPICES & FLAVORINGS

AJOWAN (1)
(Carum ajowan)
Ajowan seeds have a thyme flavor valued in Indian cooking. They are used in vegetable and lentil dishes and as a coloring agent.

ALLSPICE (2)
(Pimenta officinalis dioica)
Also known as *quatre-épices* in French, and as Jamaica pepper, allspice has a flavor reminiscent of cloves, cinnamon, nutmeg, and pepper. Most frequently used in sweet dishes and pickles, it also flavors herring and sausages.

ANISEED (3)
(Pimpinella anisum)
Aniseed's sweet, licoricelike undertones are frequently used to flavor alcohol. It is also used in Middle Eastern pastries, in French and German gingerbreads, and in some Indian fish dishes.

ANISE PEPPER (4)
(Xanthoyxlum piperitem)
One ingredient of Chinese Five Spice Powder, also known as Szechuan pepper. The whole reddish berries or powder have a piquant, peppery flavor.

ASAFOETIDA (5)
(Ferula asafoetida)
The dried, dark red resin of a plant used in small quantities to flavor Indian fish dishes and as an antiflatulent in curried legume and vegetable dishes.

BLACK CHERRY KERNEL (6)
(Prunus nigra)
This flavoring is sold as whole kernels, found inside the cherry stones. Used ground, in cakes, breads, and pastries in the cuisines of Syria, Iran, and Lebanon.

CAPERS (7)
(Capparis spinosa)
The pickled buds of a bush, originally growing wild on Sicily and Sardinia. Used in salads, fish dishes, and sauces, available salted, in brine, or in vinegar.

CARAWAY SEEDS (8)
(Carum carvi)
A favored spice of northern and eastern Europe, and of the Middle East. It is used in cabbage and sauerkraut dishes and in stews in Russia, Poland, Germany, and Alsace, and to flavor cheeses in Holland, cakes in Germany and Hungary, and many liqueurs.

CARDAMOM (9)
(Elettaria cardamomum)
Black, green, or white (sun-bleached) seed pods, or hulled black seeds. The seeds flavor Scandinavian pastries; the pods are used in Indian savory dishes, and the seeds in cakes. In the Middle East, a pod is infused in coffee before drinking.

CAROB (10)
(Ceratonia siliqua)
The pulped pods of the locust tree, also known as St John's bread. Native to the Middle East, carob is used in local soft drinks, and in Western confections as a lowfat alternative to chocolate.

CAYENNE (11)
(Capsicum frutescens)
Cayenne, the dried and powdered pods of peppers, is much used in Tex-Mex, Creole, and Caribbean cooking, in many European dishes, and in Indian curries.

CHILI POWDER (12)
In the United States, this commercial blend of chili pepper, oregano, cumin, garlic, and salt, was first made in Texas at the end of the nineteenth century. Elsewhere, however, chili powder is part dried and part ground chili peppers.

CINNAMON (13)
(Cinnamomum zeylanicum)
Available as dried bark, as peeled, sun-dried "quills," or as a powder, and used extensively in sweet and savory dishes in the Middle East, India, western Europe, and North and South America.

CLOVES (14)
(Eugenia aromatica)
Available both as hard, dried buds and ground, cloves are used in Indian, southeast Asian, and European cooking.

CORIANDER SEEDS (15)
(Coriandrum sativum)
Available both as seeds and ground, the seeds are the base of most commercial curry powders, and are paired with lamb (in the Middle East) and pork (in Greece). In the West, coriander seeds are mainly used in pickles and chutneys.

CUMIN (16)
(Cuminum cyminum)
Cumin is grown in eastern Europe, and used in charcuterie and bread. It is also used in Middle Eastern, Indian, Central American, and Tex-Mex cuisines.

DILL SEEDS (17)
(Anethum graveolens)
Used in northern, central, and eastern European and eastern Mediterranean cooking. The pungent, forceful flavor is particularly useful in pickling.

FENNEL SEEDS (18)
(Foeniculum vulgare)
The yellow seeds add an anise-like flavor to fish and Tuscan salami. Much used in French and Moroccan cooking.

FENUGREEK (19)
(Trigonella foenum graecum)
The hard, flat, brownish seeds provide essential bitterness to Indian fish curries, and are included in most curry powders. They are also common in the cuisines of Greece and Egypt.

Cloves   *Garlic grains*

Caraway

GARLIC (20)
(Allium sativum)

In medieval times garlic was carried as a protection against evil spirits and the plague. It is available in fresh bulb form, dried in granules, or powdered.

GINGER (21)
(Zingiber officinale)

An essential spice in India, China, Japan, and southeast Asia, ginger was brought to Europe by the Romans. In today's Western cuisine it is used mainly in desserts, cakes, and breads, and as a candied or preserved sweetmeat.

HORSERADISH (22)
(Armoracia rusticana)

This root gives fire to many dishes. Usually sold grated, and sometimes "creamed" as a sauce, it is also mixed into mustards and flavored butters.

JUNIPER BERRIES (23)
(Juniperus communis)

Native to the northern hemisphere, these berries infuse wines and spirits (British gin and Dutch genever) and the cooking of Scandinavia, Germany, and Alsace, especially with pork and game, sauerkraut, and other cabbage dishes.

LICORICE (24)
(Glycyrrhia glabra)

Cultivated in western Europe as an aid to digestion since medieval times. Available as sliced root or powdered, today it is used mainly in confectionery.

MUSTARD SEEDS (25)
(Brassica sinapis alba, B.s. junica, B.s. nigra)

This European and Asian native grows wild and cultivated in temperate regions. Whole seeds are used for pickles and in some eastern European and Indian dishes, but are more usually ground into a powder or made into a condiment.

NUTMEG (26)
(Myristica fragrans)

The hard fruit kernel of the nutmeg tree has both sweet and savory uses. The weblike red aril which surrounds the kernel is mace, used for more subtle flavor.

Cinnamon stick

Ginger

ONION SEEDS (27)
(Nigella sativa)

These spicy pointed seeds are used in savory Indian dishes and scattered on Middle Eastern breads and cakes.

PAPRIKA (28)
(Capsicum annuum tetragonum)

The ground pod of a dried sweet red pepper, paprika is widely used in Hungary. and by the Spanish Basques.

PEPPER (29)
(Piper nigrum)

This spice was used in Europe before the Romans. To obtain black peppercorns, berries are picked green, then allowed to dry in the sun. White pepper, made from the milder inner kernel, is picked when the berry is ripe and red, and is usually sold ground. Green peppercorns preserved in brine are also available.

POPPY SEEDS (30)
(Papaver somniferum; P. rhoeas)

Poppy seeds are a particular favorite of Jewish, Levantine, and central and eastern European pastry cooks.

PUMPKIN SEEDS (31)
(Cucurbita maxima)

Used in Mexican and Central American cooking to lend subtle flavor and noticeable texture to stews and sauces. Also toasted and eaten as snacks.

SAFFRON (32)
(Crocus sativus)

The most expensive spice, saffron scents, flavors, and colors all it infuses. Indispensable to Spanish paella, French bouillabaisse, and Italian *risotto*, saffron is probably used more in northern India than anywhere else.

SESAME SEEDS (33)
(Sesamum indicum)

A favorite in north African and Middle Eastern kitchens, sesame is toasted as a snack, decorates cakes and breads, and is the basis of halva, a sesame and nut confection. Far Eastern black sesame is used on Chinese toffee apples and bananas, and in Japanese condiments.

STAR ANISE (34)
(Illicium verum)

The dried, star-shaped fruit of an evergreen shrub, with pods containing small, peppery-anise-flavored seeds. The whole pod or the ground seeds are used in oriental kitchens, and in many *garam masalas*. In the West, it is used in liqueurs, cookies, and pastries.

SUMAC (35)
(Sumac)

The crushed berries of the sumac tree have a bitter flavor, indispensable to certain fish marinades and to chicken, lentil, and tomato-based dishes in Iran, Syria, and Lebanon.

TAMARIND (36)
(Tamarind indica)

The thick-fleshed fruit of this African tree is seeded, and the pulp dried and pressed to be sold in lumps. Indian and southeast Asian cooks soak the flesh to obtain the acid, bitter juice, used in a variety of curried dishes.

TURMERIC (37)
(Curcuma longa)

The powder from the ground rhizome is used in commercial curry powders and lends color and a mild acridity to rice dishes, condiments, and curries.

VANILLA (38)
(Vanilla plantifolia)

The cured fruit of a climbing orchid vine, most commonly used to flavor desserts, pastries, confectionery, and alcoholic and soft drinks. Sold as dried pods, vanilla extract, or as vanilla sugar.

The numbers on these pages key to the map on the previous page.

SPICE MIXES & CONDIMENTS

*T*he Romans had a passion for sauces, and their favorite was called **garum**. *The basic seasoning for much of their cooking, it reigned as the supreme condiment. Its briny, highly pungent flavor must have jaded the tastebuds, making unseasoned food seem bland.*

The odiferous *garum*, strained from a fermented concoction of herbs and the intestines of anchovies, sprats, or small mackerel, was aged and bottled in amphorae. The East had its more subtle condiments and pickles. A third-century BC Chinese poem advocates the balancing of bitter, salt, sour, and sweet flavors, and in the emperor's kitchens specialist sauce chefs worked to achieve this finesse. Soy sauce and fermented black bean sauce were staples by the second century BC, while plum sauce appeared somewhat later.

ABOVE

Jerk chicken is a dish in Jamaica, where the highly flavored, barbecued fowl is offered on roadside stalls.

RIGHT

A North African spice stall. Mixtures like ras al hanout *are made on the spot.*

These flavorings were used with discretion, not the indiscriminate enthusiasm accorded to *garum* by Roman and later Byzantine consumers.

A TASTE FOR SAUCE

During the Dark Ages, pestilence, famine, and diseased crops meant that there was little enough to sauce and most meat or fish went to the table plainly cooked. When the darkness began to lift, from about the tenth century, saucing—incorporating neglected early spices and the newly introduced spices from the Arab world—became the vogue. In the seventeenth and eighteenth centuries the refined, aromatic preparations that would eventually form the basis of today's bottled gastronomy began to appear— mayonnaise, tomato and mushroom catsups, tartar sauce.

Traditionally, European flavoring mixtures have had predominantly herbal foundations. In contrast, the Far Eastern preference is for salt and spice, but as a calculated "accent," not as a dominant note. The Middle East has produced a compromise, in which the more subtle spices—ginger, cloves, allspice, cinnamon, fenugreek—are married with a green abundance of parsley, oregano, cilantro, and mint. But when the influences of the orient and Europe meet head-on, in the mixtures and condiments of nineteenth-century, Raj-influenced England and in those of the New World, some major culinary fireworks occur.

RIGHT
One of the many brown sauces *to follow in the wake of Worcestershire sauce. They varied in strength, flavor, and consistency—in this case* goo!.

Mustard: The Pope's Condiment

Mustard has been a culinary favorite for thousands of years. First cultivated in the Levant, seeds were introduced into Egypt, where they were crushed and used in much the same way as coarse pepper is today. The Greeks and Romans ground the seeds into a powder, and it became popular in this form in Britain and the U.S.A. from the eighteenth century onward. The Romans also mixed the crushed seeds with tuna brine or with honey, oil, and vinegar, to be used as a cold sauce with meats.

By medieval times, the crushed seeds were being mixed with grape must (hence the name *moutarde*, or mustard) and various combinations of seeds, liquid, sugar, and spicing were acquiring gourmet admirers. One pope, accounts vary as to whether it was Clement VII or John XXII, was such an aficionado he was said to award titles ("the pope's mustard-maker" is still a term of derision in France) on the basis of approved recipes. Dijon, in France, with its formula for seeds crushed to a paste with sugar, verjuice (unripe grape juice), and white wine became the main center for mustard production, but there were several contenders: Orléans (smooth, with wine vinegar); Meaux (coarse seeds, bolder spicing); and Bordeaux (darker, milder, more vinous).

In time, Germans began to favor a dark, sweet-sour variation, while nineteenth-century Norwich, England, became home to a bright-yellow, hot paste developed by Jonathan Colman. By contrast, French's, the classic partner to America's hot dogs and hamburgers, is almost the same sunny color but of a surprising mildness. The mania for new styles has infected the mustard market, and there are now tarragon, green peppercorn, lemon, garlic, honey, and whiskey mustards.

SPICE MIXES AND CONDIMENTS

This map shows the world's favorite spice mixes and condiments,
which are listed by geographical region in the keybox below.
A numbered A-Z listing can be found on the following page.

■ Seasoning for cooking   ■ Condiment

(S = seasoning) (C = condiment)

Europe
Dry mixtures
BRITISH ISLES 4 *(Apple pie spice)* S; **5** *(pickling spice)* S **FRANCE 1**
(Bouquet garni) S; **2** *(fines herbes)* S; **3** *(herbes de Provence)* S; **6** *(Quatre epice)* S

Wet mixtures
BRITISH ISLES 7 *(A1/HP/Daddies/steak sauces)* C; **8** *(chutney)* C; **9** *(ketchup, tomato)* C; **10** *(horseradish sauce)* C; **12** *(mint sauce/jelly)* C; **15** *(Worcester sauce)*
S&C **FRANCE 11** *(mayonnaise)* S&C **ITALY 14** *(pesto sauce)* S
PORTUGAL 16 *(piri-piri)* S&C **SWEDEN 13** *(mustard dill sauce)* C

Middle East
Dry mixtures
IRAN 19 *(Zaatar)* C; **LEBANON 17** *(Lebanese spice mix)* S;
MOROCCO 18 *(Ras al hanout)* S **SYRIA 19** *(Zaatar)* C

Wet mixtures
MOROCCO 20 *(Harissa)* C

India, Southeast Asia,
Far East
Dry mixtures
CHINA 22 *(five spice powder)* S; **26** *(Monosodium glutamate)* S; **28** *(Shrimp powder)* S **INDIA 21** *(curry powder)* S; **23** *(Garam masala, dry)* S; **27** *(Panch phara)* S **JAPAN 24** *(Gomasio)* S; **25** *(Katsuobushi)* S & C
Wet mixtures
BURMA 32 *(fish sauce)* S; **44** *(shrimp paste)* S&C; **CHINA 29** *(bean sauce)* S&C; **31** *(Chili sauce)*, S&C; **35** *(hoisin sauce)* S&C; **39** *(oyster sauce)* S; **40** *(plum sauce)* C; **56** *(soy sauce)* S&C **INDIA 30** *(Chatni)* C; **33** *(garam masala, wet)* S **INDONESIA 41** *(sambal bajak)* C; **42** *(sambal olek)* C; **44** *(Shrimp paste)* S&C **JAPAN 34** *(gomairi-hatagorashi)* C; **36** *(mirin)* S; **37** *(miso)* S; **43** *(Shishimi tagorashi)* C; **45** *(soy sauce)* S&C; **46** *(wasabi)* C
KOREA 2 *(bean sauce)* S&C **MALAYSIA 29** *(bean sauce)* S&C; **31** *(Chili sauce)* S&C; **32** *(fish sauce)* S&C **SINGAPORE 29**
(bean sauce) S&C **SRI LANKA 31** *(Chili sauce)* S&C **THAILAND 32** *(fish sauce)* S; **38** *(Nam prik)* C; **44** *(Shrimp paste)* S&C **VIETNAM 32** *(fish sauce)* S; **44** *(Shrimp paste)* S&C

The Americas
Dry mixtures
BRAZIL 49 *(Farofa)* C **JAMAICA 50** *Jerk seasoning* S **LOUISIANA (U.S.A.) 47** *(cajun seasoning)* S **MEXICO 48** *(chili powder)* S **TEXAS (U.S.A.) 4** *(chili powder)* S

Wet mixtures
JAMAICA 52 *(Caribbean hot sauce)* S **LOUISIANA (U.S.A.) 53** *(Tabasco)* S &C **U.S.A. 7** *(A1/HP/Daddies/steak sauces)* C; **51** *(Barbecue sauce)* C

ALASKA

NORTH AMERICA

U.S.A.
7 51

LOUISIANA
47 53
53

TEXAS
48

MEXICO
48

ATLANTIC OCEAN

CENTRAL AMERICA

CARIBBEAN SEA

JAMAICA
50 52

PACIFIC OCEAN

BRAZIL
49

SOUTH AMERICA

SWEDEN
13

BRITISH ISLES
4 5 15
7 8 9 10 12 15

RUSSIAN FEDERATION

EUROPE

FRANCE
1 2 3 6 11
11

ITALY
14

ASIA

KOREA
29
29

MEDITERRANEAN

LEBANON
17

PORTUGAL
16
16

SEA

IRAN
19

SYRIA
19

CHINA
22 26 28 29 31 35 39 45
29 31 35 40 45

JAPAN
24 25 36 37 45
25 34 43 45 46

MOROCCO
18
20

MIDDLE EAST

INDIA
21 23 27 33
30

VIETNAM
32 44
44

AFRICA

BURMA
32 44
44

SOUTHEAST ASIA

MALAYSIA
29 31 32 44
29 31 44

SRI LANKA
31
31

THAILAND
32 44
38 44

SINGAPORE
29
29

INDIAN

OCEAN

INDONESIA
44
41 42 44

AUSTRALIA

NEW ZEALAND

LEFT

The vibrant yellow of mustard in bloom glows against meadow green.

LEFT

Spice dealers in India and the Middle East are family concerns.

$\mathcal{S}$OME LIKE IT HOT

Europe

Dry mixtures

BOUQUET GARNI (1)
A tied bundle of herbs added to soups and stews. The classic base herbs are bay leaf, parsley, and thyme.

FINES HERBES (2)
Finely chopped or dried chervil, chives, parsley, and tarragon.

HERBES DE PROVENCE (3)
Fresh or dried thyme, rosemary, bay leaf, basil, and savory, used especially for grilled or broiled meats and fish.

APPLE PIE SPICE (4)
A blend of ground sweet baking spices, including nutmeg or mace, cloves, cinnamon, and allspice.

PICKLING SPICE (5)
An Anglo-Saxon blend, usually containing black peppercorns, mustard seed, cloves, allspice, mace, ground ginger, and cilantro seed.

QUATRE-ÉPICES (6)
Combination of ground pepper, nutmeg, cloves, and cinnamon.

Wet mixtures

A1/HP/DADDIES STEAK SAUCES (7)
Various commercial brown sauces, used as all-purpose condiments.

CATSUP, TOMATO (8)
Developed from Italian and French tomato sauces, but with the addition of sugar, vinegar, salt, and spices. A leading condiment of the Western world.

CHUTNEY (9)
Inspired by India's *chatni*, this resembles a fruit or vegetable pickle, combining sweet (sugar) and sour (vinegar).

HORSERADISH SAUCE (10)
Commercially produced using vinegar, sugar, and milk. A traditional condiment for roast beef and smoked fish.

MAYONNAISE (11)
An emulsion of egg yolks, oil, and vinegar.

MINT SAUCE/JELLY (12)
A mixture of finely chopped mint leaves, sugar, and vinegar; traditional accompaniment to lamb.

MUSTARD-DILL SAUCE (13)
A thick emulsion of mustard, sugar, and dill, served with cured fish.

PESTO SAUCE (14)
A paste of fresh basil, pine nuts, garlic, and Parmesan cheese served tossed with pasta; widely available bottled and fresh.

WORCESTERSHIRE SAUCE (15)
Produced by Lea & Perrins since 1838 and available worldwide. The secret formula includes soy sauce, mushroom and tomato catsups, salt, sugar, sherry, anchovies, pork liver, vinegar, and a myriad of spices.

PIRI-PIRI (16)
A thin and oily hot chili sauce, used primarily with fish and chicken. Portuguese in the East Indies passed the recipe to their Dutch successors, and it traveled to South Africa with the Boers.

Middle East

Dry mixtures

LEBANESE SPICE MIX (17)
Contains cinnamon, cloves, chilies, and green cardamom pods, and is used in a variety of dishes.

RAS AL HANOUT (18)
A ground blend of ginger, allspice, cloves, black pepper, cinnamon, cilantro, and cumin seeds, and cayenne pepper.

ZAATAR (19)
A mixture of ground sumac and thyme, sprinkled over savory dishes and salads.

Wet mixtures

HARISSA (20)
A red-hot paste made from soaked and drained chilies, combined with garlic, cilantro, caraway, mint, oil, and salt.

India, Southeast Asia, Far East

CURRY POWDER (21)
Packaged mixtures containing cumin, cilantro, chili, cardamom, and other aromatic spices.

FIVE SPICE POWDER (22)
A ground Chinese mixture of star anise, anise pepper, fennel seed, cloves, and cinnamon (or cassia).

GARAM MASALA (DRY) (23)
A ground mixture, varying according to the dish; often includes bay leaf, black pepper, cardamom, cinnamon, cloves, and cilantro and cumin seeds.

GOMASIO (24)
A seasoning of black sesame seeds, coarse salt, and monosodium glutamate used to heighten flavor during cooking.

KATSUOBUSHI (25)
Dried bonito (a tuna variety), available in block form for grating, or flaked.

MONOSODIUM GLUTAMATE (26)

An extract of grains and vegetables reduced to saltlike crystals, used to enhance other flavors, and a staple of commercial Chinese cuisine.

PANCH PHARA (27)

"Five seed spice;" black mustard seed, black and beige cumin seeds, fenugreek, and fennel seeds. Added to cooking oil.

SHRIMP POWDER (28)

A fine shred of dried shrimp.

Wet mixtures

BEAN SAUCES (29)

Min sze jeung is made of mashed and whole fermented soybeans and used in cooked dishes; black bean and yellow bean sauces are saltier. *Mor sze jeung* is a sauce of ground soybeans.

CHATNI (30)

Sweet or sour relishes made with fresh ingredients, either cilantro, chopped fruit, or grated coconut.

CHILI SAUCE (31)

The Chinese style is hot and searing; the southeast Asian and Sri Lankan version is hot-sweet-sour, with ginger and garlic overtones.

FISH SAUCE (32)

The liquid obtained from drained, salted tiny fish, mixed with oil and spices. Used throughout southeast Asia.

GARAM MASALA (WET) (33)

A paste of mashed or pounded fresh ingredients; ginger, garlic, mint, chilies, cilantro, and/or fenugreek leaves.

GOMAIRI-HATAGORASHI (34)

A relish made from red peppers and their leaves crushed with black sesame seeds; served with rice.

HOISIN SAUCE (35)

A medium-thick, sweet-and-spicy, red-brown mixture of soybeans, garlic, and spices. Often used in pork and duck dishes.

MIRIN (36)

A sweet, golden, rice wine, used only in cooking, usually for grilled or broiled meats, and in cold vegetable dishes.

Chili

Garam masala

MISO (37)

A fermented, red bean paste, the base of many Japanese broths and soups.

NAM PRIK (38)

A medium-thick, very hot, red sauce of pounded garlic, dried shrimp paste, chilies, lemon juice, palm sugar, and water. An all-round dip and condiment.

OYSTER SAUCE (39)

The infused liquor from oysters cooked in soy sauce and brine. Imparts a subtle flavor to a variety of oriental dishes.

PLUM SAUCE (40)

Sweet, lightly spicy, sticky sauce made from plums, chilies, vinegar, sugar, and spices. Especially used as an accompaniment to Peking duck.

SAMBAL BAJAK (41)

A dark brown-red, medium-hot paste of chilies, onions, and spices, to accompany curries and rice dishes.

SAMBAL OLEK (42)

A very spicy, red paste of chilies, vinegar, and salt; used as above.

SHISHIMI TAGORASHI (43)

A Japanese, ginger-based relish to accompany raw fish.

SHRIMP PASTE (WET AND DRIED) (44)

Thick, gray sauce with a pungent odor. The fresh sauce is used as a base for dips and other sauces; the dried paste (*trasi*) is used in stir-fry dishes.

SOY SAUCE/SHOYU/KECAP MANIS (45)

Found throughout the Far East and southeast Asia. Chinese cooking uses light and dark soy; Japanese *shoyu* is more delicate; Indonesian *kecap manis* is sweeter and more penetrating.

WASABI (46)

A hot powder made from Japanese horseradish.

The Americas

Dry mixtures

CAJUN SEASONING (47)

A ground mixture of chilies, garlic, salt, and spices—including cilantro, cumin, and fennel seeds, and ginger—and herbs, such as oregano and marjoram. Used to flavor assorted meats, poultry, and fish.

CHILI POWDER (48)

A commercial ground mixture of several strains of dried chilies. A prime ingredient of Tex-Mex dishes.

FAROFA (49)

Ground manioc meal, sometimes mixed with pepper. It is used as a seasoning over cooked food, notably *feijoada*, Brazil's national dish.

JERK SEASONING (50)

A combination of allspice, dried chilies and pimentos, and bay leaves. Rubbed onto meats.

Wet mixtures

BARBECUE SAUCE (51)

Usually includes tomato sauce, garlic, mustard, Worcestershire sauce, brown sugar, vinegar, and "secret" spices.

CARIBBEAN HOT SAUCE (52)

A searing sauce containing Scotch bonnet (habanero) chilies.

TABASCO SAUCE (53)

First marketed in 1868. It uses a thin red variety of chili, mashed with salt and vinegar, and aged for three years in oak barrels, after which the liquid is drawn off and bottled. An essential ingredient of a Bloody Mary.

The numbers on these pages key to the map on the previous page.

SALT: OF THE EARTH & SEA

S alt, the "white gold" of the ancients, has always been the subject of fascination and conjecture, its very existence a litany of strange properties and contradictions.

The only directly edible mineral, the compound sodium chloride (NaCI), or salt, is craved by both man and beast. Our bodies require salt to live, yet saltwater is death to the thirsty. Food may seem inedible without it, yet fields can be made barren by its use. The supply of salt is inexhaustible and ever-growing, yet historically it has been a costly item—once the product of much physical labor, today of the vast expenditure of industrial energy.

BLESSING AND CURSE

Salt was once won from nature; today it is mostly farmed, like any other crop. Initially extracted from water, the resultant crystals have the power to desiccate and dry, and are thus preserved from corruption. In religious and folk custom, salt is synonymous with blessing; the rituals of both the Roman Catholic Church and the Freemasons used it to symbolize purity and regeneration, while the very word hospitality in Russian translates literally as "salt-bread." The misuse

ABOVE

A rare salt cellar from the French ceramic works at St. Porchaire, 1530-40. These works of art were made to hold a valuable work of nature.

RIGHT

Salt's many properties allowed it to grace this Renaissance herbal.

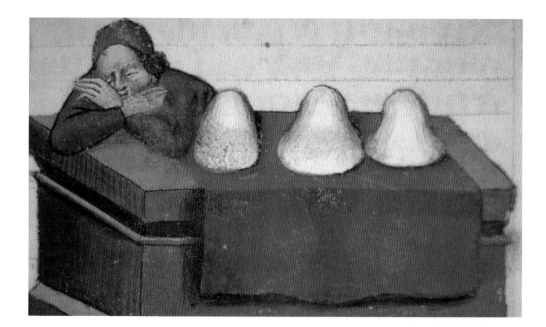

SALT CENTERS
*Many countries with
historic rock salt sources
are still producing salt on
a commercial basis, as
this map indicates. The
sea salt sources of Europe
are concentrated around
the southern French and
Spanish coasts.*

Sea salt

Rock salt and/
or salt springs

Countries with historic
rock salt sources

of such a precious commodity can bring down a curse, unless countermeasures are taken; hence the throwing of spilt salt over the left shoulder (where demons supposedly lie in wait), and the traditional presence of salt in exorcism rites.

AN HISTORIC NECESSITY

Salt is usually thought of as a condiment, rather than a spice, because it is inorganic. The word "condiment" makes it sound like an elective addition to our diet, but it has long been known that it is more necessary than any spice.

Salt workings have been discovered dating back to Neolithic times, when hunters used it to preserve game. With the advent of settled agriculture, salt became even more useful; an abundance of meat meant that some could be kept for the lean times of winter. By the Bronze Age, salt had become an important article of trade between regions. In the centuries before Roman dominance, the salt mines of Hallstatt, in Austria, enriched Celtic civilization, which traded on equal terms with Etruscans, Egyptians, and Romans. By the time of the Roman Empire, "salinators" were sent to Britain and France to

Harvesting Salt

There are three basic methods of salt extraction, all used since ancient times:

• Rock salt is mined in blocks and pulverized;
• A solution of brine is made from rock salt (or obtained from salt springs or sea water), and dehydrated in open or vacuum-sealed containers (the source of most table salt);
• Sea water is evaporated by means of a system of basins and salt pans.

Ecologically, the third is the most desirable, because it uses the drying power of sun and wind, but it is also the most costly in terms of manpower and time. Most of the prized gourmet salts are extracted by this method.

The great salt chambers of Hallstatt, in the Austrian Alps, and of Wieliczka, near Krakow in Poland, have both been worked for at least 3,000 years. They are now state tourist assets; chapels, dance halls, and hospital dormitories for sufferers of respiratory diseases like tuberculosis, emphysema, and allergies, are hewn from solid salt thousands of feet beneath the Earth's surface. In ancient times, such mines were attacked with axe and pick, but today, the majority pump water into the galleries, and evaporate the resultant solution.

ABOVE

On Bonaire, in the Antilles, solar evaporation is used to remove salt from sea water .

show the natives how to extract the precious mineral from salt springs and from sea water—by boiling it off in open pans—and to regularize the export of pure rock salt. Roman legionnaires were at first paid in salt (*sal*) and later in cash, a portion of which was used to buy this necessity, hence the origin of the word "salary." The salt industry spawned others; both ancient Egypt and Spain boasted thriving export trades in salted fish, while Roman Gaul was renowned for its salted and cured hams.

Even after the empire disintegrated, the flow of salt continued. Dry-salting, smoking, and pickling at least ensured a supply of preserved meat during the winter when fresh meat was unavilable. Even verjuice, the must produced before grape juice has fermented into wine, was salted in a vain attempt to stave off scurvy, the plague that came with the lack of fresh fruit and vegetables.

Salt enhanced flavor and disguised mold and decay. It was ubiquitous in sauces and even bread was highly salted. Norman traders plied their trade in Breton and Poitou sea salt along the Loire and the Seine, while the Poles and Germans transported their rock salt to coastal ports for trade with Scandinavia and Russia.

SALT AND CHRISTIANITY

The many days of fasting and abstinence required by the Christian Church—up to three days a week at the height of late medieval piety, as well as the forty days of Lent—meant fish was in demand. Most fish was salted, which kept it edible for several months. Salt cod, or stockfish, became the staple of the Mediterranean and Latin peoples, salted herring of eastern and northern tables.

The powers of Church and State realized salt could be made to work for them. Royal and ecclesiastical princes began to levy tolls on salt merchants under their control. At the end of the thirteenth century, the most infamous of all the many taxes levied on salt came into being: the *gabelle*. Devised by the advisors of France's Philip II ("The Fair") to fund his expansionist wars and centralist administration, it led to many rebellions, culminating in the fall of Louis XVI, and its final repeal in 1790. The impact of such taxes was a rise in price of salt, no longer to be taken as a gift of nature. The association between salt, tax, and rebellion had an eerie twentieth-century echo, when Gandhi's path to passive resistance began with a march to the sea in protest at the British government's insensitive doubling of India's salt tax in 1923.

GRAINS
& BREAD

Grains or cereals are the edible seeds of cultivated grasses such as rice, wheat and corn. The carbohydrates they contain form the staple diet of the world's population; indeed regional and national cuisines are often defined by the grains on which they are based. While most grains are ground or milled into flour to make breads, dumplings or pasta, they are also steamed, fried, stewed, and otherwise cooked. Last but not least, they are brewed into beers and wines.

FIVE HISTORIC GRAINS

*F*ive grain plants—wheat, barley, millet, rye, and oats—have defined the history of the West from neolithic to modern times. They were not "European" in origin, but were cultivated and refined by the world's first civilizations, in the Near and Far East.

The oldest recorded trove of cultivated wheat ever found by archeologists was unearthed in Jericho and has been dated to around 10,000 BC. There, and at other sites in the Holy Land, cakes of mixed wheat and barley were baked in the sun. The builders of the Egyptian pyramids existed on a muscle-sustaining porridge of the same grains. Millet flourished in China, Siberia, and India between 5,000 and 6,000 years ago, and there is evidence that wild strains of barley were undergoing hybridization in China and Japan some 2,000 years before that.

ABOVE

Found in the ruins of Jericho, this grain store, c. 8000 BC, is from a period when barley-wheat cakes were common.

THE MAINSTAY OF THE ROMAN LEGION

The improved irrigation techniques of the Greeks and the organizational competence of the Roman Empire were to make cereal farming big business in the ancient world. While little of Rome's heartland was given over to grain, it was the basis of a flourishing import industry, with laden ships from Sicily, Sardinia, and North Africa docking at Ostia, the capital's port at the mouth of the Tiber. Barley and millet were part of that cargo, but wheat soon became the favored cereal. Good bread, the fodder of the legionnaires, sustained the empire. Even the most far-flung outposts—Britain and the plains below Germany's Harz Mountains—were inducted into service as wheat-suppliers, largely for the armies of occupation. By the time the empire collapsed in the fifth century AD, reliance on a cereal diet had been well impressed on the subject peoples.

and winter barley—but by the time of the empire, barley had plunged steeply in popular estimation. As standards of living grew, wheat became the grain of choice, while barley was relegated to feeding soldiers kept under arrest. The Romans' erstwhile subjects, the Jews and Egyptians, treated barley with more respect. It became a staple ingredient of *cholent*, the traditional Sabbath meal, while the tombs of pharaohs, nobles, and workers record barley and wheat were the twin staves of life.

Barley bread fell out of favor even with the poor when the introduction of new strains of wheat and milling methods reduced its exclusivity. But the role of barley in beer manufacture, first exploited by the Gauls, and later refined by medieval monks, continues today. Brewing barley is confined to special high-starch varieties, which respond to malting; cooking barley is harder and flintier, but more nutritious. It is most commonly available as pearl barley, the trademark ingredient of Scotch broth and many other soups and stews. Infused in boiling water, sweetened, and flavored with lemon, it makes old-fashioned barley water, a highly refreshing drink. A cup of cooked barley has the protein content of a glass of milk, but its real attraction to the modern consumer is its reputation as a cholesterol-buster. Tests have shown that it seems to reduce the production of harmful Low-Density Lipoprotein (LDL), the so-called "harmful cholesterol."

WHEAT: NUMBER 1 IN THE WEST

Archeological evidence indicates that wild wheat was being eaten by the Paleolithic nomads of the central Asian steppes as early as 10,000 to 9000 B.C. Two thousand years later, the Neolithic farmers of Jericho and of the Tigris and Euphrates valleys (the "Fertile Crescent") had developed early cultivated strains, using

WORLD BEERS

Thanks to advertising and export agreements, local beers are now popular world-wide.

Europe

1. Austria: *Gösser; Schwechater*
2. Belgium: *Hoegaarden Blanche; Stella Artois; Trappish* **3. Czech Republic:** *Pilsner Urquell* **4. Denmark:** *Carlsberg; Tuborg*
5. England: *Adnams; Bass; Burton; Courage; Theakston* **6. France:** *Fischer; Kanterbraü; Kronenbourg; Pelforth* **7. Germany:** *Becks; Dortmunder Union Bier; Löwenbräu; Spatenbräu*
8. Greece: *Fix* **9. Holland:** *Amstel; Grolsch; Oranjeboom; Heineken* **10. Iceland:** *Polar beer*
11. Ireland: *Guinness* **12. Italy:** *Moretti; Nastro Azzurro* **13. Scotland:** *McEwans; Tennants* **14. Spain:** *Aquila; Estrella Damm; San Miguel* **15. Yugoslavia:** *Union*

North America

16. Canada: *Labatt (London, Ontario); Molson (Montreal)* **17. Caribbean:** *Red Stripe (Jamaica)* **18. Mexico:** *Corona; Dos Equis; Sol; Victoria* **19. U.S.A.:** *Anchor Steam beer (San Francisco); Budweiser (St. Louis); Coors (Colorado); Michelob (St. Louis); Millers (Milwaukee); Olympia (Seattle); Schlitz (Milwaukee)*

Asia

20. China: *Tsing Tao (Canton)* **21. Hong Kong:** *San Miguel* **22. Japan:** *Asahi; Kirin; Sapporo* **23. India:** *Kingfisher* **24. Malaysia:** *Tiger* **25. Philippines:** *San Miguel* **26. Taiwan:** *Tai beer* **27. Thailand:** *Singha*

Australia

28. Australia: *Castlemaine; Fosters; Swan*

Africa

29. Kenya: *Tusker, Amstel* **30. Namibia:** *Hansa Pilsner* **31. South Africa:** *Crown, Schafft*

For Poet and Peasant— Cracked Wheat

Now served in the sophisticated eateries of the West, bulgur, or cracked wheat, is the peasant dish of the Middle East. The earliest record of its use is on an Assyrian tablet of the ninth century BC. Its range as a common food extends from Tunisia and Egypt, through the Levant to Turkey, and east into Armenia and Georgia. Farther north, in Bulgaria and Byelorussia, cracked wheat features in one or two traditional dishes—probably the result of Syrian migrations over a millennium ago.

It is still made today in many Middle Eastern villages in the traditional manner, during the summer days and warm evenings. The women clean, sieve, sort, wash, and dry the new harvest of hard wheat by hand. The grain is then boiled in large tubs over dung fires and spread on straw mats to dry.

strains, using the grain whole in broth, roasted as cereal, and rough-ground in griddle cake. It has been said that wheat was the grain that encouraged the earliest cultivation, then the first civilizations; as planting, harvesting, and threshing demanded cooperation, it cemented marriages and created settled communities. The Egyptians, and subsequently the Greeks and Romans, ground it into flour to make bread, the form in which it is usually encountered in the "wheat-eating regions" of the world today. These include western Europe, North America (excluding Central America and Mexico, where corn is king), the Middle East, northern Iraq and parts of Iran, central and northern India, and northern China. It was taken to the New World by the Spanish conquistador, Cortés, in 1529, and took firm root there; today, the U.S.A., together with the Ukraine and the Confederation of Independent States (part of the former Soviet Union), leads the world in production figures.

Common wheat (*Triticum aestivum*) is the most versatile grain, available as whole husked kernels ("wheat berries"), as bulgur (parched, steamed, and ground kernels), as

THE FIRST CEREALS

The history of wheat and barley cultivation dates back 12,000 years. This map shows the original areas of cultivation, in Central Asia and the Holy Land respectively. The subsequent spread of the cereals, to the Far East and northern Europe, can be traced by following the numbers, which refer to the explanatory chronology (below).

🌾 → Wheat   𝌆 Barley

WHEAT
10,000 BC	**1**	*Growing wild in Central Asia*
10-7000 BC	**2**	*Cultivation in Holy Land*
5000 BC	**3**	*Cultivation in Egypt*
200 BC	**4**	*Cultivation in North Africa, Sicily, Sardinia for Roman Empire*
AD 200	**5**	*Cultivation spreads to Britain, France, lower Germany*

BARLEY
10,000 BC	**1**	*Growing wild in Holy Land*
5000 BC	**2**	*Cultivation in Egypt*
3000 BC	**3**	*Cultivation in China and Japan*
500 BC	**4**	*Cultivation in Ancient Greece*
AD 300	**5**	*Grown in Scandinavia, northern Germany, Scotland*

Meanwhile, outside the sphere of Roman influence, the Scandinavians, Scots, and northern Germans were forced by their climates to rely on cakes and gruels made from barley or oats. The Gaulish tribes, despite imperial sway, continued to cherish their barley beer—a spiced, fermented brew of barley, oats, rye, and sometimes wheat, aged in pottery casks. The recipe survived to be passed onto the monks who came with Christianity.

PITILESS NATURE

Europeans found that their daily bread was dependent on the combination of microclimate and soil quality that characterized each region. Wheat grew only on rich earth, where both summers and winters were mild. Rye and barley were more adaptable, and could be grown under more extreme temperatures in less fertile terrain, while oats survived the worst that nature could bring, particularly in rocky, mountainous regions.

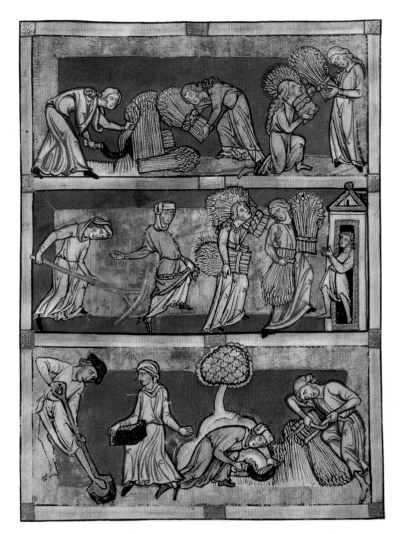

The twelfth-century German manuscript, The Mirror of the Virgin, *held at Bonn's Rheinisches Landesmuseum, provides a delightful record of medieval life, including the reaping, threshing, collecting, and sowing of grain.*

Real wheat bread was a luxury, reserved for the nobility and grander clerics and abbots. When times were good, *maslin*—a bread made of flour ground from wheat, rye, and barley—was the fare of the common man. However, the proportion of wheat in the mixture diminished with social status. "Gruel bread," made from rye, barley, and dried legume flour, was the fare of destitution and famine. Millet, a staple of the poorest districts and a standby for periods of fasting prescribed by the Church, was a nutritious alternative grain, boiled into a porridge—sometimes left to harden into a "cake"—and flavored with butter, lard, olive oil, or milk.

By the sixteenth century, in the homes of wealthy Russians and middle Europeans, there were as many as 20 varieties of porridge, made from wheat, barley, oats, and legumes, which were served with or without meat. Even in the nineteenth century, the European country kitchen was still based on grain. Vegetables were not prized, but were viewed as a stop-gap until the new season's grain was ripe for harvest. Meat was destined for sale and only coincidentally for subsistence; chickens were for eggs. Only grain could guarantee a full belly. Slowly, buckwheat and the potato were to replace millet in the West, and although rye was retained, it was for its flavor, not for survival.

WHEAT & BARLEY: EARLY GRAINS

ABOVE

Chapattis are flat, unleavened Indian bread, made from whole-wheat flour. Here, they are being prepared for breakfast.

RIGHT

The golden, feathery ears of barley have a short growing season, but can withstand disease and weather better than wheat.

*I*n the New Testament, the Third Horseman of the Apocalypse measures out portions of wheat and barley, together with wine and oil, to ensure famine does not rise from injustice—an indication of the importance of these two grains to the ancients.

Barley was, without doubt, one of the foundations of civilization throughout Asia, and had been known in China since the third millennium B.C. Together with wheat, it can trace an even earlier pedigree in the Middle East and the eastern Mediterranean. Its robust character—it is capable of surviving frost, flood, and drought—meant it could be grown from the equator to the southern limits of the Arctic.

Among the Greeks, barley was valued: the Spartans, who upheld strength over finesse, looked to barley porridge to nourish their young men; Olympic competitors were allotted a measure of barley meal, and a stew of barley and roast vegetables was the daily meal of the professional gladiators of Thessaly. The early Romans knew two kinds of the grain—primitive double-row barley

extracted wheatgerm (the untreated embryo—a health-food supplement), and in a variety of flours (from finest white bread flour and powdery cake flour to stoneground wholewheat). One of 14 existing species, common wheat divides farther into *hard* wheat, whose dry, tough kernels need thorough milling, making the best bread flour, and *soft* wheat, which has less protein content, and is therefore a more workable flour, better for cakes and pastries. Amber or durum wheat (*Triticum durum*), the basis of semolina and pasta, is an exceptionally high-gluten species, requiring warm, dry growing conditions. It thrives mainly in the Mediterranean and in the Great Plains of the U.S.A., where it became an economically important grain after Italian supplies were disrupted during World War I. These two species account for almost 100 percent of commercially grown wheat.

Wheat is exceptionally nutritious. The husked grain (the kernel or wheat berry) is rich in protein, carbohydrates, B vitamins, phosphorus, calcium, mineral salts, and seven essential amino acids. In health-conscious Western countries, particularly the U.S.A., crunchy

Tabbouleh—Lebanese Cracked Wheat Salad

Variations of this salad are popular throughout the Middle East, from Turkey to Egypt.

SERVES 4 TO 6
1 cup (6 oz/175 g) bulgur
l large bunch fresh parsley leaves, trimmed from stems and minced
4 tablespoons minced fresh mint leaves
½ cucumber, peeled, seeded, and finely chopped
½ red bell pepper, cored, seeded, and finely chopped
6 green onions, trimmed and finely chopped
1 large tomato, seeded and finely chopped
⅔ cup (5 fl oz/150 ml) lemon juice
⅔ cup (5 fl oz/150 ml) olive oil
Salt and freshly ground pepper to taste
Fresh mint leaves, to garnish

Soak the bulgur in a bowl of cold water for 30 minutes. Drain and strain it thoroughly, squeezing out excess moisture by hand.

In a serving bowl, combine the bulgur, parsley, mint, cucumber, pepper, onions, and tomato; toss well using your hands. Add the lemon juice and oil; combine well. Chill the tabbouleh, covered, for 2 to 3 hours. Before serving, add seasoning to taste and garnish with the fresh mint leaves.

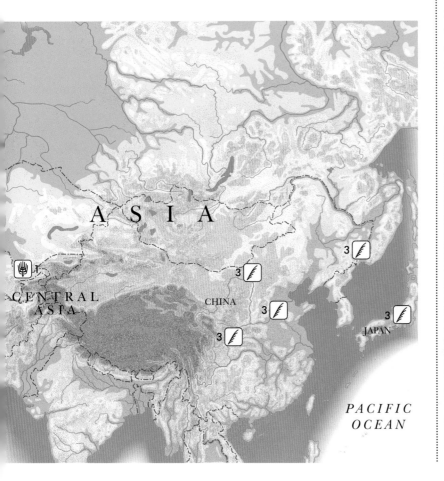

RIGHT

Wheat began as a wild grass but evolved into a nutritious plant.

TRADE ROUTES

By the end of the fifteenth century, grain had reached the Ukraine.

germinated wheat is recommended for salads and homemade breads, while cooked kernels are used in salads, stews, and pilafs. Wheat in this whole grain form, however, has not taken off commercially, and can only be found in wholefood and health-food stores. Cracked wheat, or bulgur, boasts a long history in the Middle East, and is enjoying huge success in the U.S.A. and Europe. But bread and pasta are still the forms in which most people in the world eat their wheat.

🌾	Wheat

Spread of wheat
- AD 528
- AD 737
- AD 1028
- AD 1478

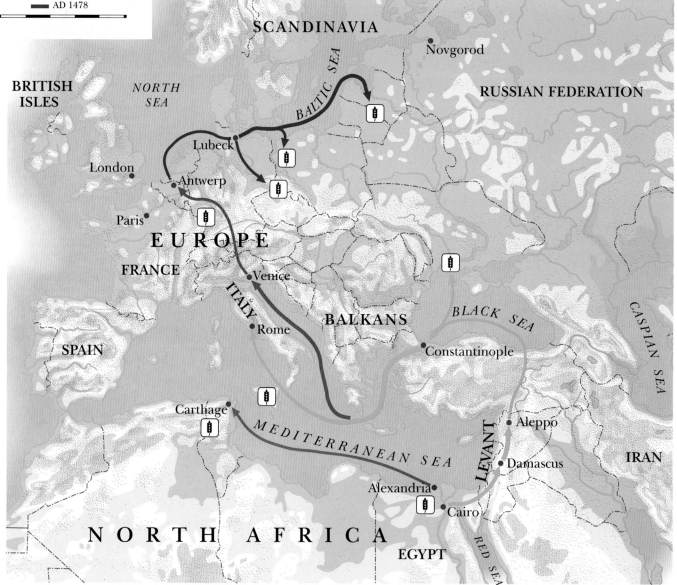

SCANDINAVIA

Novgorod

RUSSIAN FEDERATION

BRITISH ISLES

NORTH SEA

BALTIC SEA

London

Lubeck

Antwerp

Paris

EUROPE

FRANCE

Venice

BALKANS

BLACK SEA

Rome

Constantinople

CASPIAN SEA

SPAIN

Carthage

MEDITERRANEAN SEA

LEVANT

Aleppo

Damascus

IRAN

Alexandria

Cairo

NORTH AFRICA

RED SEA

EGYPT

BUCKWHEAT, OATS, & MILLET

*T*hese three plants are peasant foodstuffs, once cultivated as bulwarks against hunger in the most difficult of climates and on the most unrewarding of soils, the resort of the desperate.

OATS: THE CELTIC GRASS

Despised by the Egyptians as a weed of the wheat fields, and regarded by the finicky Romans as fit only for animal fodder, it was Bronze Age Gaulish and Germanic tribes who appreciated that the common oat (*Avena sativa*) could be cultivated for the benefit of man. They, and the fabled Mongolian warriors of the East, were said to feed their young men on a gruel of oats to keep them fighting fit.

By the Iron Age, the feathery grain had made its way across the English Channel. Like their cousins on the bleak west coast of France, the Celts in the northern British Isles developed a particular respect for ground husked oats. This "oatmeal" lacked enough gluten to make leavened bread, but it could be griddle-baked as filling, nutritious cakes, or mixed with water and salt and slowly heated until it thickened into a gruel or porridge.

BELOW

An early nineteenth-century Yorkshire mother offering her children hot oatcakes. Behind her can be seen the hotplate over the open oven, into which coals or peat was shoveled.

BUCKWHEAT, OATS, AND MILLET

This map shows the areas where three staple cereals originated. Their spread through Asia and Europe can be traced by following the numbers which refer to the chronology (below).

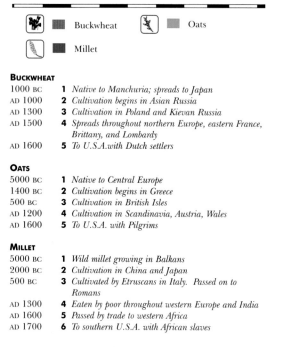

Buckwheat · Oats · Millet

Buckwheat

1000 BC	**1**	*Native to Manchuria; spreads to Japan*
AD 1000	**2**	*Cultivation begins in Asian Russia*
AD 1300	**3**	*Cultivation in Poland and Kievan Russia*
AD 1500	**4**	*Spreads throughout northern Europe, eastern France, Brittany, and Lombardy*
AD 1600	**5**	*To U.S.A.with Dutch settlers*

Oats

5000 BC	**1**	*Native to Central Europe*
1400 BC	**2**	*Cultivation begins in Greece*
500 BC	**3**	*Cultivation in British Isles*
AD 1200	**4**	*Cultivation in Scandinavia, Austria, Wales*
AD 1600	**5**	*To U.S.A. with Pilgrims*

Millet

5000 BC	**1**	*Wild millet growing in Balkans*
2000 BC	**2**	*Cultivation in China and Japan*
500 BC	**3**	*Cultivated by Etruscans in Italy. Passed on to Romans*
AD 1300	**4**	*Eaten by poor throughout western Europe and India*
AD 1600	**5**	*Passed by trade to western Africa*
AD 1700	**6**	*To southern U.S.A. with African slaves*

The relative lightness of the grain to transport and its ease of preparation, made it the ideal fare for crusading knights. By the time the Crusades were over, its health-giving properties had been more fully realized, and oats became a native ingredient of Austrian, Scandinavian, Welsh, and northern English cooking. It became most associated with the Scots: oatmeal porridge, called *fuarag* (from the Gaelic for "cold") in the Highlands, and *crowdie* in the Lowlands, was the Scottish national dish.

ABOVE
An early depiction of Mr. Quaker Oats.

From these British roots, the grain made its way with the Pilgrims to New England. Pilgrims and porridge became virtually synonymous, and this dependence was passed onto the Quaker brethren. Their devotion to oatmeal porridge was commemorated by name and logo when the U.S.A.'s first trademarked cereal, Quaker Oats, reached store shelves in 1877. Today we are beginning to recognize scientifically what our forebears knew intuitively; a diet rich in oats nutritionally outranks a wheat-based one, in terms of protein, fat, and B-vitamins, as well as contributing to lower cholesterol levels.

Three grades of oats are usually available: the finest is traditionally used to thicken soups and stews, for coating fish (usually herring or brook trout), and for mixing with wheat flour for scones. A medium grade, often rolled oats (which keep better than stoneground), is used for porridge. The stoneground variety is reserved for fresh bannocks, made with buttermilk, baking soda, and salt. The coarsest grade of stoneground meal traditionally makes the best haggis and the best oatcakes, signature dishes of the true Celtic cook.

Old-Fashioned American Oatmeal Cookies

MAKES ABOUT 6 DOZEN

2¼ cups (1 lb/450 g) packed brown sugar
1 cup (8 oz/225 g) lard or shortening
½ cup (4 fl oz/125 ml) buttermilk
1 teaspoon vanilla
½ cup (4 oz/125 g) sultanas
4½ cups (12 oz/350 g) rolled oats
1¾ cups (9 oz/250 g) all-purpose flour
1 teaspoon baking soda
¼ teaspoon salt

Heat oven to 375°F/190°C/Gas mark 5.
Thoroughly mix together the sugar, lard or
shortening, buttermilk, and vanilla. Stir in the dry
ingredients. Using your hands, shape the dough
into golf-ball-sized balls. Place 3½ inches (9 cm)
apart on ungreased baking sheets. Flatten into
3-inch (7.5 cm) cookies, using the back of a spoon
dipped in water. Bake the cookies in batches until
golden, about 10 minutes. Remove from the sheet
immediately and leave to crisp on wire racks.
Store for up to 3 weeks in an airtight container.

BUCKWHEAT—THE MOOR'S CORN

Buckwheat is not a member of the cultivated grasses
(*Graminaceae*) to which the other grain cereals belong but,
as *Fagopyrum esculentum*, it is rather a relative of rhubarb
and sorrel. Its fruiting seed has a dark beige, three-
cornered husk; when this is dried and split, the inner
"groat" is extracted. Groats can be dried, then cooked and
used as a starchy substitute for rice or semolina products,
or toasted until they attain a dark color and a nutty flavor,
becoming the *kasha* so beloved of Polish and Russian
cuisines. The husked groats are available either whole
(toasted or plain), or ground into meal, which is classed
into grades from coarse- to fine-ground. Whole groats (or
coarse-ground) is the best grade for classic Slavic dishes;
the finer grades are used in northern Italy to make a
buckwheat *polenta nera* and dumplings in both Austrian
and Alsatian cooking.

The dried or toasted kasha is also ground into a gray-
white flour. This is the basis, along with wheat flour, of
Russia and Poland's famous blinis, the classic
accompaniment to caviar or smoked salmon. Larger,
earthier variations of these plump little yeast cakes are

Soba Noodles: Japan's Dark Secret

In Japan, the word *soba* is synonymous with both buckwheat and buckwheat noodles. The making of fresh *soba* noodles is a highly regarded artisanal activity, and its survival in a commercially minded world is protected and promoted by the Japan Buckwheat Association. While the hand-rolled-and-cut fresh variety (*kisoba*) accounts for only a small part of consumption, its continued production by a devoted coterie of small farmers and manufacturers is a source of national pride. These producers beat the grain by hand, spread it out to dry naturally outdoors, and mill their flour using an old-fashioned grinder through which the grain is passed several times between siftings. These time-consuming techniques conserve the delicate flavors otherwise lost using more modern methods.

Before cooking, fresh *soba* noodles are a pale gray-black, veiled by a light dusting of buckwheat flour. After boiling, they are a pale translucent tan, and are slightly chewy. Traditionally, they are served at room temperature with a *dashi* dipping sauce; the cooking water is drunk afterward to ensure all the goodness in the buckwheat (which has more protein than soybean) is consumed.

Brittany's unleavened buckwheat crêpes and the stacks of buckwheat pancakes dripping in butter and syrup found both north and south of the Mason–Dixon line in the U.S.A. Lombardy in Italy has its *pizzocheri*, made with buckwheat noodles; but it is the Japanese who have really made an art, and a cult, of buckwheat noodles. Originally from the north of Japan, *soba* noodles can now be found everywhere where Japanese food is appreciated.

For a grain with such a varied heritage, buckwheat has a surprisingly confused and unreliable history. Its earliest appearance in Europe was at some point in the late fourteenth century. Since the grain was known in Manchuria during the first millennium BC, and was probably first cultivated in China, it would seem likely the Tartars introduced buckwheat during their sporadic raids on Kiev and the surrounding countryside. The North African Moors were traders in grain, as in everything else, and buckwheat is still known in France as *sazzarin* ("Saracen's corn"), a name it was also known by in much of Renaissance Europe. The English name, however, is a derivative of its Dutch soubriquet, *boek weit* ("beech wheat"), itself a translation of its Chinese name, reflecting the shape of the husk, which is reminiscent of a beech nut.

Buckwheat is a crop of nutrient-poor soil and requires little rainfall, so it thrives on steppes, rocky plains, and on rugged mountains. The stems and leaves become fuller in rich, dark soils, but the seed harvest is not increased. Buckwheat has the same caloric value as wheat and a high protein content, but it has virtually no B vitamins and loses its potassium when roasted. So nutritionally, buckwheat must be treated with more caution in a subsistence diet than wheat, barley, oats, and millet.

LEFT
Golden heads of millet shine against the green of foliage. While the Western world knows millet mainly as birdseed, it is a vital grain for much of the Third World.

MILLET—NUTRITION FOR MAN AND BIRD

A prehistoric food, millet has been relegated in the West to the status of birdseed—a protein-rich carbohydrate that increases the laying power of domestic fowl and is reputed to restore voice to a mute canary. But in other, less wealthy, parts of the world, particularly in Asia and Africa, it is still used whole or roughly cracked, boiled into porridge or mixed into stews. It is also ground into a flour which can be used on its own or combined with other flours to make a nutritious unleavened bread.

Sixth-millennium-BC Balkan sites have yielded traces of wild millet, and it is known that ancestors of this large family, which includes many strains of modern millet and sorghum, were cultivated by the Japanese and Chinese three millennia later. In fact, the Chou emperors believed "Prince Millet" to be the celestial forebear of their dynasty, and enrolled it among the five sacred crops. It suited those uncertain times, as it suits war-torn and famine-hit areas today, for millet has keeping qualities which far surpass those of wheat and most other cereals—it can be stored for up to 20 years in dry, dark conditions.

The Etruscans were among the first Europeans to acknowledge millet as a principal element of their diet; it may have been from them that the Roman legionnaires gained their affection for a ground millet porridge, *pulmentum*, served hot or left to congeal into a heavy cake. From the Middle Ages onwards, millet was the grain of serfs, indentured farmers, and peasants, used to feed both man and beast. With so many species and subspecies, at least one could be found to suit any soil type, from rock hard to marshy. Millet also enabled peasants to avoid tolls exacted by landlords for using communal mills and ovens, a necessity for baked breads. By the early twentieth century, however, millet in Europe had become little more than a folk memory, preserved in some regional recipes

Today, there are certain regions of the world where life could not survive without millet. In southern India, finger millet (*Eleusine coracana*) is combined with *dal* flour to make *dosa*; in other parts of India, great millet (*Panicum majorum*) is used for *chapattis*—both of these are the flat breads of the common people, sometimes the main food in the poorest households. In east Africa, from the Sudan to Zimbabwe, finger millet is also an important crop. In Nigeria, Ghana, and other west African coastal states, it is surpassed in importance by pearl millet (*Pennisetum glaucum*), bulrush millet (*Pennisetum typhoideum*), and sorghum, or Guinea corn (*Sorghum vulgare*), and it is used to make a gruel or a kind of wet pilaf. In this latter variation it appears as "mealies" or "millies" in the Gullah cooking of the southern states of the U.S.A. This "soul food" of the Georgian and Carolina offshore islands descends from the slaves brought in chains from Africa's Dahomey coast.

Ukranian *Kasha* and Onions

SERVES 4

½ cup (3½ oz/100 g) toasted buckwheat groats
⅓ teaspoon salt
3 tablespoons (1½ oz/40 g) butter
1 large onion, chopped
2 hard-boiled eggs, chopped
Pepper to taste
Sour cream

Bring ⅔ cup (5 fl oz/150 ml) salted water to a boil in a large saucepan. Add the toasted groats (if plain *kasha* was purchased, the grains can be roasted in a dry skillet for a few minutes). Bring back to a boil, lower the heat, skim the surface of scum, and cover the pan. Simmer for 30 minutes, or until the groats are soft and the water absorbed. The *kasha* should be on the dry side. (If desired, the *kasha* can be more fully cooked by leaving it in a 350°F/180°C/Gas mark 4 oven for 10 to 15 minutes longer.)

Meanwhile, melt 2 tablespoons (1 oz/30 g) butter in a skillet. Add the onion and sauté until it is translucent and turning golden, about 8 minutes. When the buckwheat groats are ready, stir in the onions, the remaining butter and the chopped eggs; adjust the seasoning. Pile into a serving dish and serve with sour cream on the side.

$\mathcal{M}$AIZE: THE NEW WORLD'S GIFT

*H*istorically, the term "corn" has been used to denote any grain which was the mainstay of a particular nation or area. But the culture of maize was so important to the New World that finally the archaic term "corn" was assumed by the yellow grain.

ABOVE

A majolica tile by Minton & Co, c. 1855, from a series on fruits and grains produced by the company. Five species of maize supply cornflour, cornmeal, hominy, grits and popcorn, as well as fresh sweet corn.

Today, the word "maize" (from the West Taino Indian *mahiz*) remains the chosen term of historians and botanists but, to the contemporary English-speaker, "corn" now means only one thing. Corn is second only to rice in tons of grain harvested worldwide, yet many Europeans have little idea of just how important corn is in other parts of the world. In the U.S.A., the corn crop is equal to the combined harvest of wheat, barley, oats, rice, rye, and millet; it is the staple grain of Mexico, Central America, and parts of South America; while central and southern Africa rely on "mealies" (corn porridge) to survive.

FROM THE NEW TO THE OLD WORLD

The real importance of this huge international harvest is somewhat distorted by the fact that a large proportion is grown purely as animal fodder. Until recently, to the Belgians, Germans, Swiss, Italians, and the majority of the French and Spanish, the idea of eating corn in any form was risible—it was the fare of poultry and cattle, or the pitiably poor. Only now, largely due to successive waves of mainstream American, Tex-Mex, and Mexican restaurants in places like London, Paris, and Berlin, have the attractions of eating corn-on-the-cob, corn relish, cornbread, tacos, and other corn-based recipes found favor.

Corn (*Zea mays*) is the only grain native to North America, a genus all to itself, and the only species in its genus. It is really a giant grass, of which no wild forms exist today. Because of its uniquely evolved seedhead (the corn-on-the-cob), corn cannot seed itself without human intervention; it has been so for thousands of years. The earliest whole specimens discovered date from 5,600 years ago and were the remnants of a Mexican cave-dweller's meal. Other evidence indicates that in the intervening years, the plant was cultivated and the cob grew from a minuscule ½-inch/1-cm to the 8-inch/20-cm average we now expect on our plate; the largest specimen is the gigantic 2-foot/60-cm-long cob produced by a type of soft corn in Mexico's Jala valley. The corn plants grown by the Aztec, Mayan, and Inca civilizations were the forerunners of the plants farmed today by the people of Mexico, Bolivia, Ecuador, Peru and Brazil.

When Columbus landed in Cuba in 1492, he and his men discovered the Indians used this new grain much as the Europeans used wheat. They took corn samples back to their sponsors, Ferdinand and Isabella. On his return to Spain in 1527, Cortés brought back additional strains, so that by the early sixteenth century, the value of this new crop was established. However, Charles V, the subsequent ruler, thought it a heathen's grain unfit for Christians, so it was firmly relegated to duty as animal feed.

A GROWING MARKET

It needed the impetus of the Venetian traders and the Turkish overlords who ruled the eastern Mediterranean to follow the lead of the New World and make corn a meal fit for Europeans. The Venetians, ever open-minded and available to trade, were the first of the western European nations to cultivate corn. In the eastern Mediterranean, it seems to have taken root in the Nile valley and in Lebanon in the early sixteenth century, perhaps by way of Portuguese traders along the east African coast, or by courtesy of the Venetians. Either way, by the mid-seventeenth century it had spread though the Balkans and along the Danube to find favor in Romania and Hungary.

LEFT

In Guatemala women still clean and prepare corn the traditional way.

Corny Facts

There are hundred of varieties of corn, but ultimately all are members of one of five families:

Flint corn This, with dent corn, makes the best meal for cornbread. Traditionally, flint cornmeal was more popular in the northern states, where it made the dense breads and johnnycakes preferred there. However, it is a low-yielding corn, and hybrids of dent are fast replacing it. It is still grown in Africa, where its disease-resistant qualities are appreciated.

Dent corn Now the most commonly grown commercial corn, so-called because the kernels have a dimple. This produces the traditional southern-style sweet, starchy cornmeal.

Popcorn The hardest-hulled corn, another favorite of the Native Americans, grown for celebration and decoration. Heating the grains in oil causes the starchy inner core to burst through the shrinking outer skin.

Soft corn This is not grown on a commercial scale, but is cultivated by some specialist growers. Known as "squaw corn," it was the familiar type grown by Native Americans, both for hand-ground meal and cooking, and comes in a variety of colors, including red and blue. It is now found mainly in western South America and some parts of Mexico.

Sweet corn Pale yellow cobs with milky kernels, this is the one corn which will not dry successfully. If not cooked (either boiled or roasted) and eaten immediately, corn should be frozen as soon as possible after cooking; the sugar content decreases with age. It was not exploited until the 1820s–40s, when it began to be grown for the table and canning. There are always new varieties appearing which promise extra sweetness.

RIGHT

A night at the movies!

Polenta with Italian Sausage

Polenta may be fashionable in the United States now, but it has been a longtime staple from Piedmont, west of Venice.

SERVES 4

1 teaspoon salt
1 cup (4 oz/115 g) fine yellow cornmeal
2 tablespoons olive oil
1 lb/450 g sweet Italian sausages
l large onion, chopped
1 garlic clove, chopped
28 oz/800 g canned plum tomatoes with juice
¾ cup (4 oz/115 g) Fontina cheese, cubed
Minced fresh flat-leaf parsley

In a large, heavy saucepan bring 3¾ cups (1½ pints/750 ml) water and the salt to a boil. Add the cornmeal in a thin stream, whisking constantly. Cook the *polenta* over medium heat, stirring continuously, for about 40 minutes, or until the mixture pulls away from the side of the pan. (This can also be made using instant *polenta*, following directions.) Cover and keep warm.

Heat the olive oil in a heavy skillet. Add the sausage and brown; remove and reserve. Sauté the onion until golden and translucent, about 10 minutes. Add the garlic and cook for 1 minute; remove the onion mixture and reserve.

Return the sausage to the pan. Stir in ½ cup (4 fl oz/125 ml) water, cover, and simmer 10 to 15 minutes until the sausage is cooked through and the water has evaporated. Remove the sausage and discard any fat in the pan. Slice the sausage and return to the pan, with the onion mixture and tomatoes, breaking up the latter with a wooden spoon. Cover the pan and simmer 30 minutes.

Just before serving, stir the cheese into the warm *polenta*. Stir the parsley into the meat sauce. Serve each portion of the cheese *polenta* accompanied by the tomato-sausage sauce.

CORN COUNTRY

It was in North America, however, that both natives and settlers were able to make the most of the wonderful grain. The early colonists were awed by the thick, almost impenetrable fields, where corn did indeed seem to "grow high as an elephant's eye." Captain John Smith, the founder of Virginia's Jamestown colony in 1608, had been impressed by the provisions of corn carefully laid away by the local tribe against the hard winters. In the spring following the arrival of the *Mayflower* in 1620, the friendly natives who welcomed the Plymouth colony also instructed them on the planting and nurture of the vital crop. The first Thanksgiving witnessed the success of that fall's harvest, while the invited native guests introduced another delicacy at the feast—popcorn.

The Native Americans also showed the colonists how to cook fresh corn in vegetable stews, as well as how to roast and grind it to make cornmeal, adding ash to soften the kernels to make the meal more digestible (the addition of ash-lye releases the niacin trapped in the kernel). Although corn is rich in complex carbohydrates, potassium, and magnesium, its lack of essential amino

LEFT

Fields not too different from these must have greeted the eyes of sixteenth-century conquistadors looking for Eldorado—the "Cities of Gold"—on the North American continent. Instead they discovered a strange grain that could also be eaten as a vegetable.

A Corn-ucopia of Traditional American Dishes

Corn dogs Hot dogs impaled on a stick, coated in cornmeal batter and deep-fried.
Corn oysters Corn kernels, cornmeal, wheat flour, and eggs combined to make fritters.
Corn pudding Creamed corn batter which is baked in the oven.
Fried cornmeal mush Hasty pudding (*see below*), dipped in egg and fried in bacon fat.
Grits A classic southern breakfast dish, made of white cornmeal and usually served with sausage gravy or redeye gravy.
Hasty pudding Made famous in the song "Yankee Doodle" and by the Harvard Club of the same name, this simple cornmeal mush is enriched with cream and molasses.
Hush puppies Deep-fried corn dumplings.
Indian pudding A cornmeal and milk porridge, enriched with cinnamon, ginger, and molasses, served with cream and nutmeg.
Succotash A version of a Native American dish combining corn and lima beans said to have been served at the first Thanksgiving.

CORNBREADS
Classic cornbread Plain, crumbly bread, made with mixed cornmeal and wheat flour, milk, eggs, butter, and a dash of sugar.
Corn pone Cornmeal, water, and salt cooked over an open fire; of Native American origin.
Cracklin' bread Cornbread made in an iron skillet with pork crackling.
Hoe cakes Small, flat breads, originally baked on a spade over an open fire.
Johnnycakes A Rhode Island specialty, made with flint cornmeal and either water or milk.
Santa Fe cornbread A classic cornbread with added corn kernels, hot chilies, and cilantro.
Scrapple Scrap ends of butchered pork are combined with cornmeal to make a congealed pudding, which is then sliced and fried.
Spoon bread A custardlike cornbread, made with meal from dent corn.
White corn cake A southern variation containing egg whites, often partnered with southern fried chicken and gravy.

acids means it had to be partnered with other vegetables, and meat, to form a balanced diet. For this reason, the Indians usually planted corn, beans, and squash together in drills; these partners in the field were also partners in the pot. Such nutritional limitations were less understood when corn was first adopted by enthusiastic European and African societies, and virulent outbreaks of pellagra, a deficiency caused by a lack of niacin (nicotinic acid), followed. It was not until 1937 that the cause of the disease was actually established.

Today, more than half the world's maize is grown in the U.S.A. "Corn Belt"—the states of Iowa, Ohio, Indiana, Illinois, Nebraska, and South Dakota. The grain known to the Indians as "The Sacred Mother" and "The Provider of Life" is one of the most important buttresses of the international economy: the ultimate livestock and poultry feed; the source of cornmeal, corn oil, corn syrup, and cornstarch; a dehydrated or hydrogenated ingredient in numerous commercial soft drinks, ice creams, breakfast cereals, bottled sauces, canned fruits and vegetables, and candies, and a constituent polymer in many plastic, cardboard, and paper products.

GRAIN OF EASTERN PROMISE: RICE

R*ice is the most significant grain grown worldwide—both in terms of actual tonnage harvested, and in the utter dependence its cultivation engenders. It is the staple starch of more than half of the Earth's population.*

ABOVE

Rice paddies must be flooded for two or three months, so the surface must be flat, even if on a hill or steep incline.

There are probably some 10,000 historical and contemporary rice varieties, of which only about 1,000 are in cultivation today. Selective breeding and hybridization have concentrated on improving yield proportion, often at the price of flavor and quality. In areas where rice is the primary foodstuff there are marked preferences for the type and quality used in traditional local dishes. The U.S.A. is the world's largest rice exporter, but it produces only 2 to 3 percent of the world's crop; the rest is largely eaten where it is harvested. In order of importance, the largest consumers are: China, India, Indonesia, Japan, Bangladesh, South and Central America, and Africa. In China, average rice consumption reaches 300 pounds/135 kg a year (compared to 2–3 pounds/900 g–1.3 kg a year in parts of Europe and the U.S.A.).

BLOWN BY THE WIND OF HISTORY

It is uncertain whether rice first appeared as a wild plant in southeast Asia or in Africa. Certainly, its initial taming and cultivation was the work of the Chinese, who by 3000 BC had recorded its place in local agronomy; but it was the equally sophisticated Hindus who developed the potential of the grain. By 2000 BC it had spread eastward along trading routes to the Philippines, arriving in Indonesia about 1000 BC. It passed westward along the Silk Route into the hands of Arab and Hebrew traders, and through the latter's exile into Egyptian grain stores, but it was not until Alexander's conquest of Persia and India that it became an important grain in Byzantine court circles.

This plutocratic association has persisted in the eastern Mediterranean until modern times. There, rice is still regarded as the grain of the wealthy or of special occasions. It reached its pinnacle of reverence in Iran, source of the

Native Americans along the Canadian border have seen wild rice develop from a local foodstuff, harvested and threshed by hand, into an expensive gourmet delicacy, and finally into a supermarket item produced to commercial specifications.

word and the technique for pilaf, and a rich repertoire of Persian rice recipes still survives.

THE RICE TRAIL WEST

By the eighth century, the Moors were transforming Roman Spain into Allah's garden, blooming with sugar cane, saffron, citrus trees, and *arroz* (rice, from the Arabic *al-raza*). The dissemination of culture and learning in the Renaissance assisted the spread of the grain to France and Italy, where it was served as either a savory course, with or without meat, or a dessert. Before the debacle of the Armada, Spain had begun to export its Valencian rice to England, and the taste caught on, although the British climate was too cold to allow the seed to germinate. Rice pudding, still popular in England today, is a direct descendant of the rice steeped in sweet almond milk and cinnamon enjoyed in Tudor times.

There are several legends that credit a kind of "Johnny Rice-Seed" sea captain with the coming of the grain to the U.S.A.; none can be verified. It is certain that rice was growing in the Carolinas by 1685, and within 40 years South Carolina was exporting 4,500 tons to Britain. For the next 200 years, the state remained in the forefront of American production, although by the early nineteenth century, every southern state east of the Mississippi, with the exception of Louisiana, was in the market. Texas

Wild Rice

Also known as Indian rice, wild rice (*Zizania aquatica*) is native to the northern U.S.A. around the Great Lakes, notably the states of Minnesota, Michigan, and Wisconsin. It is not a true rice, but actually a lush aquatic grass with long, feathery plumes whose pointed brown-black seeds require long cooking. It has a distinctive nutty-smoky flavor that goes particularly well with game and poultry.

It was an important foodstuff for the Sioux and Chippewas before the days of the pioneers, and today Native Americans are still the only legal harvesters of the expensive, true "wild rice," which must be gathered and husked by hand and yields one pound/450 g of grain to every three harvested. However, there are now cultivated paddies in the U.S.A. and the Far East, which supply a less costly, more uniform, mechanically harvested grain.

Hot Fried Rice, Thai Style

SERVES 4

3 tablespoons peanut oil

2 onions, minced

1 green chili and 1 fresh red chili, seeded and chopped

1 pork steak, about 4 oz/125 g, finely chopped

1½ cups (8 oz/225 g) raw shelled shrimp or prawns

1 cup (6 oz/175 g) chopped white crabmeat or
  chicken meat

3 eggs, beaten

2 cups (10 oz/300 g) cold cooked rice (dry-boiled or
  steamed)

Salt and freshly ground pepper to taste

2 tablespoons nam pla (fish sauce)

1 tablespoon nam prik (chili sauce)

1½ tablespoons tomato paste

6 green onions, trimmed and chopped

3 tablespoons chopped fresh cilantro

Heat the oil in a wok and stir-fry the onions and chilies over medium heat until the onions are soft and very lightly colored, about 6 minutes. Turn up the heat slightly and add the pork; stir-fry for 3 minutes. Stir in the shrimp and crab or chicken, and continue stir-frying 3 minutes longer.

Pour the eggs in the center of the wok, and season to taste. Stir the eggs into the mixture until just beginning to set. Stir in the rice. Toss and stir the mixture until well combined and heated through; sprinkle the fish and chili sauces over, stirring all the time. Stir in the tomato paste and finally the green onions. Stir thoroughly. Spoon into a serving dish and sprinkle the chopped cilantro over.

joined the rice race only in the early twentieth century. Today, Louisiana and Texas are main growers, along with California and Arkansas. It is fitting that these regions, with large Creole and Hispanic populations, are America's rice basket. Both ethnic groups are enthusiastic consumers of rice, a legacy of the Spanish, who brought their taste for rice to the Caribbean and Central America.

ORIENTAL SPECIALISTS

China, Japan, southeast Asia, and India are generally considered the pivotal rice cultures. A Chinese emperor in the third millennium BC is supposed to have conceived the idea of the dyked, flooded rice paddy, designed to control the irrigation of the water-loving grain. The Indonesians perfected the technique of terracing, maximizing the use of a mountainous, rugged landscape which is divided between thousands of small farmers—the average plot in these populous islands is only one acre/0.5 hectare. These astounding rice terraces, with their vertiginous paddies rising almost 3,000 feet (914 meters) into the clouds, are sometimes known as "The Eighth Wonder of the World."

In India, one-third of all arable land is given over to rice; Uttar Pradesh, the huge coastal province, is known as "the rice bowl of India." Ironically, one of the best rice-growing regions, Gujarati, has a wheat-based (bread) cuisine, and the fine, separate-grained rice grown there is treated as a delicacy. In southern India, by contrast, rice is an everyday partner to soupy vegetarian and fish curries, and must have the requisite absorbent consistency.

Less rice per head is consumed in Japan than in Indonesia and China, but it is of higher quality and treated with great respect. The rice harvest in November is the signal for regional festivals, and the new rice is considered a seasonal delicacy, like the first wild grouse or late summer blueberries in other cultures.

RICE - A UNIVERSAL GRAIN

Rice is available in three stages of refinement:

PADDY RICE
Unhusked raw rice, found only in the Far East, where it is cooked as is (glutinous black rice) or treated for specific recipes.

BROWN RICE
Only edible husk removed, leaving outer shell (bran) intact. Higher fiber and vitamin content than white rice. Uncooked it is light brown; retains nutty flavor and some bite when boiled (cannot be fried). Long-, medium-, and short-grained varieties.

WHITE RICE
This is brown rice which goes through more treatment to remove the germ and bran, resulting in a white grain. Most white rices are *pearled* or *polished*, which removes any rice flour still clinging to the kernel. *Unpolished* white rice has not gone through this process.

The above rices are further divided into the following types (see map):

LONG-GRAIN RICE
The aristocrat of rices, used for pilafs, stir-frying, and other dishes in which dry, separate grains are desired. The description applies to varieties in which the grain is three times longer than it is wide. These include:

1 American aromatics Domestic hybrids with quite strong flavors, including Della, popcorn, and Wehani rices.

2 American-style domestic rices Hybrids of Carolina rice, named after the one-time rice state. This is one of the most popular, if unremarkable, rices in the Western kitchen.

3 Patna rice An Indian original, though now grown in the U.S.A. and elsewhere.

4 Punjabi basmati A highly regarded white variety, with low moisture content.

5 Surinam rice A delicate rice, with particularly long, thin grains—a continental European favorite.

6 Thai jasmine An elegant Thai fragrant white specimen.

7 Texmati A hybrid of American domestic and aromatic rices, not as bland as the former nor as delicate as the latter. Available in white and brown.

MEDIUM-GRAIN RICE
Slightly shorter and plumper than long-grain, these rices absorb more moisture in cooking. They are generally used where stock flavors the rice or a creamier texture is desired. Varieties include:

8 Italian risotto rices These are traditionally white, with a high enough level of starch (amylopectin) to make the interior of the grain retain a slight bite, while the outer coating melts into the stock. Mainly a product of northern Italy, the preferred types are *arborio*, followed by *carnaroli* and *vialone*.

9 Spanish Valencia-style rice This is the *arroz* used in classic *paella*, the dish of seafood, sausages, and sometimes meat or poultry made in a special copper pan, and in other Spanish-style dishes. The grains of this rice should stay fairly separate, but they are cooked thoroughly so they "bloom." This is also the type of rice preferred in Central and South America.

10 Sushi rice An Asian-style rice (*see above right*) of medium length, but high in amylopectin so it sticks together.

SHORT-GRAIN RICE
The shortest varieties, often appearing almost round. They include:

11 Asian-style rices The "sticky" or glutinous rices popular throughout the Far East. They are high in amylopectin, which allows the rice to be rolled into a ball to be eaten, be used as stuffing for lotus leaves, or sweetened and used in desserts. They are generally available only in oriental markets. (There are a few long-grained glutinous varieties, but these are only available in the East.)

PUDDING RICE
Most commonly the polished white rice used in a range of European puddings. Health-food stores stock brown varieties.

SPECIAL TREATMENTS
Certain rices are subjected to processes designed to make them easier to cook:

Converted or parboiled rice. The rice is industrially soaked, steamed, and dried before it is husked and milled. This process forces the vitamins and minerals from the outer layers into the kernel, thus conserving most of the brown rice nutrients in white rice.

Instant or minute rice This process, introduced in 1949, mills the rice, cooks it under pressure, and then dehydrates it. It takes only a few minutes to cook, making up in time what it lacks in flavor.

Easy-cook rice. A variant of the above, which has not been subjected to the same amount of processing; it requires more cooking than minute rice, but has more flavor and texture.

American aromatics

Brown rice

Sushi rice

THE WORLD'S RICE BOWLS

Rice is available in three stages of refinement, and there are several different regional types, as this map shows. More detailed descriptions can be found on the preceding page. Many countries have evolved their own classic rice dishes; some of the most famous examples are listed in the keybox (below).

■ Long-grain ■ Medium-grain

☐ Short-grain ◯ Classic Rice Dishes

④ **INDONESIA** *Rystaffel* "Rice table" (a medley of spiced fish, meat, and vegetable dishes centered around rice) ① **CHINA** *Lotus rice* (glutinous rice wrapped in lotus leaves) ⑮ **THAILAND** *Coconut rice* (fragrant rice cooked in coconut milk) ⑧ **JAPAN** *Sushi* (steamed sticky rice wrapped with fresh new fish and/or seaweed) ③ **INDIA** *Biryani* (rich Mogul rice *pilau,* mixed with spices, meat, or poultry and nuts) ⑤ **IRAN** *Pollo* (lamb or poultry pieces and rice baked with pomegranate juice or sour cherries and walnuts) ⑯ **TURKEY** *Pilau* (version of sautéed rice, mixed with cooked meats or poultry, diced fruit, and spices) ⑥ **IRAQ** *Timman* (boiled or steamed rice with *smen* [clarified butter]) ⑩ **LIBYA** *Riz el Tammar* (rice with chopped date, pistachios, and orange water) ⑨ **JORDAN** *Riz bi Sh'Riyah* (rice mixed with vermicelli and pine nuts) ⑬ **SAUDI ARABIA** *Dajaj M'Ashi* (chicken stuffed with rice, garlic, and almonds) ⑫ **MOROCCO** *Poulet farci* (chicken stuffed with rice, tomatoes, and cilantro) ⑦ **ITALY** *Risotto* (short-grained rice cooked with stock, fish, or vegetable, leeks, and cheese) ⑭ **SPAIN** *Paella Valencia* (spicy rice sautéed and baked with a selection of shellfish and/or poultry, rabbit, and sausage) ②
ENGLAND *Rice pudding* (rice cooked in milk with spices and raisins) ⑪ **MEXICO** *Arroz con frijoles* (rice and beans in tomato sauce) ⑰ **U.S.A.** *Boiled rice* (usually served as a side dish to poultry)

BELOW
Risotto uses rice as its basic ingredient. This recipe for Artichoke Risotto comes from Sicily.

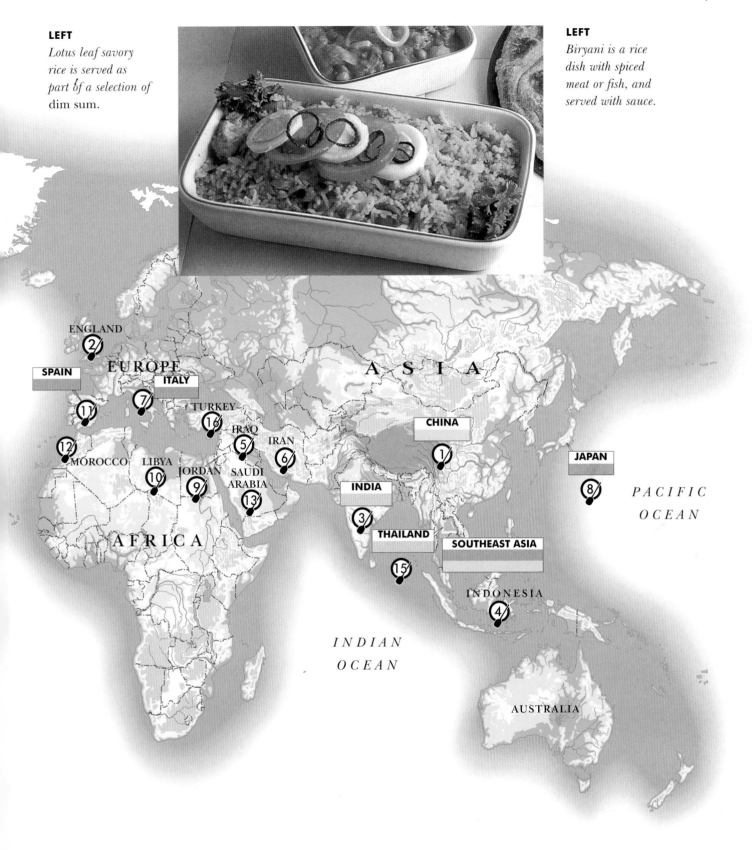

ENGLAND
②

SPAIN

EUROPE

ITALY
⑦

①

TURKEY
⑯

IRAQ
⑤

IRAN
⑥

SPAIN
⑪

⑫
MOROCCO

LIBYA
⑩

JORDAN
⑨

SAUDI
ARABIA
⑬

A S I A

CHINA
①

JAPAN
⑧

INDIA
③

THAILAND
⑮

SOUTHEAST ASIA

INDONESIA
④

AFRICA

PACIFIC
OCEAN

INDIAN
OCEAN

AUSTRALIA

PASTA & SEMOLINA

Cereal flour is generally used in one of four ways: as baked or fried bread; as a porridge; as boiled or baked pasta or dumpling; or as a steamed couscous. Pastas and couscous made from durum-wheat semolina combine lightness with notable character.

BELOW
"Branches" of tagliatelle dry in the open air outside a small local factory in a northern Italian town.

The Chinese and Italians have long disputed the invention of pasta, a foodstuff of which both can boast a long and innovative history. For many years the introduction of pasta to Italy was attributed to the Venetian explorer, Marco Polo. He did mention sampling pastalike (the Italian word pasta merely means "paste") concoctions in the East, but descriptive records from the thirteenth century, before Polo returned from his travels, show that northern Italians were already eating something resembling today's lasagne and macaroni. There may even be an argument for a Middle Eastern origin, since contemporaneous Syrian cookbooks mention both couscous and a type of "soup noodle."

Implements for pasta and noodles

All pasta or noodles are boiled or left to steep in boiling water until they are cooked through.

Cutting wheel There are special cutters for ravioli, and pastry wheels are used to create a decorative edge.

THE PREMIER ITALIAN DISH

Whatever the true derivation, the Italians' appreciation and development of the form is undisputed. To date, there are some 200 shapes of Italian pasta cataloged, while certain regions claim particular pasta types as their own: the Neapolitans *maccheroni* (macaroni); the Romans ravioli and fettucine; the Bolognaise *tortellini*; the Genoese *trenette*, and the Tuscans *penne*—to say nothing of the complementary sauces devised by these and many other regions of Italy.

By the sixteenth century, pasta was becoming an art form in Italy. Catherine de Medici introduced it to France, although it did not make much impact at the time. It took Napoleon's imperial conquests to bring Italy closer to France and macaroni and *vermicelli* into French cookbooks. Macaroni in a cheese sauce was a dish familiar to eighteenth-century English and American cooks (the pasta appears in the ditty "Yankee Doodle" and was served by Jefferson at the White House). However, it was not until the fashion for the Grand Tour reached its zenith in Regency England, and the flood of Italian immigration began in late-nineteenth-century America that spaghetti and its cousins came into the national consciousness and kitchen. By the 1930s and 40s Italian pasta had taken the U.S.A. by storm.

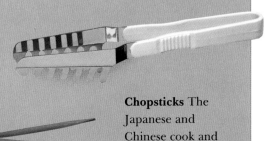

Tongs In Europe, special pasta spoons, that look rather like tongs, are used to lift and serve pasta.

Chopsticks The Japanese and Chinese cook and turn noodles in boiling water with chopsticks.

Steamer In Japan a bamboo strainer or basket, known as a *zaru*, is used to drain the noodles, and in China a finely meshed deep drainer.

Cannelloni, Catalonian Style

SERVES 6

¼ cup (2 fl oz/60 ml) olive oil
1 onion, chopped
8 oz/225 g ground lean veal
8 oz/225 g ground lean pork
6 chicken livers, trimmed and chopped
1 sweet Spanish (or Italian) sausage, about 6 oz/175 g, chopped
3 tomatoes, peeled, seeded, and chopped
2 teaspoons ground cinnamon
Salt and freshly ground pepper to taste
12 fresh sheets or rolls of cannelloni dough
2 tablespoons (1 oz/25 g) grated Manchego or other sharp, hard cheese

SAUCE

3 tablespoons (1½ oz/40 g) butter
2½ tablespoons flour
3¾ cups (1½ pints/750 ml) milk
Salt and freshly ground pepper to taste
2 egg yolks, beaten

Heat 3 tablespoons of oil in a heavy skillet. Add the onion and cook until it is translucent and soft, about 5 minutes. Add the remainder of the oil, heat it, and add the meats, livers, and sausage. Fry for about 20 minutes, stirring constantly, until brown and cooked. Stir in the tomatoes and cinnamon. Continue cooking until the tomatoes are soft and have broken up. Using a slotted spoon, transfer the meat mixture to the bowl of a large food processor (for a smaller machine, do this in batches). Process briefly to combine and finely grind, but do not make a paste; season to taste. When cool, stuff the cannelloni sheets or rolls. Place in an oiled baking dish in one layer.

To make the sauce, melt the butter in a saucepan. Stir in the flour and cook for 1 minute. Stir in the milk slowly until the sauce is smooth. Season to taste and add the egg yolks. Cook over low heat until just thickened.

Pour the sauce over the cannelloni, sprinkle with the grated cheese. Bake for 20 to 25 minutes until bubbling and browned.

REGIONAL PASTA DISHES

*The main regions of Italy are shown
on the map. Each region has a
numbered symbol relating to a pasta
dish that is typical of the area.*

Pasta Dishes

① CAMPANIA

La Pommarola *(Pasta served with fresh tomato
sauce)*

② THE VENETO

Pasta e fagioli *(Pasta and beans)*

③ CALABRIA

Spaghetti al ragù di totano *(Spaghetti with
cuttlefish sauce)*

④ SICILY

Pasta coi broccoli arriminata *(Pasta with tossed
broccoli)*

⑤ EMILIA ROMAGNA

Pasta alla Bolognese *(Pasta with Bolognese sauce)*

⑥ MARCHE

Vincisgrassi *(Chicken lasagne)*

⑦ PUGLIA

Orecchiette con braciolette *("Little ears" pasta
with pork)*

⑧ ABRUZZI

Ravioli all'Abruzzese *(Ravioli Abruzzi style)*

⑨ SARDINIA

Culigionis *(Ravioli made with pecorino Sardo)*

⑩ LIGURIA

Pansoti *(Cheese ravioli served with a nut sauce)*

⑪ UMBRIA

Pasta con salsa di tartufi *(Pasta with truffle
sauce)*

⑫ LAZIO

Bucatini all'amatriciana *(Pasta with bacon and
tomato sauce)*

⑬ LOMBARDY

Tagliatelle con salsiccia e panna *(Tagliatelle
with sausages and cream)*

⑭ TUSCANY

Ravioli con spinaci *(Ravioli stuffed with spinach
and ricotta)*

LEFT
*The colorful combination of black
tagliolini, leeks and oranges,
creates a dramatic looking dish.*

TOP LEFT
*Tomato spaghetti is combined with
dried cèpes, red onions and fresh
sage for a flavorful meal.*

TOP
*This simple pasta recipe is made
from peppers, bacon and pine nuts.*

ITALIAN PASTAS

Italy is the king of the pasta cultures, with an ever-growing variety of flat, round, tubular, shaped, and stuffed options. The dough is almost always made with durum-wheat (semolina) flour, and sometimes eggs (which give fresh pasta malleability). The dough may also be flavored with vegetable paste (spinach, tomato, herb and garlic, beet, chili) or squid ink. Thickness and shape of pasta affect flavor and sauce-holding ability.

PASTAS FOR SOUP

These go under the generic term *pastina*; many are miniature versions of larger shapes; most names are self-explanatory. They include *anellini* ("little rings"), *conchigliette* ("little shells"), *nocchette* ("little lumps"), *semini de melo* ("little melon seeds"), *perlini* ("little pearls"), *ruotellini* ("little wheels"), and *vermicelli* ("little strings").

PASTAS FOR BOILING

These are unstuffed pastas, sometimes flavored with vegetables extracts, squid ink, or herbs, or enriched with eggs.

Bignoli *A long, thin tubular pasta, popular in the Venice region.*

Bucatini *A large macaroni.*

Capelli d'angello *"Angel hair"—thin, delicate strings.*

Conchiglie *"Conch shells."*

Ditali *Very small macaroni.*

Farfalle *"Bows."*

Fettucine *Long ribbon noodles, the Roman version of tagliatelle.*

Fusilli *"Little spindles," spirals.*

Laganelle *Ruffled strips from southern Italy.*

Lasagnette *Ruffled strips.*

Linguine *"Little tongues;" slightly thicker ribbon noodles.*

Macaroni *Pasta tubes of many sizes.*

Orecchiette *"Little ears."*

Paglia e fieno *"Straw and hay;" very thin ribbons of plain and spinach pasta cooked, and sometimes sold, together.*

Penne *"Quills;" tubular pasta with pointed ends; particularly popular in northern Italy.*

Rigatoni *Large "ridged" tubes, also called grosso rigato.*

Ruote *Spoked "wheel"-shaped pasta.*

Spaghetti *"Little strips;" comes in several thicknesses.*

Tagliatelle *"Little ribbons;" slightly wider than fettucine.*

Trenette *Long, thin straight noodles, like flattened spaghetti.*

Zite *Long, thick tubular pasta—zitone is even thicker.*

STUFFED PASTA FOR BOILING

There are many regional variations, but these are the most widely encountered. The most common traditional fillings are meat, pumpkin, or a spinach and cheese mixture, but today there are many imaginative alternatives, including smoked salmon, mushrooms, or puréed artichokes.

Agnolini *Much the same shape as a ravioli.*

Agnelotti *Said to resemble a "little fat lamb," nose between hooves—more like a tortellini, from Tuscany, Liguria, and Piedmont.*

Capellini *Stuffed "little hats."*

Ravioli *Usually square, with a crenellated edge; originally from the Genoa area.*

Tortellini *Bolognese specialty now widely popular. Crescent-shaped with ends twisted to meet.*

Tortellone *are even larger, usually 2 or 3 to a serving.*

STUFFED PASTA FOR BAKING

These pasta shapes (and in the case of lasagne—sheets) must be partially cooked or softened in water before stuffing and baking, using a recipe which contains adequate sauce to continue cooking the pasta.

Cannelloni *"Big pipes." These pasta cylinders are usually stuffed with a meat-and-tomato or a cheese-and-spinach mixture, and baked in a béchamel sauce.*

Lasagne *Pasta sheets baked in a pie layered with a meat, vegetable, or seafood filling. Sheets are available in plain or green (spinach) pasta.*

Lumache *"Snail shells." These are stuffed and baked up-ended in a sauce.*

Manicotti *A tubular pasta rather like cannelloni, very popular with Italian-Americans. Manicotti are usually stuffed with beef and cooked in a tomato-mozzarella sauce.*

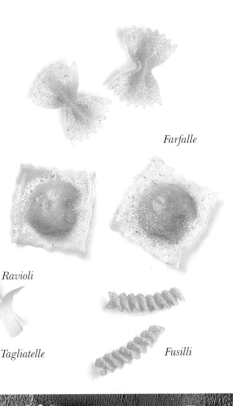

Farfalle

Ravioli

Tagliatelle

Fusilli

More Western Pastas

SPAIN

Cannelloni The Catalans claim to have invented these meat-stuffed pasta tubes. Most common fillings are chicken and veal, rabbit, and variety meat.

FRANCE

Nüdeln Alsace shares the German affection for noodles and dumplings. Often served with poultry (goose and duck), beef, pork, or veal.

GERMANY, AUSTRIA, AND HUNGARY

Nüdeln Ribbon pasta, made with egg and ordinary hard wheat, to accompany roast meats *Sauerbraten*, and stews.

Spätzle "Little sparrows"—egg dough forced through a strainer, then boiled, to accompany roast goose and goulash. In Hungry called *csipetke*.

POLAND

Kolduny Meat or cheese ravioli in clear chicken or meat broth.

Uszka "Little ears," stuffed pasta named for its shape, usually filled with wild mushrooms.

RUSSIA AND THE REPUBLICS

Pierogi Meat-filled Russian egg-dough squares, served in broth or moistened with meat juices.

Galouski Small egg-dough dumplings, a specialty of the Ukraine and relative to *spätzle*.

Manty A specialty of Uzbekistan. Steamed wheat-and-water dough packets filled with minced lamb.

ISRAEL, THE LEVANT, AND IRAN

Calsones A Sephardic cheese-filled ravioli; boiled and served with butter.

Rishta Noodles, originally from Persia, made with eggs, water, and durum wheat. If made in the Arabic manner, the pasta is baked (after boiling) with meat or vegetables.

USA

After Italy, the U.S.A. is the prime producer and per capita consumer of pasta. Canned pasta in tomato sauce and several shapes owe their invention to American ingenuity.

GNOCCHI: LITTLE LUMPS OF GOODNESS

Traditionally shaped and ridged using a fork and spoon, these "little lumps" or "little knots (of wood)" have traveled over much of Italy. Although they have been considered a specialty of the northwestern reaches of Italy (Liguria and Piedmont) and their border neighbor, the district around Nice, for several centuries, their history is actually more complicated. The earliest references to gnocchilike dumplings are in recipe books from the kitchens of classical Rome. In Rome today, gnocchi are made from semolina, milk, and eggs, much like those earlier versions must have been; then, Romans gratin the freshly made dough in a rich butter and Parmesan sauce *alla Romana*.

Eastern Pastas

Pasta has existed in southeast Asia and the Far East at least as long as it has in the West. The flour may be ground from grains or plants, and mixed with water, oil, or eggs. Many types should be soaked before boiling.

Buckwheat noodles These are Japanese *soba* noodles, straight and gray-brown. Fresh noodles are only available in Japan.

Corn noodles Called *bijon*, these thin, long, round noodles are made in southeast Asia with fermented corn mash. Sold dried, they are used in special Malay and Indonesian dishes.

Egg noodles Flat or round, made of plain wheat bound with egg, these are staples of Chinese cooking, available in a variety of widths and colors: from pale beige to bright yellow (the more egg the brighter the color). Usually sold dried; "fresh" versions can sometimes be found in oriental markets and stores. After boiling they are usually used in a stir-fry dish.

Konnyaku flour noodles Called *shirataki* ("white waterfall") in Japanese. The *konnyaku* flour is derived from the devil's tongue plant (*Amorphopallus rivieri*). The noodles are most commonly used in *sukiyaki*.

Mung-bean paste noodles Delicate, almost flavorless noodles used in China and Japan.

Rice noodles Made with rice flour. Rice vermicelli, most common in Cantonese and Malay cooking, are thin, white, and almost translucent. Somewhat thicker, round, long noodles are also used in Chinese dishes. Thai and Malaysian rice "sticks" are off-white and flat.

Wheat noodles The most common are of Japanese origin and include *somen* (thin, delicate white noodles, usually served cold) and *udon* (like very narrow tagliatelle, served hot in meat and vegetable recipes). The Szechuan cuisine of western China also uses white, flat, ribbonlike wheat noodles.

In other regions, however, gnocchi are more often treated like dumplings. Shaped into ridged ovals or crescents, potato-and-flour gnocchi are first boiled then bathed in pesto (Liguria) or coated with tomato sauce and baked (Naples and Nice). In Piedmont, cooks make both potato and semolina gnocchi, often coating the latter in spiced Fontina cheese and deep-frying them, while the Veronese deep-fry their potato gnocchi.

Today, spinach is sometimes added to semolina dough, although this is not traditional. Although vacuum-packed gnocchi in plastic packages are widely available in delicatessens and supermarkets, their rubbery consistency cannot duplicate the melt-in-the-mouth perfection of the "real thing."

Couscous with Garbanzo Beans and Cilantro

SERVES 6

4 cups (1¹/2 lb/675 g) couscous
2 large sweet onions, cut into quarters
1 sprig fresh thyme
¹/2 teaspoon ground cumin
1 can /14 oz/400 g) garbanzo beans drained
* and rinsed*
¹/2 cup (4 oz/115 g) clarified butter, melted
2 tablespoons olive oil
Salt and freshly ground black pepper to taste
Harissa (Moroccan hot-pepper sauce)
3 tablespoons chopped fresh cilantro

Place the couscous in a large bowl and cover with cold water. Drain immediately, return to the bowl and stir with a fork. Let the grains rest 15 to 20 minutes, until they swell.

Bring 5 cups (2 pints/1.2 litres) water to boil in the bottom of a *couscoussière* or steamer. Add the onion, thyme, and cumin. Line the top of the steamer with cheesecloth. Add the couscous. Turn down the heat to simmer, and steam until the couscous is tender. During the last 10 minutes of cooking, add the garbanzo beans to the boiling water in the bottom of the *couscoussière*.

Transfer the couscous to a serving dish. Drain the garbanzo beans and onions. Toss the couscous with the clarified butter and oil, salt, and pepper, a dash of *harissa*, and 2 tablespoons cilantro. Top the couscous with the garbanzo beans and onions, and scatter the remainder of the cilantro over. Serve immediately.

LEFT
Couscous is the staple carbohydrate of much of North Africa. It is usually cooked by steaming in a special pot with a fitted strainer known as a couscoussière.

COUSCOUS: NORTH AFRICA'S ANSWER TO PASTA

Couscous acts as the pasta or bulgur of Morocco, Algeria, Tunisia, and parts of Libya, and can be found in other parts of French Africa, Syria, and Palestine. It is an everyday starch, used to absorb the flavors of meat and vegetables cooked in broth or, tossed with oil and lemon juice, and served as a cold salad. The term has also grown to include dishes made with it, the most famous being couscous royale—a lavish, celebratory mound of semolina particles crowned with lamb, *mergez* sausages, and a medley of vegetables, served with *harissa* on the side.

Although the couscous we see in Moroccan restaurants is always made of durum-wheat (semolina) flour and is certainly the best-known variety, in fact, the term "couscous" refers to the treatment given the flour, rather than to the type of flour used. Historical versions use barley, millet, or corn flour, or varied mixtures of all three. Couscous was once made from the fresh, coarsely ground grain. But, probably in the thirteenth century, at about the same time that pasta became widespread in Italy, the technique of turning ground durum flour into separate "grains" evolved. Unlike pasta, couscous is not kneaded, rolled, or boiled, but steamed. This steaming conserves the shape and thus the nutrients; otherwise the semolina particles would disintegrate into a gruel.

THE MILLER'S TALE: BREAD

*B**read is the basic food for the majority of nations, the most economical use of grain in most societies. Generally speaking, the more sophisticated and affluent a culture, the more types of bread—and the more alternatives to it exist.*

The earliest bread was a flattish affair, a mere cake of compressed ground grains—most commonly barley, wheat oats, or rye (or in the Americas, corn)—baked on a flat stone or an iron griddle. In time, certain peoples preferred slightly puffed breads, the result of natural fermentation, baked in a wood-fired oven. Variations of this bread can still be found in many rural societies, mainly those of north Africa, the Middle East, and the Indian subcontinent.

THE FLOWERING OF THE GRAIN

Leavened, or double-rising, bread was the delayed result of ancient Egyptian ingenuity. While making barley loaves, they discovered this particular grain fermented quickly and at a controllable rate, producing a yeast which could be isolated, grown, and introduced into other foods. This inspiration saw the birth of the crafts of baker and brewer, though it would take additional centuries and other nations to develop both trades.

Yeast-assisted baked bread could only be made when grain could be crushed finely enough to become flour; "cracked" or crushed grain made too rough a mixture to leaven. It was the invention of the rotary mill, in which two stone wheels were adjusted so grain could gradually be ground finer and finer, that allowed culinary experimentation to flourish.

In Western society during the Middle Ages, bread was truly the staff of life. Although mixed-meal *maslin* was the daily ration of the laborer and servant, wheat breads were the staple of the nobility and monasteries. It is likely that, at medieval dinners, a coarse, heavy wholewheat loaf was used as a "trencher"—an edible dining plate that absorbed the juices of roasted meats and vegetables. The finest white flour was reserved for *paindemaine* ("the Lord's bread") eaten at the best tables and with the most refined dishes.

A WORLD OF BREAD

Bread is a staple food all over the world, and many regional specialties have evolved, exploiting a wide range of available grains, and even potatoes. This map highlights the countries with special bread recipes; the breads are described in the more detailed A–Z listing below.

1 Breads of the world

AUSTRIA *Kugelhopf*: Sweet bread with raisins. **1** **CHINA** *Bao*: Dim sum steamed buns, with filling. **2** **ENGLAND** *Crumpets*: Thick batter cooked on a griddle in round rings. **3** *Muffins*: Bread dough is cut into rounds and cooked on a griddle. **4** *Scones*: Savory or sweet, pieces of unleavened dough are baked in the oven. **5** **FINLAND** *Barley bread*: Sweetish bread with a soft texture. **6** *Rieska*: A flat rye bread. **7** **FRANCE** *Baguette*: Bread stick. **8** *Brioche*: A buttery bread. **9** *Pan de campagne:* Sour, crusty bread. **10** **GERMANY** *Potato bread*: Potatoes are added to dough with herbs. **11** *Pretzels*: Dough knots sprinkled with salt. **12** *Pumpernickel*: Dark, moist rye bread. **13** **INDIA** *Chapatti*: Flat whole-wheat bread. **14** *Dosa:* Thin pancake made with gram flour. **15** *Kulcha*: Oven-baked square-shaped flat bread. **16** *Nan*: Tear-shaped flat bread. **17** *Paratha*: A flat, unleavened bread, cooked on a griddle. **18** **IRAN** *Lavash*: A large type of flatbread. **19** **IRELAND** *Soda bread*: Bread leavened with baking soda and buttermilk. **20** **ISRAEL** *Bagels:* Dense, chewy dough circles. **21** *Challah*: Braided egg bread sprinkled with poppy seeds. **22** **ITALY** *Ciabatta*: Flat bread made with olive oil. **23** *Focaccia*: Bread flavored with herbs and olives. **24** *Grissini*: Thin, crisp bread sticks. **25** **MEXICO** *Bolillos*: Large, tapered crusty rolls. **26** *Tortilla:* Cornmeal flat bread. **27** **MIDDLE EAST/NORTH AFRICA** *Barbari*: Olive oil bread. **28** *Khobz*: A type of pitta. **29** **POLAND** *Rye bread*: Plain or caraway. **30** *Potato bread*: Silesian bread. **31** **RUSSIA** *Black bread*: Molasses rye bread. **32** *Pryanik*: Spice bread. **33** **SCOTLAND** *Bannocks*: Flat oatmeal loaves baked on a griddle. **34** *Griddle scones*: Dough rounds cooked on a griddle. **35** *Oatcakes*: Thin, crisp biscuits cooked on a griddle. **36** **SWEDEN** *Flatbrod*: A crunchy, salty unleavened bread. **37** *Limpa*: Rye bread, flavored with anise and caraway. **38** **USA** *Boston brown bread*: Dark, sweet bread. **39** *Cornbread*: Quickbread made from cornmeal, with cheese or bacon. **40** *New York bagels*: Onion, raisins, poppy seeds and cinnamon are added to dough. **41** *San Francisco sour dough*: A slightly sour bread. **42** *New England Buttermilk rolls*: Light rolls with a fine crumb. **43**

BREAD OF ANGELS

By the thirteenth century, London could boast two separate guilds, for the bakers of white and of brown breads, while "brewer's yeast" was sold by the ale-maker's wife in the marketplace. Since it took a manor of some size to brew its own beer and bake its own bread, the spread of communal mills and ovens in parts of Europe meant villagers could also expect a certain standard of bread. In England in 1266, the Assize of Bread fixed the price of loaves in relation to weight; similar laws were enacted in other European countries. Even today in France, while costs are not fixed, the flour type and weight of all loaves must be displayed, together with respective prices.

Through the next centuries, the baking of bread in cities, towns, and villages became more and more the work of master artisans, while in the countryside the homemade loaf was the test of a capable housewife. It was regarded as the most nourishing of everyday foods.

NORTH
AMERICA

U.S.A.
39 40 41 42 43

MEXICO
26 27

ATLANTIC

OCEAN

BELOW *Bagels and rye bread originated in Eastern Europe.*

ABOVE *Scones and English muffins make a perfect tea-time treat.*

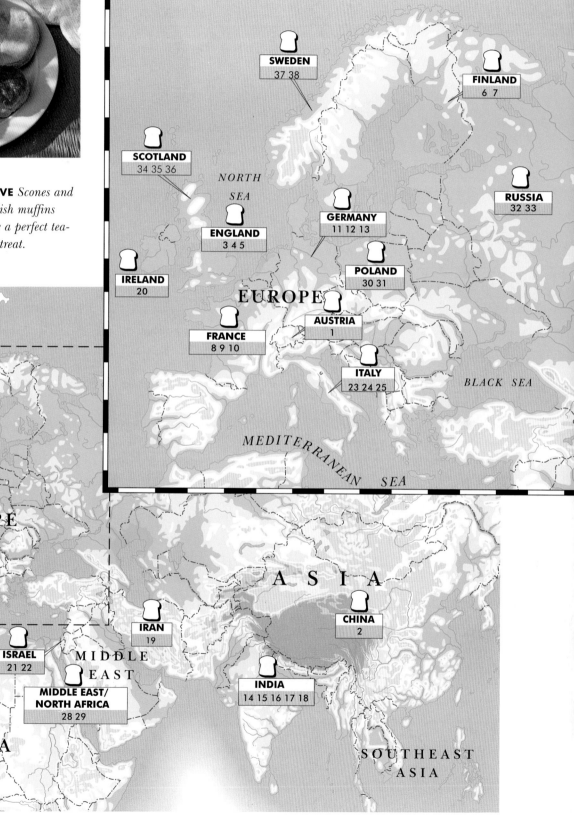

SWEDEN
37 38

FINLAND
6 7

SCOTLAND
34 35 36

NORTH SEA

GERMANY
11 12 13

RUSSIA
32 33

ENGLAND
3 4 5

EUROPE

POLAND
30 31

IRELAND
20

AUSTRIA
1

FRANCE
8 9 10

ITALY
23 24 25

BLACK SEA

MEDITERRANEAN SEA

EUROPE

ASIA

IRAN
19

CHINA
2

ISRAEL
21 22

MIDDLE EAST

MIDDLE EAST/
NORTH AFRICA
28 29

INDIA
14 15 16 17 18

AFRICA

SOUTHEAST
ASIA

Russian Barley-Wheat Bread

The cracked barley and wholewheat flour can be replaced with 3½ cups (8 oz/500 g) barley flour.

MAKES 2 LOAVES

1½ teaspoons active-dry yeast
3 tablespoons honey
1¾ cups (12 oz/350 g) cracked barley
1 cup + 3 tablespoons (6 oz/175 g) wholewheat flour
2 teaspoons salt
1½ cups (12 fl oz/350 ml) milk, lukewarm
2 tablespoons sunflower or vegetable oil
2½ cups (12 oz/350 g) white bread flour
1 egg

Dissolve the yeast, together with 1 tablespoon honey, in ½ cup (4 fl oz/120 ml) lukewarm water in a small bowl. Cover the bowl and leave in a warm place for 20 minutes, or until foamy and almost doubled in volume.

Meanwhile, in a blender or food processor fitted with the steel blade, grind the barley in batches, as finely as possible. Transfer to a large bowl and add the wholewheat flour and salt. Slowly beat in the yeast mixture, the remaining honey, the lukewarm milk, and the oil. Add as much of the white flour as needed to make a soft, malleable dough. Transfer the dough to the floured counter and, adding a little more white flour all the time, knead until it is shiny and elastic, about 10 minutes. Remove to an oiled bowl, cover with a dishcloth, and allow to rise in a warm place for 1 hour, or until doubled in size.

Punch down the dough, knead for another 5 minutes and form into 2 round loaves. Place them on a lightly floured baking sheet and leave, covered, for another hour, or until well risen.

Meanwhile, heat the oven to 400°F/ 200°C/Gas mark 6. Make an egg wash by beating the egg with 1 tablespoon water. Brush the loaves with the wash, prick the tops with a fork, and bake 15 minutes. Lower heat to 350°F/180°C/Gas mark 4 and continue baking for 30 to 35 minutes, or until the loaves sound hollow when tapped on the bottom. Cool the bread on wire racks and serve with unsalted butter.

ABOVE
Old village bread ovens such as this one are fired by wood; the bread is baked with the embers. The process requires deft timing.

But in many societies the majority of breads continued to be those which did not require an additional leavening agent or purpose-built ovens. Basic dough, made from flour and water, could be varied by the style of cooking and the grain from which the flour was made. Thus, Indian *chapattis* are made from wholewheat flour, Scottish oatcakes from oatmeal (of varying fineness), and Mexican *tortillas* from fine ground limed cornmeal—all three are dry-baked on a griddle. If chapattis are spread with *ghee* (Indian clarified butter), folded and fried, they become *parathas*; if they are made from barley-wheat dough, spread with *samneh* (clarified butter) and fried, they are Yemeni *bint-al-sahn*; if made from rice flour and crushed *dhal* (lentils) and fried in oil, they are South Indian *dosa*.

Even where ovens are used, the breads may remain simple, requiring limited baking and no forms or loaf pans. The wheat flour *nan* of India and the *khoubz* of the Levant and Morocco are both single-rising yeast breads baked in earth ovens. But while the Arab bread is passed into and out of the oven by a paddle, *nan* is traditionally baked on the walls of the Indian clay oven, or *tandoor*.

FISH
& SEAFOOD

The life of fisherfolk has traditionally been a hard one, with sometimes weeks, even months, spent away from home, and a safe return far from assured. Yet historically fish has been an essential source of protein for inland as well as coastal societies. Today much fish and shellfish has

reached the status of luxury food. Oysters, once the tavern snack of the urban poor, are a gourmet treat; deep-sea fish like turbot and halibut are more expensive than steak.

EARLY FISHING

The water that covers more than 70 percent of the surface of the earth teems with so many good things to eat that fish and shells became symbols of creation, fertility, and wealth.

Every ancient civilization caught fish, first by hand, later with lines and hooks, and then with nets and from boats. Archeological evidence shows that fish were smoked and dried as early as the Stone Age. Even land-locked peoples chose to eat fish when it was available. Fossil remains of fish bones in a cooking pot, thought to be 5,000 years old, were found in central Africa, despite the fact local game was plentiful.

Written evidence of the Spanish salt fishing industry, from the Roman historian Strabo, dates back to the first century BC. The Chinese are known to have been breeding carp for 3,000 years. In his treatise on the correct principles of eating and drinking of 1330 BC, Hu Sihui, an imperial dietician, gave a recipe for sliced raw carp flavored with radish, ginger, chives, basil, and peppered knot grass that would not look out of place on a modern menu.

BELOW

Fish from the Nile were an important food in ancient Egypt. This relief from the tomb of Meresanka in Saqqara shows a fisherman and his catch.

THE FISH WE EAT

Both ancient and modern peoples eat relatively few of the approximately 20,000 existing fish species. The most popular fish, such as cod, haddock, halibut, salmon, and several species of tuna and whale, have been overfished and are now in such serious danger of extinction that in many parts of the world quotas have been imposed. Yet, salmon, for example, was plentiful up to the Middle Ages and was the most popular freshwater fish for luxurious eating, followed by pike, perch, trout, turbot, and eel.

The earliest ocean fisheries were in the settled coastal areas around the Mediterranean Sea. Later the Atlantic, North, and Baltic Seas were exploited, and were greatly to influence the spread of trade during the Middle Ages and the colonization of the New World. Fishing for cod, which may have begun as early as the tenth century in Newfoundland, was certainly well established by the sixteenth century when Sir Walter Raleigh encouraged Queen Elizabeth I to secure Newfoundland and its rich cod-fishing industry. Dominated by the French in the early 1500s, by the middle of the sixteenth century, fish from the North Atlantic had become a major source of wealth for England.

Climatic changes also influenced fish consumption. The Little Ice Age began at the end of the thirteenth century and lasted until about 1700. Colder weather all over Europe made the growing season shorter, which meant there was less fodder available for the livestock that was overwintered for breeding purposes. As meat was both expensive and rare, fish became a significant trade item. Strict regulations regarding fishing in ponds and lakes made it difficult to obtain fresh fish. James IV of Scotland, who reigned from 1488 to 1513, passed a law making a second salmon poaching offense a capital crime. It was in the interests of the maritime nations to encourage fish eating; salt and dried fish were relatively cheap and easy to transport, and thus became an important part of the European diet.

Brain Food

Seafood has always been thought to be good for the brain. Modern research has confirmed this long-held belief. *Homo sapiens* is the only land mammal which evolved retaining a large brain in relation to body weight; the only other species which did so are aquatic. Human brain development, and that of the dolphin, requires a one to one ratio of the omega-3 family of fatty acids, present in seafood, and the omega-6 fatty acids, found in seeds. This critical balance of food was only available where the land and sea met, and this has led some scientists to speculate it was there that the human species evolved. The very earliest settlements were near water, and all five of the civilizations which first developed a written language did so on rivers or estuaries: the Yangtse in China, the Indus and Ganges in India, the Nile in Egypt, and the Tigris and Euphrates in Mesopotamia.

Seafood is important in the modern Western diet because, unlike meat and dairy products, it is low in fat and cholesterol, contains many valuable trace elements which are not easily found in other foods, and is very easy to prepare.

Fasting and Fish Days

Every religion has rules governing the consumption of food; some demand total abstinence from certain foods, while others require avoidance of particular foods at specified times. The Lenten fast of forty days before Easter dates back to the fifth century and commemorates Christ's fast in the desert.

At its strictest, fasting meant one meal a day and a meager one at that, often only bread and water. Until the middle of the sixteenth century, eating meat on a Friday in England was a hanging offense. Fish was consumed in place of meat, and at times dairy products, on Wednesday, Friday, and Saturday and during the forty days of Lent. Another forty meat-less days were observed during Advent. Eggs, frogs, beaver, unborn rabbits, and chicken (decreed to be aquatic) were allowed, but the main meat substitute was fresh or, more frequently, salted fish.

Good cooks could prepare salt fish well but it could also be monotonous and unpalatable. A fifteenth-century primer must have drawn an appreciative response from the schoolboys who read this passage: "Thou wilt not believe how weary I am of fish, and how much I desire that flesh were come in again, for I have ate none other but salt fish this Lent, and it hath engendered so much phlegm within me that it stoppeth my pipes that I can neither speak or breathe."

THE SHOALS OF HERRING

Herring was the single most important fish used for salting from the thirteenth to fifteenth centuries. The most active fishing centers in the North Sea were Yarmouth and Scarborough in England and Brielle in Holland. Most of the cod caught in the Atlantic were also preserved by salting, while oil was extracted from the fish's liver.

In the thirteenth century, a tidal change swept herring from the North Sea into the Baltic. The city of Hamburg was founded as a herring port and several northern German fishing towns, which had previously been members of various smaller trading associations or *hanses*, formed themselves into the more powerful Hanseatic League between 1250 and 1350. The league protected and advanced their common commercial interests, notably herring fishing, curbed piracy on the Baltic and North seas where the fish were plentiful, passed laws, provided navigational charts, and secured mercantile concessions for its members. It was at its most influential from 1350 to 1500, when it dominated commerce in the Baltic. In 1447, thirty-nine towns were members, but there were just nine when the league last met in 1669. In the fifteenth century, the currents shifted again and the fish moved south toward Holland. As a result the Dutch fishing fleet expanded into a powerful navy and Holland became a major player in world trade and colonial expansion.

LEFT

A Byzantine mosaic depicting the miracle of the loaves and fishes. The fish was already a lucky symbol when it was adopted by the early Christians. Later, fish was eaten on fast days for symbolic reasons and also because it was in the commercial interest of maritime nations to encourage fish eating.

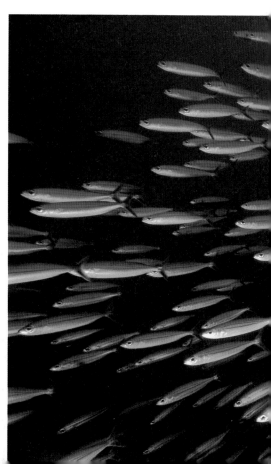

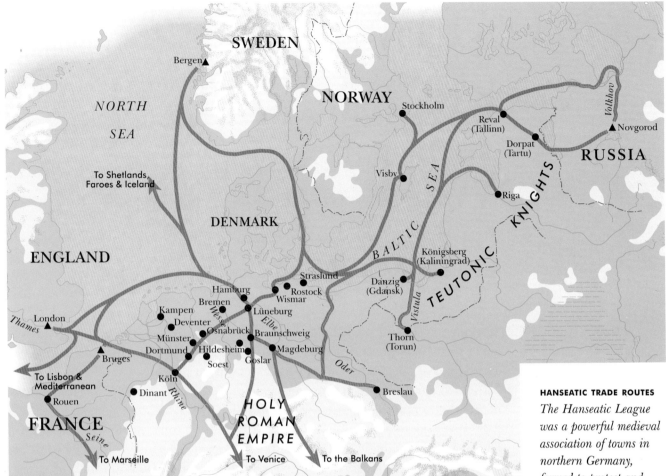

HANSEATIC TRADE ROUTES
The Hanseatic League was a powerful medieval association of towns in northern Germany, formed to protect and control trade.

● Major Hanseatic League town

▲ Trading outpost

▬▬▬ Hanseatic trade route

LEFT
In the early days of fishing huge shoals of many species thronged the oceans. Today, overfishing has caused a crisis in the industry, and stringent quotas have been imposed by every nation with a shoreline which has been exploited.

SUSTENANCE FROM THE SEA

While in some regions, fish are still caught with nets, hooked lines, and traps as they were in the ancient world, the world's oceans are being effectively strip-mined by factory ships which employ crews of 500 to 600 fishermen and huge drift nets.

BELOW

Brightly colored fish from warm tropical waters, which are still well stocked, are caught and transported to the far corners of the world.

Two main groups of sea fish are harvested. The pelagic (herring, tuna, salmon, anchovies, pilchard, sardines, menhaden, and mackerel) live near the surface. The demersal species live near the ocean bottom; the most commonly consumed species are cod, sole, and halibut. Cod is the name for a large family of fish that is still the most harvested in the world.

In 1948, the total world fish catch was 19 million tons. By the early 1990s it had increased dramatically to 97 million. The world's major fishing grounds are in the north Atlantic, North Sea, the waters over the continental shelf of Iceland and Norway, the Barents Sea, north Pacific, the Bering Sea, Gulf of

Alaska, the Peruvian coast, the shores of the southeastern United States, and the Pacific waters off the coasts of China, Malaysia, and Japan. The Japanese continue to eat more fish than any other country in the world. The brilliantly colored tropical fish from waters off the coast of Africa, until now relatively underexploited, are air freighted around the globe.

ABOVE

Fishing boats are now often huge floating factories, and their catches are enormous. Fishermen still brave the elements and go out in small boats to put fish on the menu.

Fabulous Fish Eggs

One of the most luxurious and desirable foods in the world is caviar, the preparation of lightly salted fresh eggs, or roe, of the sturgeon. Described in China before the tenth century, this delicacy is particularly associated with imperial Russia and Persia. Caviar is graded according to the size of the eggs. The largest and most expensive comes from the fish called beluga, the second largest from the ostra, which some consider to have the most refined flavor, and the third and least expensive from the sevruga. The salt content also affects the price; mallossol is the least salty. The very best caviar is fresh but some is pasteurized to keep it longer, which affects the taste. Slightly damaged eggs are pressed into a paste which has much of the flavor if not the elegance of whole eggs and is half the price.

The striking translucent red roe of the salmon is also delicious and far less expensive than sturgeon caviar. Lumpfish roe from Scandinavia, which is almost always dyed black or red, is not of comparable quality but is inexpensive and useful in the kitchen, and an excellent accompaniment to scrambled eggs or melted cheese. Other roes of interest to the cook are the soft roes of herrings, which can be lightly cooked in butter and oil and piled on toast, and the smoked roe of the cod which is widely available and is often used to make the popular Greek paste called *taramasalata*. It can also be thinly sliced and seasoned with lemon juice and black pepper. Less common is the smoked roe of the gray mullet, dark in color and almost as firm as a salami, which is very popular in the Mediterranean, where it is used in the same ways as smoked cod's roe and makes a fine partner for fresh figs.

RIGHT

A tin of Russian caviar, one of the most luxurious foods in the world.

MAIN FISHING GROUNDS, MAJOR CATCHES, AND DEPLETED FISH STOCKS AROUND THE WORLD

Over the counter fish are becoming ever more expensive as overfishing continues to decimate the world's stocks.

Main commercial fishing grounds

Major catches

Depleted stocks

ARCTIC OCEAN

GREENLA

CANADA

U.S.A.

PACIFIC OCEAN

ATLANTIC OCEAN

CARIBBEAN SEA

SOUTH AMERICA

PERU

CHILE

CRAB, SHELLFISH

PACIFIC PERCH, KINGCRAB, SALMON

MACKEREL

PACIFIC SALMON

LOBSTER

ATLANTIC COD, HADDOC

COD, HERRIN HADDOCK

FLOUNDER SOLE, PLAICE

ATLANTIC REDFIS MENHADEN

HAKE

MACKEREL

SOUTH AMERICAN PILCHARD

PILCHARD, ANCHOVY, HERRING

PRAWN, SHRIMP

RIGHT

Shrimping vessels spend days and nights on the open sea with nets spread.

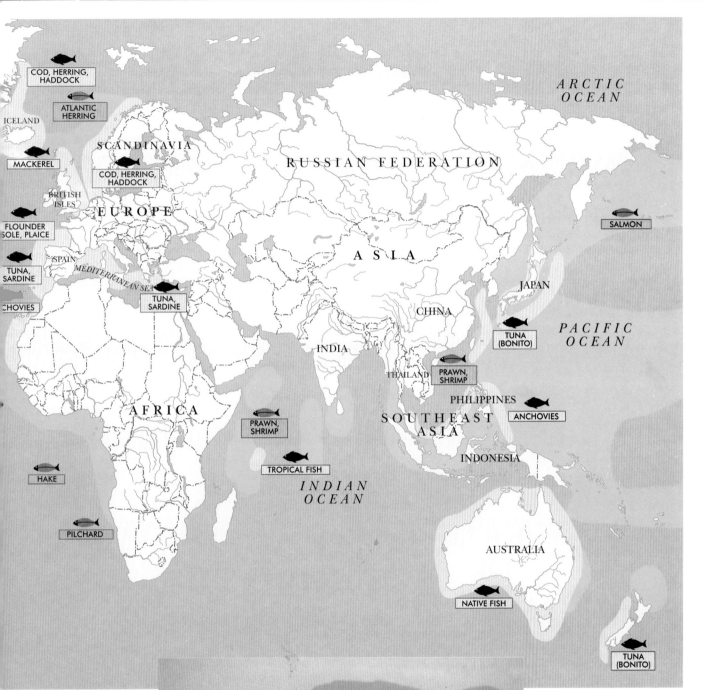

COD, HERRING, HADDOCK

ATLANTIC HERRING

ICELAND

MACKEREL

SCANDINAVIA

COD, HERRING, HADDOCK

BRITISH ISLES

EUROPE

FLOUNDER SOLE, PLAICE

SPAIN

TUNA, SARDINE

MEDITERRANEAN SEA

CHOVIES

TUNA, SARDINE

AFRICA

HAKE

PILCHARD

RUSSIAN FEDERATION

ARCTIC OCEAN

ASIA

SALMON

JAPAN

CHINA

INDIA

TUNA (BONITO)

PACIFIC OCEAN

THAILAND

PRAWN, SHRIMP

PHILIPPINES

ANCHOVIES

SOUTHEAST ASIA

INDONESIA

PRAWN, SHRIMP

TROPICAL FISH

INDIAN OCEAN

AUSTRALIA

NATIVE FISH

TUNA (BONITO)

LEFT

Fish auctions, whether at London's Billingsgate or in a small port, always take place in the early morning.

LEFT

Native fishermen take in their boats and nets on Lake Chappala, Mexico's largest lake.

An A - Z of Sea Fish

BARRACUDA
(Becune, sea pike)
Found worldwide in temperate and tropical seas, barracudas range from 1 to 5 feet/30–150 cm, but retain the firm white flesh of small fish.

BASS
(Sea perch)
Found in tropical and temperate seas, bass are usually cooked whole, although they can weigh up to 20 lbs/10 kg. The delicate flesh must be cooked with care.

BLUEFISH
Found in the Mediterranean and North Atlantic, this carnivorous, oily game fish is best broiled or baked. Can be cooked as herring, mackerel, or pompano.

BONITO
(Skipjack tuna)
Found in warm tropical seas worldwide, this fish has a strong, meaty pale flesh.

BREAM
(Dentex, porgy)
Found in the Atlantic, the bream is usually sold whole and has sweet, delicate flesh.

BRILL
A large flatfish found throughout the Atlantic and most often sold whole. Can be cooked as turbot or sole.

Red snapper

COD
Found in the North Atlantic, cod is tusually sold as cutlets or steaks, but young whole codling are a delicacy, as are cod cheeks. It is a robust fish which can be cooked in almost any way.

FLOUNDER
Found worldwide, though most abundant in temperate water.. It can be cooked whole, skinned or unskinned, and is often filleted.

GRAY MULLET
Found worldwide, but not related to the red mullet, it looks and tastes similar to the sea bass. Most usually cooked whole.

GROUPER
This large family of warm-water fish is found in the Caribbean, Gulf of Mexico, and tropical and temperate seas. It has an exquisite flavor and can be cooked almost any way because the flesh is robust and firm.

HADDOCK
One of the best loved north Atlantic fish of the cod family. Small haddock are a delicacy, but cutlets and fillets from larger fish are excellent fried or broiled.

HAKE
Found throughout the Atlantic, the hake's delicate white flesh requires careful cooking and is often wrapped in leaves or paper for steaming or baking.

HALIBUT
A large north Atlantic fish which lives deep in the ocean depths. The flesh is firm and white.

Mackerel

HERRING
Found in the North Atlantic and North Sea, herring are usually broiled and served with horseradish sauce or a strong mustard or braised in white wine.

MACKEREL
An Atlantic and Pacific fish which is usually sold whole. The flesh is dark and oily with a strong meaty flavor. It can be fried or broiled and is most often served with a robust sauce. Mackerel goes particularly well with tart fruit, such as rhubarb, cranberries, or gooseberries.

MONKFISH
Fishmongers usually spare us the sight of the huge ugly head of this fish, found in the Mediterranean and Atlantic. It has finely flavored, dense white flesh and can be cooked in almost any way.

POMPANO
Found in the Mediterranean, Caribbean, and along the Florida and Louisiana coasts, this warm water-fish is much loved in New Orleans, where it is cooked in paper to prevent the slightly dry flesh becoming too tough.

RED MULLET
Found in the Mediterranean and Atlantic, the golden mullet is slightly redder than the red mullet but both are true red mullets and are among the most prized fish in the world. They are often cooked whole with the liver intact.

SALMON
Found in the Atlantic and Pacific, this popular fish is now mostly farmed. The firm, pale pink flesh has a distinctive flavor. Smaller fish can be cooked whole. Larger fish are often cut into steaks.

SCROD
The New England name for a split and boned young cod (or young halibut), found in the Atlantic. It is cooked as cod.

SHARK

One of the most meatlike of fish, usually sold in chunks or steaks. It is found worldwide, but is most abundant in tropical and subtropical seas.

SKATE

Found in the Pacific, the skate has sweet, fine-textured flesh.

SNAPPER

Found throughout subtropical and tropical waters, the best known of this family is the red snapper which has agreeable firm flesh.

SOLE

Found in temperate and tropical waters, this flatfish is much valued for its delicate white flesh.

SPRAT

Found in European coastal waters, this small fish of the herring family is usually cooked ungutted and broiled or fried.

SWORDFISH

Because the firm meaty flesh can be dry, it is usually marinated before baking or broiling.

TUNA

(Albacore, bluefin, skipjack, yellowfin) The flesh of fresh tuna is firm and slightly oily with a strong flavor. It can range in color from light pink to dark meaty red. Tuna steaks should be basted with fat or oil to prevent dryness.

TURBOT

A large flat fish with a delicate taste which should be subtly seasoned.

LEFT
Turkish fishermen are seen here preparing their nets. In days gone by, their catch would have would have fed the local community. Nowadays, improved storage enables them to sell their fish further afield.

WHITING

A small relation of the cod with fragile flesh and an unassertive flavor.

Gozitan Salmon Baked in Pastry

This dish is good hot or chilled. Any firm-fleshed fish, such as swordfish or cod, can be used. Sage or mint can be used instead of dill and fennel

SERVES 4 TO 6

1 salmon steak, 2½–3 lbs/1.1–1.3 kg, in one piece
1 bunch fresh dill or fennel fronds, minced
4 tablespoons (2 oz/60 g) butter, at room temperature
Sea salt and ground black pepper
8 oz/225 g frozen puff pastry dough, defrosted

Heat the oven to 425°F/220°C/Gas mark 7. Grease a cookie sheet. Remove the center bone and skin from the fish. Beat the herbs with the butter and season with salt and pepper. Fill the fish cavity with all but 1 tablespoon of the butter, which should be spread on the top and bottom of the fish.

Roll out the dough thinly in a single piece. Put the fish in the middle of the dough and wrap it up, pinching the ends together to seal them. Put this package on the cookie sheet, seam side down. Bake for 20 minutes. Reduce the heat to 375°F/190°C/Gas mark 5 and bake for 30 minutes longer. To serve, cut it into ½-inch/1 cm slices.

A TREASURY OF SHELLFISH

Vast mounds of oyster, clam, scallop, and other shells that were gathered for food provide spectacular evidence of just how much shellfish prehistoric humans consumed.

Shells had many uses in the ancient world. They were traded as currency, as the cowrie still is in parts of Africa. Scallop shells were employed as cooking utensils and the ancient Greeks used ostrakon, or oyster shells, for inscribing the names of people to be exiled, or ostracized. The imperial purple of ancient Rome was a dye made from the murex shell and the finest came from the city of Tyre on the coast of Lebanon. Conch shells blown like a trumpet are still used in Buddhist and Jewish religious ceremonies (although for both the Egyptians and the Jews, creatures from water which had neither fins nor scales were seen as an anomaly and classified as unclean and taboo).

BELOW

An array of freshly caught shellfish is on display at this open air market.

MOLLUSKS AND CRUSTACEANS

The general term "shellfish" refers to two distinct types. Mollusks have shells, and this group includes bivalves, such as abalone, oysters, clams, mussels, scallops, cockles, winkles, whelks, and the sea urchin, an echinoderm. Aquatic creatures with a hard, jointed outer skeleton, such as crabs, crayfish, lobsters, and shrimp, are crustaceans, and various species live in both salt and fresh water. They regularly grow out of their shells, which are then shed.

Shrimp and langoustine, also known as Norway lobster and Dublin Bay prawn, are the scavengers of the sea. Fresh local shrimp are prized wherever they live, but much of the shrimp available now has been frozen and some will have traveled half-way across the globe before they reach the kitchen.

THE CLAM FAMILY

Clams are the most common North American shellfish, and they are now farmed.

CRUSTACEAN COUSINS

The flesh of the lobster is rich and dense with a subtle but distinctive taste, and is one of the most sought-after treasures from the sea. They are harvested in the summer months when they migrate from the ocean depths to the coastal waters

A WORLD OF SHELLFISH

Many countries and regions of the world are famous for their shellfish dishes, as can be seen from this map. In addition, several major cities have become associated with specific dishes. The geographical key (below) lists these regional specialities.

⬢ Countries with famous shellfish dishes

⬢ Cities associated with famous shellfish dishes

① **AUSTRALIA** *Big muddy crabs; Moreton Bay bugs; Queensland raw oysters; Yabbies* **②** **BRAZIL** (Northeast) *Frittada de Mariscos* (deep fried and battered shellfish) **③** **BRITISH ISLES** *Beefsteak and oyster pie; Cockles; Dressed crabs; Potted shrimps; Raw oysters on the half shell with lemon and chili vinegar, brown bread, and butter; Scallops and bacon; Winkles and whelks* **④** **CHINA** *Crab with black bean sauce; Jellyfish with mustard sauce; Prawn toast; Stir-fried prawns with chili* **⑤** **FRANCE** *Coquilles St. Jacques; Lobster bisque; Lobster Thermidor; Moules a la marinière; Plat de fruit de mer; Shellfish à la nage* **⑥** **GREECE** *Raw sea urchins; Squid stew* **⑦** **INDIA** (Bengal and Goa) *Giant prawns with spice, cream, and poppy seeds; (Kerala) Prawns poached in coconut milk with chili and coriander* **⑧** **IRELAND** *Oysters, brown bread, butter, and stout* **⑨** **ITALY** *Grilled scampi; Spaghetti con vongole* **⑩** **JAPAN** *Prawn tempura; Shellfish sashimi* **⑪** **LEVANT** *Horseshoe crabs; Sea urchins* **⑫** **SOUTH AFRICA** *Rock lobster* (grilled or barbecued) **⑬** **SOUTHEAST ASIA** *Prawns in green curry sauce; Prawn satay with peanut sauce* **⑭** **SPAIN** *Deep fried calamari; Seafood paella* **⑮** **U.S.A.** (East Coast) *Deep fried clams and oysters; Shrimp cocktail; (Louisiana & New Orleans) Oysters Rockefeller; Seafood gumbo; Shrimp jambalaya; (Maryland) Maryland crab cakes; Soft-shell crabs; (New England) Boiled Maine lobster; Clam bake; Clam chowder; (Oregon to Alaska) Dungeness crab*

⬢ **Dublin:** *Grilled Dublin Bay prawns* (scampi)
⬢ **Hong Kong:** *Deep fried soft-shell crab*
⬢ **New York City:** *Lobster Newberg; Manhattan clam chowder*
⬢ **San Francisco:** *Cioppino* (fish stew containing shrimp, crab, mussels)
⬢ **Shanghai:** *Clams in custard; Shanghai hairy freshwater crab*

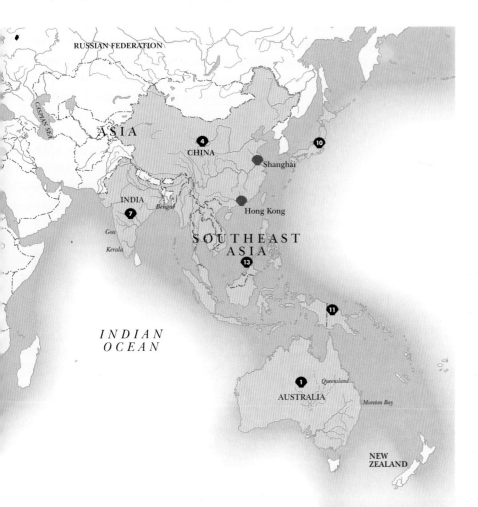

RIGHT

*The witty surreal
lobster telephone
was made by
Salvadore Dali in
1936 and is now in
the Tate Gallery in
London.*

stretching from Labrador to Delaware in North America, they are caught in traps baited with fish. They weigh between 1–1½ pounds/450–675 g on average, but lobster have been known to reach 30 pounds/13.5 kg, and these large specimens could be as much as 50 years old. Those only weighing a pound are sometimes called "chicken lobster."

Shrimp and Scallop Soup

Using the shrimp shells for the initial cooking improves both the color and flavor of this simple but elegant soup.

SERVES 4 TO 6

8 oz/225 g unpeeled raw jumbo shrimp
8 oz/225 g unpeeled raw small shrimp
4 sea scallops, halved
⅔ cup (5 fl oz/150 ml) dry or medium sherry
1¼ cups (10 fl oz/300 ml) skim milk
2 tablespoons sour cream
Salt and ground black pepper
Dill or chives, to garnish

Place the jumbo and small shrimp in a blender or food processor. Add 2½ cups (1 pint/600 ml) water and process. Pour the mixture into a saucepan and bring to a boil over medium heat. Reduce the heat and simmer for 30 minutes. Take the pan off the heat and set aside to cool. When it has cooled, blend or process it again. Strain the mixture through a fine strainer, discard the broken shells, and reserve the purée.

In the saucepan in which the shrimp was cooked, poach the scallops in the sherry for 1 minute. Stir in the shrimp purée and the milk and heat slowly until it reaches a boil. Remove from the heat and stir in the sour cream. Season to taste. Serve hot, or chilled. Garnish with a sprig of dill or snipped chives.

The crab is related to the lobster and there are hundreds of different varieties, found in both salt and fresh, cold and tropical waters. The smallest is the tiny pea-sized oyster crab that lives inside oyster and other shells, and one of the largest is the Pacific Alaskan crab, a spider crab which can weigh as much as 10 pounds/4.5 kg with an 11-foot/3.3-m leg span. Some species are eaten just before they molt when their shells are soft. Soft-shelled crabs, eaten when the old shell has been shed, but before a new shell has been formed, are very popular in the U.S.A.

KILLING THEM KINDLY

Lobster Look for the lobsters that seem the most lively. The most humane method of killing lobster is to plunge it into boiling salted water. It will only stay alive for about 15 seconds, and the noise it makes, which sounds to some like a scream, is actually the result of air inside the shell being forced out by the sudden change in temperature. Cook it for 11 minutes per pound/450 g; lobsters of 1 pound/450g or less should be cooked slightly longer. When a recipe calls for raw lobster meat, immobilize the lobster with a blow to the head, then cut it into pieces which will kill it. The only parts of the lobster which are not good to eat are the small transparent stomach sac and the thin intestine. This looks like a dark string which runs down the center of the body and can be removed with the point of a sharp knife. The soft gray-green liver, or tomalley, has a marvelous flavor, and a female lobster may contain an orange coral that is also edible.

Crab When choosing a live crab, look for an active one which feels heavy; shake it and if you hear the sound of water inside the shell, reject it. It will probably have recently molted and will be watery and flabby. Crabs should be cooked in salted water, with a generous ½ cup (6 oz/175 g) salt to 2½ quarts (4 pints/2.4 litres) water. The crab will expire as the water comes to a boil and should be simmered for 15 minutes per pound/450 g.

Extract the cooked crabmeat from the shell by hitting the underside sharply with your fist, then, standing the crab on edge with the shell facing you, brace your thumbs on the body and pull it away from the shell. Twist off the tail and discard it. Remove the legs and claws and crack them open to extract the meat. Pull off and throw away the gills along the side of the body. Split the body open with a sharp knife and remove the meat. Scrape the brown curd from the shell and use it in the dish or to make a sauce. Soft-shelled crabs can be pan-fried or sautéed, and eaten "shell" and all.

OYSTERS OF THE WORLD

Pacific oysters reached European waters clinging to the ships of the sixteenth-century Portuguese navigator, Magellan. Atlantic and Pacific oysters can be eaten all year round, but the eating season for native European varieties are restricted to months with an "r" in them.

There are three main species of oysters and many sub-species. The main species of Atlantic North America is *Crassostrea virginica*. Some of the better known Americans are the Bluepoint from Long Island, Rappahannocks, Choptanks, and Fire Island salts. The rock oysters of New South Wales in Australia originally came from New Zealand and are similar to the American and Portuguese varieties. Large, rough-shelled Pacific oysters are quite

Implements for fish

The items shown here are not essential for eating lobster and oysters but are extremely useful and make the presentation more stylish. They are inexpensive and worth buying if you eat shellfish often.

Lobster crackers are the most efficient way of cracking the claws so the meat can be extracted.
Lobster forks whose small pointed tines can reach into tiny crevices to pry out the sweet cooked flesh.

Oyster knife The safest tool to use to open oysters. Grip it firmly and twist to open the shell.
Oyster plate The indentations hold the oyster shells in place so that they do not slip as they would on an ordinary plate.

LEFT
Oysters farmed in the nearby estuaries are being sold in the Quimper market in Brittany by a stall-holder wearing traditional Breton costume.

RIGHT

RIGHT

Oysters are elegant fare. This grand supper of oysters was painted in 1735 in Paris by Jean François de Troy. The painting is entitled Le Déjeuner d'huîtres.

Tentacles and Tender Flesh

Cuttlefish, octopus, and squid have neither fins, scales, nor shells, but sweet delicate flesh. Tender squid is generally widely available. Very small squid can be quickly fried, while the larger varieties can be stuffed and braised or gently fried. The sepia-colored ink is used to color and discreetly flavor rice and pasta.

To clean squid, rinse it and then grasp the head and gently squeeze the hard part to pop out the round beak between the tentacles. Discard. The tentacles should be cut off so they are attached by a ring. Rub off the purple skin. Pull the head away from the body along with the innards. They can be used for stock. The ink sac looks like a silvery streak and can be eased free with a sharp knife and set aside. Ensure that the body cavity is empty and skinless, cut away the two finlike flaps, and pat it dry. The sac can then be stuffed or, if the squid is large, cut it into two triangles and score it with a knife in a diamond pattern to tenderize. Squeeze the ink into a strainer or put directly into the dish and strain after cooking.

different from the British and French natives (the belons, Marennes, Colchester, Whitstable, Pyefleet, and others).

The waters in which oysters live affect their flavor. Since the emperor Nero, oyster connoisseurs have claimed, like wine buffs, they can identify oysters from anywhere in the world by their taste. Oysters are graded by quality and size and there are wide variations. Europeans tend to think American oysters are too large and not as finely flavored as their European relations. William Thackeray, the English writer, wrote that eating an American oyster was like swallowing a baby. Americans, in turn, sometimes remark that foreign oysters have a metallic taste.

Although oysters are often used in cooking in soups, stews, and even in the British classic beefsteak and oyster pie, they will become tough if not heated very carefully. The best-quality oysters are usually eaten raw in their shells with a squeeze of lemon juice and, at the most, the merest scrap of cayenne pepper or a few drops of hot-pepper sauce. Broiled oysters can taste superb, provided great care is taken not to overcook them.

LEFT

A small squid which has been grilled on a skewer is being consumed with relish by this young girl in the town of Hakkodate in Hokkaido in Japan.

STORED GOODNESS: PRESERVED FISH

Modern methods of refrigeration and canning mean fish no longer need to be cured by salting, smoking, drying, and pickling to sustain people during long hard winters, or to supply fish to land-locked regions.

BELOW

Native American smoked salmon, one of the most ancient ways of preserving any oily fish.

Traditional preserving processes are still used because people like the taste of them. A well-stocked larder in the developed world would always include salted anchovies, and small dried fish are much used in the East. In the British Isles, the traditional breakfast or high tea often features one of the many kinds of smoked herring. People all around the globe eat salt cod because they appreciate its unique flavor and texture, and it is the main ingredient of many classic Mediterranean, Caribbean, and African dishes. Smoked salmon is a glamorous addition to any meal. The Scandinavian method of pickling salmon, called gravlax, is widely used.

Haddock is also preserved and flavored by smoking. The fish are gutted, brined for a few minutes, drained, and lightly smoked as the fish color quickly. The town of Arbroath in Scotland has given its name to the Arbroath smokie, a small haddock or whiting which is gutted, decapitated, and soaked in a strong brine for less than an hour. The haddock are then hung in pairs which are wood-smoked until they are brown. Discerning consumers choose smoked fish which has not had artificial coloring added. Fish which take on color from the smoking process only, are much paler than the dyed ones.

One Fish, Many Names

The numerous and versatile herring is preserved in many different ways, each with a subtly different taste. The various treatments add flavor and are not done primarily to preserve the fish. They can be eaten on their own or added to salads, such as a Swedish version that combines kippers with lettuce, onion, and chopped apple. Pickled herrings can be eaten on their own or served as part of a mixed hors d'oeuvres.

Rollmops are herring fillets stuffed with onion, pickles, and spices and marinated in salted vinegar.

Bloaters are not gutted, which gives them a slightly gamy taste. They are briefly salted and lightly smoked. They were once a specialty of Great Yarmouth, U.K., and bloater paste sandwiches were a tea-time favorite. The French version is called *bouffi*, *craquelots*, or *demi-doux*.

Buckling from the United Kingdom and Holland are lightly salted, and the flesh is cooked by hot smoking so they do not need any additional preparation, except the removal of the tough skin.

Kippers are gutted, briefly soaked in brine, and then wood-smoked. They are often referred to by the place where they are made. The **red herring** of the Middle Ages, which continued to be made up to the beginning of this century, were much more heavily salted. They are now very rare but English-speakers recognize a reference to a red herring as meaning a false lead—because of their powerful smell they were once used to create a trail of scent in a drag hunt for the dogs to follow instead of a fox.

Bismark herring are marinated in vinegar with onions and spices.

Matie or **green herring** are young herring, very lightly brined with saltpeter and sugar, and eaten raw with chopped onion in Germany, Belgium, and Holland.

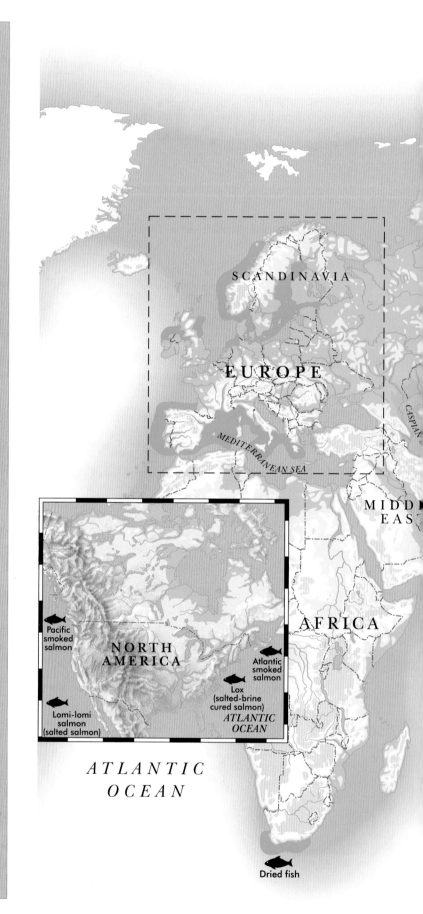

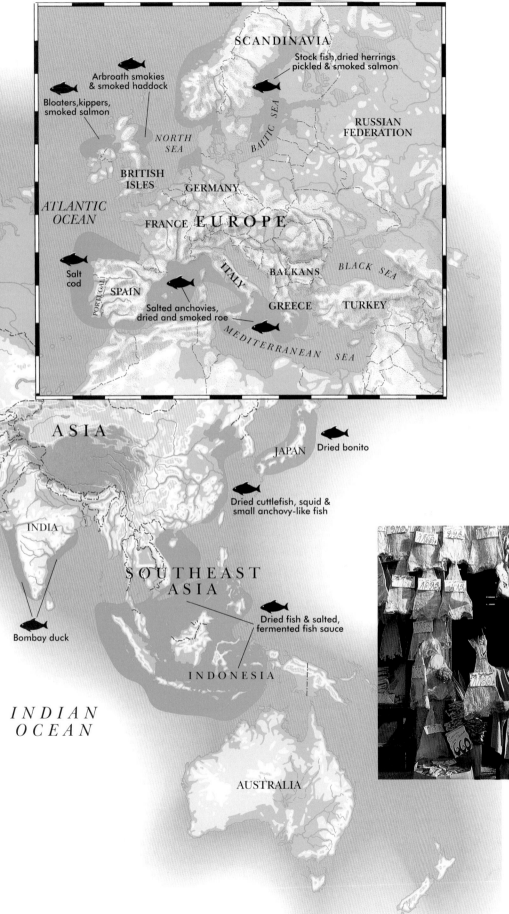

SCANDINAVIA

Stock fish, dried herrings
pickled & smoked salmon

Arbroath smokies
& smoked haddock

Bloaters, kippers,
smoked salmon

*NORTH
SEA*

RUSSIAN
FEDERATION

BRITISH
ISLES

GERMANY

*ATLANTIC
OCEAN*

FRANCE EUROPE

BALTIC SEA

Salt
cod

PORTUGAL

SPAIN

ITALY

BALKANS

BLACK SEA

Salted anchovies,
dried and smoked roe

GREECE

TURKEY

MEDITERRANEAN SEA

ASIA

JAPAN   Dried bonito

Dried cuttlefish, squid &
small anchovy-like fish

INDIA

SOUTHEAST
ASIA

Dried fish & salted,
fermented fish sauce

Bombay duck

INDONESIA

*INDIAN
OCEAN*

AUSTRALIA

PRESERVED FISH

*Most of the world's main
fish-eating areas have
developed ways of
preserving fish. While
once this was to ensure a
nutritious food supply
through lean periods,
preserved fish specialties,
highlighted on this world
map, have now become
sought after in their own
right and, in some
cases—for example the
salt cod of Portugal—
indispensable to national
cuisine.*

Fish producing
areas

Preserved fish
Specialities

ABOVE

*A shopkeeper in
Porto with a huge
piece of stiff salt cod
which is used as the
basis for a wide
variety of dishes.*

Greek Taramasalata

Cod's roe skin gives this taramasalata attractive flecks of color and a very intense flavor, which is far more robust than most commercial versions.

SERVES 4 TO 6

1 lb/450 g smoked cod's roe
Finely grated peel and juice of 1 lemon
2 cloves garlic
1¼ cups (10 fl oz/300 ml) olive oil
Ground black pepper

Put the cod's roe, with its skin, and the lemon peel and juice and garlic into a blender or food processor and process until it forms a mass. Add the olive oil gradually until a soft paste forms; you may not need all of the olive oil. Spoon the mixture into a serving bowl and adjust the seasoning. Serve immediately with pita bread, thin toast, or plain crackers, or cover and chill.

LEFT
Sardines are canned all over the world. These packs show a classic design of fishing boats.

DRIED AND SALTED SNACKS AND CONDIMENTS

Even though cured fish were usually eaten in Europe hen other food was scarce, and are associated by many with poverty and slavery, people around the globe eat tough, salty, dried fish for pure pleasure. Cinemas in Asia reek of pungent salty seafood and resound with the crunch of brittle fishy morsels being consumed with relish. Canned Bombay Duck or *bummalo*, a wind-dried tiny fish with a powerful high fish odor and taste from the Arabian Sea off the coast of India, is eaten crumbled over curries or nibbled as a cocktail snack.

In Scotland's Shetland Islands, sticks of rock-hard sillocks, salted and dried young cod, were not so long ago eaten uncooked with a piece of oatcake. Christmas in Scandinavia is unthinkable without *lutefisk*; the dried cod called stockfish is soaked for a week then treated with lye and soaked for another week before being boiled with salt until the texture is like jelly. Even flavored with bacon fat, mustard, and cheese, *lutefisk* has few fans who are not Norwegian, Swedish, or Finnish. South African *bokkem* is of Dutch origin; salted and wind-dried bass, horse mackerel, shad, or mullet are said to taste similar to the dried meat called *biltong*, and are respected and appreciated as a culinary national treasure.

CANNED SEAFOOD

Many fish and shellfish are most commonly encountered in cans. Anchovies, sardines, pilchards, tuna, some types of salmon, minced clams, mussels, and smoked oysters are invaluable kitchen cupboard standbys. The canning process involves heat and this will slightly change both the taste and texture of the fish. The bones in salmon, for example, become soft when the fish are canned, and need not be discarded.

There is a great variety to choose from. Some fish are simply packed in brine or oil, but tuna and pilchards are often canned in various sauces. Plain fish or shellfish can be quickly cooked with a few other ingredients to make an almost-instant pasta sauce, or used to make a salad into a more substantial dish. Tuna or anchovies with sliced onions, black olives, and capers can be cooked in minutes and poured into pasta; tuna and salmon both make excellent fish cakes; sardines, mackerel, and pilchards can be simply piled on hot buttered toast or quickly mashed into a paste with a few flavoring ingredients, such as onions, capers, mustard, or lemon juice.

FISH FROM FRESH WATERS

*F*ish from lakes, streams, and rivers are still something of a luxury. Although many species are now farmed, the best are still caught by sporting fishermen. Pollution is becoming a serious problem, and fish such as pike are now fairly rare.

BELOW

There is no more thrilling sight to a sporting fisherman than a splendid mature salmon leaping upstream on its way to spawn. This fish is one of the most finely flavored in the world.

Almost all freshwater fish are more delicate than saltwater varieties, and are said to have more finesse. Those fish which live in swiftly moving water, the vigorous swimmers such as salmon and black bass, are thought to be finer in flavor than fish which inhabit sluggish waters, such as the slower moving catfish and gar. The lively trout who sparkle and dart in clear water have a more refined and superior flavor to fish which thrive in muddy water like the carp. Even in the same species, colder waters produce a more assertive flavor than warm water.

Before modern refrigeration, freshwater fish would have been caught and eaten quickly because they did not keep and could not be transported for any distance. Many freshwater fish, such as carp, catfish, tilapia, and trout, are

Mysterious Eels

Exactly how eels reproduce was a subject of much speculation, all of it mythic and completely erroneous, until the Danish biologist Johannes Schmidt studied the life cycle of European and American eels for 25 years. He discovered they are all born in the Sargasso Sea between Bermuda and Puerto Rico. Ten-year-old mature eels make the long journey back to where they were born to spawn and die, and their tiny offspring disperse in all directions to begin the arduous and dangerous migration back to the rivers and streams of Europe and America. It takes the European eels a year to reach home.

Many slim young glass eels or elvers are scooped up for food before they mature and they are an exquisite delicacy. Both conger eel and the freshwater eels of the Indo-Pacific are fished commercially and many varieties are farmed.

There are numerous ways to cook larger eels, but they must be kept alive until just before cooking because once they are dead the flesh disintegrates very rapidly. For many cooks, lightly smoked eel or a plate of quickly cooked elvers is a more practical option than killing a live eel.

RIGHT
Eels are considered a great delicacy. The flesh of young eels is delicate and sweet.

farmed, but few of them are oily enough to withstand most preservation methods. Trout can be very lightly smoked, mainly for flavor, but this is a fairly recent development.

FESTIVE CARP

All the carp family are attractive fish, and many carp are swimming decoratively in ornamental ponds—the goldfish are perhaps the most familiar. Some carp still live in the wild where they can survive to a great age and can weigh up to 50 pounds/22.5 kg. Freshwater carp are eaten for celebratory meals in China, France, eastern Europe, and even the Ivory Coast where the fish is dried. They have always been a favorite Jewish fish, and in Catholic countries carp is eaten on Christmas Eve and Good Friday. It is said to be at its best from late fall until early spring. It is almost always sold whole and has firm, slightly sweet flesh and very few bones, but it should be cooked gently to keep it succulent.

EARLY AMERICAN FAVORITE

Shad, a herringlike fish which lives in both salt and fresh water, were plentiful when America was first settled. The Dutch in New York City called them "eleven" fish because the first spring shad were caught on March 11, and cooked on a plank of wood—a method, legend has it, that was taught to them by Native Americans. George Washington ate fish caught on the Potomac, and baked shad is reputed to have been one of his favorite dishes. Shad are now quite rare but similar fish such as salmon or small cod can be cooked on a well-oiled piece of wood, put into a cold oven which should then be heated to 400°F/200°C/Gas mark 4. When the plank is hot, put the fish on it and bake it for 10 to 15 minutes per pound/450 g, basting the flesh frequently with melted butter.

VEGETABLES
& FUNGI

Thanks to improved techniques for storing and trasporting food, the choice of fruits and vegetables in our supermarkets spans the globe. New varieties of potatoes and onions are sharing shelf space with older varieties, still valued for their flavor. We are also learning new or foreign

ways with old favorites: serving lightly cooked

rather than limp vegetables, and using raw green-leaf varieties like spinach and endive in salads, and many more pulses, in the Indian, Middle Eastern and Central American way.

THE ORIGINAL VEGETABLES

Our hunting and gathering ancestors spent much more time gathering wild food than they did hunting game. Food-gatherers need skill and knowledge; they have to identify and remember what is edible and what is toxic, where things grow, and how to treat them.

It has been suggested that gathering was mainly the work of women, but it is now thought all the able-bodied members of prehistoric communities were involved initially in communal gathering and subsequently in primitive agriculture. On every continent, people gradually settled together to prepare land and plant seeds, with the exception of Australia, where the indigenous peoples continued to hunt and gather with extraordinary expertise until the arrival of Captain Cook in 1770.

ABOVE

The settlers who followed Captain Cook to the Antipodes ignored the native flora and fauna exploited by the aboriginal population and imported all their food with disastrous results in the early years.

RIGHT

Christopher Columbus with the King and Queen of Spain who helped finance his attempt to discover a new trade route to India.

LEFT
When the painter Arcimboldo devised this fanciful head of vegetables around 1573, the ear of Indian corn was a recent arrival from the New World.

For the first farmers, the process of agriculture was mysterious and magical. Major crops were invested with religious significance and complicated rituals were employed to ensure a good harvest. A vegetable staple on which a people depended for survival, such as corn in the Americas, grains in Europe, and rice in the Far East, was worshipped and believed to be of divine origin, a gift from the gods.

MOVABLE FEASTS

Since the beginning of time, foods have been migrating. Seeds and plants were carried randomly by ocean tides and established themselves on distant continents, or were carried by people over land and water, first as sustenance, and then for trade. Some plants quickly adapted to the local growing conditions and changed, forever, the eating habits of the world. In the modern era, two of the most notable successes are the potato and the chili, both from the New World.

Implements for Vegetables

A very basic assortment of simple tools are all that are necessary for preparing fresh vegetables quickly and easily providing the blades are sharp.

Knives A small selection of very sharp knives are essential for slicing, chopping, and peeling thin-skinned vegetables.

Peelers A fixed or swiveling blade peels thin skin from vegetables such as potatoes and carrots quickly and neatly.

Grater Some have a choice of blades for fine or coarse grating.
Masher Boiled potatoes, celeriac, and other root vegetables are pounded while still warm into a smooth purée with butter and other flavorings added during mashing.
Steamer The basket holds food in the steam above, not in, the boiling water to cook it with mimimal loss of nutrients.

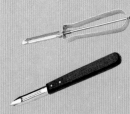

European colonial expansion was responsible for the widest dissemination of plants and foodstuffs the world has ever known. The early explorers and conquering soldiers not only took their own food with them for sustenance on long and dangerous voyages, they returned home bearing new and exotic foods. At first, these new foods were treated as curiosities at court and in aristocratic circles and, more generally, were regarded with some caution and considerable suspicion. However, many foods introduced from the New World, for example corn and potatoes, were eventually to find their place as the staple foods of the poor.

RIGHT
Seaweed being gathered from the beach on the island of Jersey off the French coast.

THE DISPERSION OF VEGETABLES AND LEGUMES BETWEEN THE OLD AND THE NEW WORLDS

Explorers were initially responsible for the discovery and introduction of new foods to their native lands.

Exchange between New and Old worlds
Exchange between Old and New worlds
Tomato
Pepper
Avocado
Corn
Chili
Potato
Squashes
Black-eyed bean
Haricot bean
Chayote
Okra

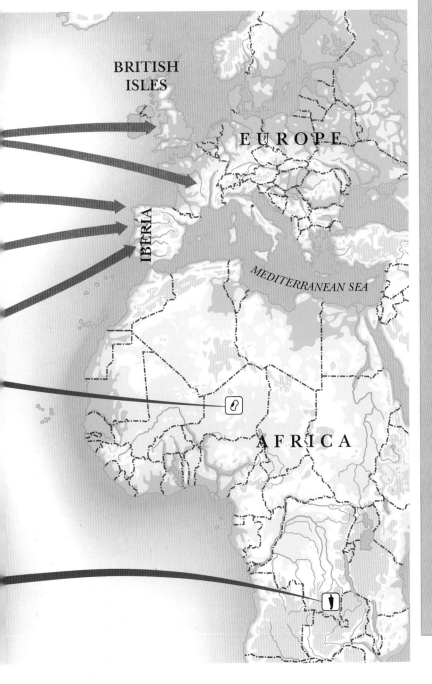

Seaweeds: Vegetables from the Sea

Seaweeds are a valuable source of vitamins—the B complex, C, E, and K—and are rich in minerals, especially calcium, iodine, iron, magnesium, potassium, sodium, copper, and zinc, as well as high-quality protein. Most are sold in dried form, while some are finely shredded and can be sprinkled over salads and cooked dishes to give them a tangy, salty flavor. In Japan, seaweeds are one of the most essential cooking ingredients. They are particularly recommended for cleansing the body and are even said to have the ability to remove toxins, especially heavy metals.

Agar-agar is a useful vegetarian alternative to gelatin, usually sold as thin, transparent sheets or flakes.

Arame has a delicate flavor and is very rich in calcium. It must be soaked and simmered for 30 minutes and is used in Japanese *miso* soup.

Dulse is found all along the Atlantic coast. It has a strong flavor and can be eaten raw, used as a garnish, or dressed as a salad. It is eaten in Ireland with buttered mashed potatoes in the dish called "dulse champ."

Kelp grows all over the world and is called *kombu* in the East. It has the ability to soften other foods and is excellent with legumes.

Laver or **Nori** is best known in the Celtic regions of Ireland, Scotland, Cornwall, and Brittany. After rinsing, soaking, and lengthy cooking it is puréed to make laver bread, and can also be formed into cakes and fried. In Japan, dried nori sheets are used as the wrapping for sushi rolls. They can also be lightly toasted and then shredded or crumbled and used as a garnish.

Samphire grows along the shoreline, but retains the salty tang of the ocean. It is a rare treat which goes particularly well with fresh fish or shellfish and should be rinsed and then boiled until tender. It is often dipped in melted butter and eaten with the fingers as a sort of sea asparagus and has something of the same exquisite pungency.

EARTHY DELIGHTS: ROOTS, TUBERS

Every traditional cuisine is constructed on foundations of a staple starch. Starch is rich in energy-giving carbohydrate, fiber, and essential nutrients, filling, and easier to store than more perishable green vegetables.

The seventh-largest world food crop, a tuber variously called manioc, cassava, and tapioca, is a staple starch. A South American native, it was one of the first plants to be domesticated in the New World and traveled via Europe to Africa, where most of it is now grown. Since several species of manioc contain the bitter poison hydrocyanic acid, which has to be removed by soaking, its widespread cultivation is a tribute to human ingenuity.

Yams are also an important tropical root crop, growing in all of the warm temperate areas of the world. Another edible tuber is the taro, a tropical arum. The wetland taro is cooked to remove its bitter taste and is then ground and fermented into a paste called *poi*, which is served as a festive food in Polynesia, east Asia, and Hawaii. The upland taro, or *dasheen*, produces a corm which serves as a potato in Japan, China, and the West Indies.

THE DISCOVERY AND RISE OF THE POTATO

The Andean potato, frozen and dried and used to feed slaves working in the Inca silver mines, greatly impressed the Spanish conquistadors, who found such an inexpensive source of food to feed cheap labor irresistible. It was also ideal fodder for the ships' crews who traveled back to Spain laden with New World booty.

The original vegetable would be unrecognizable to today's potato-lovers. Its descendants are still dried in South America and look more like dried mushrooms than potatoes. As with every new food, when it was first brought to Europe, the potato was regarded as a novelty by the upper classes and with deep suspicion, even fear, by ordinary people. Indeed, anyone with botanical knowledge would have been foolish not to be wary of this new vegetable, since it is a member of the *Solanum* family which also includes belladonna, the deadly nightshade. In common with many rare and expensive foods, it was designated an aphrodisiac, or at the very least a tonic and restorative. The early small, dark potatoes seemed to resemble truffles, and were called by the same or similar names in several languages. Potato is, in fact, closer to its original name.

BELOW

A wild potato —descendant of those eaten by New World natives when the first Spaniards arrived.

POTATO DISHES

The potato plays a part in many European cuisines. This map highlights some of the more famous national potato dishes, which are described in the geographical key (below)

🍴 Potato Dishes

BALTIC STATES/POLAND: 🍴⑩ *Latkes* (grated, fried pancakes) **BELGIUM:** 🍴③ *Pomme frites* (deep fried sticks) **CZECH REPUBLIC:** 🍴⑥ *Poached dumplings* (made with flour, egg, and fat) **ENGLAND:** 🍴① *Baked* (unskinned and oven-baked); *Roast* (peeled, quartered, and basted with fat from a joint) **FRANCE:** 🍴⑦ *Dauphinois* (slices baked with milk and cheese); *Lyonnaise* (slices sautéed with onion and butter); *à la Parmentier* (cubes cooked in butter) **GERMANY:** 🍴⑧ *Bratkartoffel* (sliced, fried with onions in fat) **GREECE:** 🍴⑤ *Skordalia* (puréed with garlic and olive oil) **IRELAND:** 🍴② *Colcannon* (left-over mash fried with cabbage) **ITALY:** 🍴④ *Gnocchi* (small poached dumplings made with flour and egg) **SPAIN:** 🍴⑪ *Patatas bravas* (cubed and fried in a garlic sauce) **SWEDEN:** 🍴⑨ *Jansonn's Temptation* (sliced, baked with cream and anchovies)

Potato Varieties

There are more than 400 varieties of potato, a nutritious and extremely satisfying food, rich in fiber, vitamin C, and trace minerals, especially when fresh and quickly cooked. This most versatile of tubers comes in all sizes, shapes, and colors. One of the most important world food crops, commercial growers divide them into "earlies," or new potatoes, which are harvested from late May, and "main-crop," available from September through the winter and spring until June. The early varieties are dug up when they are still very small and are cooked in their thin skins.

Potatoes, like all vegetables, are at their peak when they have been freshly dug from the ground. Potatoes do keep, which is why they have been such a resounding success, but some varieties keep better than others. The old method of soaking potatoes in water is now known to leech out much of their nutritional content; they should be scrubbed or peeled and very quickly rinsed, not soaked. For dishes where it is essential that they are completely dry, they can be patted gently with a paper or cloth towel.

Three varieties of potato make up 60 percent of the U.S. crop: the late maturing Russet Burbank grown in Idaho and Maine; the mid-season to late Katahdin from Maine and New York; and the Kennebec, a mid-season, all-round potato from Maine, Minnesota, and North Dakota.

The best-known European potatoes are the King Edward, good for roasting; the second early Maris Peer and main-crop Maris Piper; the red-skinned Desirée, an excellent potato for baking, mashing, and salads; and the fine-flavored Pink Fir Apple, a main-crop variety which tastes more like a new potato. Belle de Fontenay and Charlotte are superb salad potatoes, and the Duke of York is one of the best for mashing.

The Spanish started growing potatoes in Spain in the middle of the fifteenth century and they were common in Italy by the early 1700s, but the French continued to resist them—they were thought to be dangerous, and until the eighteenth century were seen as a cause of leprosy. Although the Swiss did eat potatoes, they were warned that overindulgence caused scrofula, while the Germans refused to eat them even in times of famine. In fact, some Protestant sects regarded them as ungodly because they were not mentioned in the Bible. In eighteenth-century England they were only grown as animal fodder.

But by the nineteenth century, the British, and even the French, had succumbed to the potato's attractions. Indeed, the poor of Ireland found them so easy to grow that they ate them to the exclusion of almost everything else, with disastrous consequences. When the entire Irish potato crop was wiped out by successive blights between 1845 and 1847, more than a million people perished of starvation or fever, and another million emigrated to North America and Australia.

LEFT

The Irish peasant family in this picture, painted in the last century, would have lived on a diet of potatoes boiled over a peat fire and buttermilk from the family cow. It is a tribute to this simple fare that travel writers of the period often remarked on the beauty and fine complexions of the poor of Ireland and their robust health.

Swiss Potato Cakes

A similar potato cake is called *latke* in Yiddish. Potato cakes vary slightly all over northern and eastern Europe and are often eaten with a dollop of sour cream.

SERVES 4

1 lb/450 g waxy potatoes
2 medium eggs
1 tablespoon all-purpose flour
Salt and ground black pepper
4 tablespoons vegetable oil

Peel the potatoes and grate them into a bowl of cold water. When they are all grated, drain and squeeze the potato pieces with a cloth. Mix the potato with the eggs, flour, and seasoning.

Heat 1 tablespoon of the oil in a skillet. Divide the potato mixture into quarters. Spread one quarter of the mixture over the bottom of the pan with the back of a spoon or a metal spatula. When the underside is crisp and golden, turn it over and brown the top; remove and keep warm while you make the rest.

FAMILY MEMBERS

Another member of the same family which comes from India is the eggplant. It was brought to Europe by the Moors who later colonized Andalusia, Sicily, and southern Italy. North of the Moorish strongholds, the eggplant (or "aubergine," a word of Sanskrit-Arabic-Catalan-French derivation), was thought to be just as alarming and dubious as the potato. Thomas Jefferson, U.S. President from 1801–09, delighted in unusual plants, and grew eggplants at his country estate, Monticello, but he was an exception. Eggplants have not been generally accepted until this century. There are several varieties in the Middle East and Asia, including a small white variety which does resemble an egg, but the large purple eggplant is the most commonly used in cooking, both in America and Europe.

Other family members which are classified as fruits are the garden huckleberry, which probably originally came from Africa, the native American ground cherry or *physalis*, the Cape gooseberry, an African *physalis*, and the Mexican *tomatillo*, or jamberry.

Iced Russian Borscht

SERVES 4

1 lb/450 g beets, unpeeled
Salt and ground black pepper
2 tablespoons (1 oz/25 g) butter
1 large onion, sliced
8 oz/225 g raw potatoes, peeled and sliced
2 cups (16 fl oz/450 ml) milk
1 teaspoon cumin seeds, or ½ teaspoon ground cumin
2 chicken stock cubes, crumbled
Juice of ½ lemon
¾ cup/⅓ pt/190 ml cream
1¼ cups (10 fl oz/300 ml) sour cream
1 tablespoon chopped fresh dill

Scrub the unpeeled beets. Place them in a saucepan with a good pinch of salt and 2½ cups (1 pint/ 600 ml) water. Bring to a boil. Reduce the heat and simmer for 3 hours, or until very tender. Remove the beets from the water; set aside the cooking water. Peel the beets, discard the skins.

Melt the butter in a heavy saucepan. Add the onion and fry until just beginning to color. Add the potatoes and cook over low heat for about 5 minutes. Stir in the milk, cumin, and chicken stock cubes. Continue simmering until the potato is tender.

Place the beets with their cooking water in a blender or food processor and purée. Add the potato mixture in the pan and purée again. Transfer to a bowl and stir in the lemon juice. Season with pepper and salt if needed.

Cover and chill well. Serve with a spoonful of sour cream in the middle of each bowl and sprinkle dill over the tops.

SWEET ROOTS

Both the leaves and the root of the beet are edible. The Greeks ate the leaves as a vegetable but only used the red root as medicine. The Roman recipe writer, Apicius, used beets in a salad dressed with oil, vinegar, and mustard—if he had added honey it would be very like the American classic dish of Harvard Beets.

All beets have a natural sweetness and in l747 a German chemist isolated sugar from the large white sugar beet. By 1880, more sugar was being extracted from beets than from sugar cane—a consequence of the abolition of the African slave trade which up to this point had fueled the cane sugar plantations of the Caribbean. Over the last century, sugar consumption has rocketed. In eighteenth-century France, for example, annual sugar consumption averaged a little over 2 pounds/900g, an amount currently estimated to be the average weekly consumption in the United States.

MANY-COLORED ROOTS

The *Umbelliferae* family includes delicious stalwarts such as the carrot, parsnip, fennel, celeriac, and celery, and their deadly relation, the hemlock. The original carrots came from Afghanistan, and were yellow, lilac, or purple. Seeds of both red and white carrots were introduced to Spain by

the Moors. White, yellow, and purple carrots were still available in the nineteenth century; Alexandre Dumas, writing in the 1870s, said the pale white or yellow varieties were the best.

There are several native varieties of parsnip in North and South America, but the European parsnip probably came originally from the Caucasus. The Roman Emperor Tiberius was very fond of parsnips from the Rhine area, and the Romans introduced them to their colonies of Gaul and Britain. Although the sweet flesh of the parsnip is still a valuable winter vegetable, particularly in Europe where it is roasted and served with meat or game, it was supplanted in popularity by the potato. Celeriac or celery root, at its best from November to February, is a useful winter vegetable, very rich in iron with a faint taste of celery. It can be grated and served raw and is often boiled and combined with potatoes for mashing.

JERUSALEM ARTICHOKES

This New World tuber was called the "Canada" or "French" potato when it first arrived in Europe, but in Italy it was named *girosol articocco*, meaning the sunflower artichoke, and in English this was corrupted into "Jerusalem." Perhaps the reason why it did not become as popular as the potato is because it contains large quantities of inulin, which causes a violent reaction in many people. John Goodyear, the gardener who was one of the first to grow it in England, wrote that "they stir up and cause a filthie loathsome stinking winde within the bodie," and thought them suitable only for pig food. Today, they are roasted, boiled, and made into a soup called Palestine, which dates to the eighteenth century.

ABOVE
In the developed world, governments have tried to encourage their over-weight populations to eat more vegetables.

ROOTS AND TUBERS
This map shows the countries and regions where the major roots and tubers originated. In most cases, they have been transported all over the globe and are cultivated commercially, and have become staple food crops, in areas far removed from their original homes.

manioc: **CENTRAL AND SOUTH AMERICA** *yams:* **SUB-SAHARAN AFRICA** *taro:* **SOUTHEAST ASIA** *potatoes:* **WESTERN SOUTH AMERICA** *eggplant:* **INDIA** *carrots:* **AFGHANISTAN** *parsnips:* **CAUCASUS** *turnip:* **TURKEY, LEVANT, GREECE, ITALY** *beetroot:* **GREECE, ITALY** *swedes:* **BOHEMIA (CZECH REPUBLIC)** *Jerusalem artichoke:* **NORTH AMERICA**

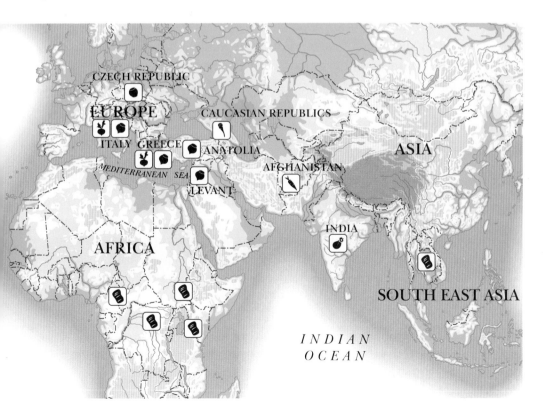

ℋEALTHY BOUNTY: LEAFY GREENS

*G*reen leafy vegetables, including both the extensive lettuce family and the ancient and useful brassicas, are one of the most important elements of a healthy diet.

The best-known brassica, the cabbage, is one of the oldest European foods and now comes in all sizes, shapes, and colors. Brassicas are rich in the B vitamins and sulfur, which, although it is very good for the body, also gives these vegetables their characteristic smell when cooking, particularly when it is prolonged. For this reason, cabbage has never been considered a particularly refined or elegant vegetable. Cabbage is very low in calories and renowned as a blood purifier. It is also said to be beneficial for those suffering from skin problems, ulcers, kidneys, diabetes, and asthma.

The most famous American dish of raw cabbage is coleslaw, from the Dutch word for salad and *cole* or *colewart*, the old name for cabbage. When fresh and properly made it can be a dish of refreshing sophistication, although, because it is sometimes made with mayonnaise, it is not especially slimming. The addition of an acid element, such as lemon juice or good vinegar, and the accent of an aromatic seed, such as caraway or cumin, also complements the flavor.

The most familiar cabbages are the white, red (particularly rich in vitamin C), and round, green, smooth-leaved varieties. Other popular cabbages include the crinkly-leaved Savoy, and the pointed European spring and Chinese cabbages. Kale is dark green and curly, while Brussels sprouts are actually budding cabbage stems.

Both broccoli and the cauliflower (which Mark Twain said was cabbage with a college education) are dense inflorescences of cabbage. Broccoli and cauliflower are equally delicious eaten raw or cooked, and Brussels sprouts have a fine, fresh flavor when they are grated, or finely sliced and cooked very quickly in a skillet with a little olive oil and sharp seasonings such as black pepper or mustard seed. In Europe, whole Brussels sprouts are often cooked with chestnuts and are part of the traditional British Christmas dinner.

LETTUCES AND THEIR RELATIVES

The large lettuce family includes many common garden flowers such as asters, marigolds, and zinnias, as well as the varieties grown for their edible leaves. These beautiful leaves come in many colors and shapes, and, in general, the darker they are the more nutrients they contain. Their nutritional value is also affected by how and where they are grown and how fresh they are. When they begin to turn yellow and limp they are well past their prime.

Most lettuces (an exception is the modern iceberg) are rich in powerful antioxidants and contain valuable quantities of iron, calcium, phosphorus, potassium, as well as the vitamins A, C, and E. The leaves should always be torn and not cut. Cutting the leaves breaks down the cellular structure and makes them go limp more quickly, as well as hastening the oxidation process and the resulting loss of nutrients.

Other edible dark green leaves, such as spinach and chard, belong to the beet family. Watercress is classed botanically as a nasturtium and is almost always eaten raw. When spinach and chard are young and tender they are also delicious uncooked.

OKRA

Also known as "ladies' fingers" and "gumbo," this tropical African native is a member of the mallow family; its botanical name is *Hibiscus esculentus*. Cotton, kola nuts, and several flowers belong to this family but okra is the only vegetable. Okra came to Brazil in the seventeenth century and later to the southern United States with the slave trade, and it is still popular in the south. Okra is often cooked in stews (called "gumbo"), and it combines especially well with tomatoes. Okra is rich in calcium, magnesium, potassium, phosphate, vitamin C, and carotene. It is sold fresh and canned.

Sauerkraut

One of the most ancient foods in the world is cabbage preserved in brine, known as sauerkraut or *choucroute*. Immersion in brine over a period of time causes fermentation, which prevents the cabbage from decaying and also destroys potentially dangerous microbes. Cabbage is rich in phosphorus, potassium, and vitamins, particularly vitamin C, and these are preserved by the fermentation process. The process also produces benign bacteria, necessary for a healthy colon.

One of the first foods to be processed on an industrial scale, in Germany in the seventeenth century, sauerkraut was invaluable as a ship's store. Captain Cook swore by it and during his first expedition in 1769 the ship's doctor used compresses of cabbage leaves to treat sailors wounded in a terrible storm, saving them from gangrene.

Sauerkraut is still primarily a manufactured product but it is very easy to make. Finely shredded cabbage is packed in layers, each one generously sprinkled with sea salt (this can be done in a plastic bucket), weighted and covered, then stored in a cool place for six weeks. Any cabbage which has rotted, and the excess juice from the top, is discarded and the sauerkraut is then packed into jars. The salt content can be reduced by rinsing it before using. It can be served hot or cold and is very digestible.

LEFT
A Portuguese cook, who may shop for fresh seasonal produce every day, has plenty to choose from even in a stall as tiny as this one in Lisbon.

EDIBLE LILIES: THE ONION FAMILY

T*here is hardly a cook in the world who would not find it an almost impossible task to prepare a main meal without using one or more potent bulbs of the allium family.*

Onions, garlic, shallots, chives, and leeks are members of this group, which botanically comes between the lilies (*Lilaceae*) and the *Amaryllidaceae*, a family which includes the flowers amaryllis, narcissus, and snowdrop.

Both onions and garlic are especially rich in powerful natural antiseptics and their health-giving properties were well known in the ancient world. They are still recommended for heart disorders and arthritis, and are said to reduce blood pressure and blood sugar levels. Throughout the centuries they have been eaten by rich and poor alike. The laws of Hammurabi, which were evolved in Mesopotamia between 1792 and 1750 BC, provided a monthly ration of bread and onions for citizens in need. The Roman historians, Pliny and Juvenal, claimed, without citing any conclusive evidence, that the onion was worshipped in Egypt.

ABOVE

On this Gascon farm, small white onions have been tied up in bunches to dry in the fresh air.

RIGHT

Sweet red onions, violet shallots, and fresh garlic on sale in a French market are only a few of the alliums essential to the cook in France.

LEFT

Once onions have been harvested, if properly stored in a dark, cool place such as a dry cellar or garage, they will keep for several months and are available all through the year.

Onions come in many sizes, colors, and flavors, and have numerous names, not all of them accurate. The tree onion, for example, which the French call "Egyptian," was unknown in ancient Egypt and, in fact, comes from Canada. Some onions, such as the Spanish variety and the Vidalia from Georgia, are milder than others. Shallots are smaller and milder than the larger members of the family, while the scallion, or green or spring onion, is more delicate still, but contains more calcium, vitamin C, and potassium than ordinary onions. Chive leaves and not the bulb are eaten and these have the most elusive onion flavor of all.

The leek looks like an elongated onion and is grown with soil heaped up around the lower part of the plant to exclude light and keep the edible stem white. Leeks are a much-loved vegetable in Europe, widely used in soups and often served as a separate dish, hot with melted butter, and tepid or cold with a vinaigrette.

Know Your Onions . . .

Onions are both antiseptic and diuretic. Roasted onions have been used to cure earache and a syrup of onion juice is a remedy for colds and coughs. Crushed raw onion used externally acts as a local stimulant and can be used for cuts, acne, as a lung poultice to relieve inflammation, and is even thought to make hair grow. When eaten, they have a mild laxative effect and will help clear up sinus conditions. Steeped in gin, onions are said to be useful in cases of gravel and dropsy. Moles are reputed to dislike the smell so much that if onions are planted in their runs they will leave and never return.

$\mathcal{P}$ODS, PEAS, & LEGUMES

T*he humble legumes, full of starch and essential nutrients, are the most sustaining vegetables. The seeds which grow in pods—beans, lentils, peas, and peanuts—are all called "legumes," from the Latin root* lego, *meaning to gather or select.*

ABOVE

The Italian painter, Annibale Carracci, painted this peasant eating black-eyed peas, a pulse well known in the ancient world, in the sixteenth century. Cultivated in Africa, it came to the New World with slavery.

The legumes form the second largest food group, only the grasses are more numerous. The soybean, which takes on many forms, is more widely consumed than any other food in the world.

The variety of the legumes is vast and their history is as old as time. They play a major role in every traditional cuisine and there is hardly a country in the world which does not have a beloved national bean dish. The Egyptians have been eating *ful mesdames* since the time of the pharaohs. Northern Italians eat so many beans they used to be known as "bean eaters." Many towns in France claim to make the only true *cassoulet*: in one, it is sacrilege not to use preserved duck or goose; another stipulates pork; in Toulouse, breast of mutton and sausage are allowed; and in Corbières, it must include salted pigs' tail and ears. But every *cassoulet* contains beans. The Dutch make superior dried pea soup and Indian cuisine makes spectacular use of lentils. In the Middle East, a meal is not considered to be complete without a dish of hummus or falafel made with garbanzo beans. In the Far East, soybeans appear in one or more of their myriad incarnations at every meal, including breakfast.

When dried, these beans are also referred to as pulses, from the Latin which means paste (or porridge). They need to be soaked and cooked in liquid to rehydrate them and, because of their high protein content, they form a solid mass when cooked and mashed. From the New World, the haricot family includes the kidney, lima, and the green or yellow long-podded beans, called French beans in Europe. Old World families include the fava, the European broad beans, black-eyed peas (or beans), lentils, green peas, and garbanzo beans.

LEFT

The Yankee bean, coooked in tomato sauce and sold in cans, is one of the most popular bean dishes in the world. Cheap, filling, and slightly sweet, it is a universally loved comfort food which appeals to young and old alike.

All come in many sizes and colors; red, pink, creamy white, pale green, purple, brown, beige, striped, spotted, and marbled. For most members of this group, it is the seeds rather than the pods which are eaten, more often dried than fresh. But fava beans and peas are eaten both ways (and a special pea called the *mange tout,* or snow pea, is eaten pod and all). Green and runner beans are grown primarily for their pods, which are eaten young and green, but the clever gardener who allows them to dry on their stems instead of discarding the withering pods will discover within them delicious plump seeds. Beans have always been valued because they keep. But in countries where they are really appreciated the young, new season's dried beans, sometimes called "half-dried," are more expensive than older beans and are treated as a delicacy. As beans age, they become tougher and take much longer to cook.

It is a curious phenomenon of culinary fashion that every few years a peasant food is elevated to gourmet status. It is not easy in urban areas thousands of miles from the land to eat as well as many peasants do. A lunch that a Tuscan farmer would take for granted would be expensive to reproduce in the fashionable restaurants of Manhattan and San Francisco: salad picked a few minutes before it reaches the table and a dish of fresh legumes, both dressed with the first pressing of local olive oil, freshly carved slices of home-cured prosciutto made from pigs who have grazed on chestnuts, and salami made from wild boar hunted on the surrounding hills, all washed down with locally produced wine. It is no wonder creative chefs and cooks at home eagerly embrace the latest fashionable tiny lentil or beautifully colored bean to satisfy an atavistic longing for this kind of food.

Fabled Beans

Beans were common in the classical world and the poor must have eaten more of them than any other class, but from the writings which survive, beans appear to have aroused disconcertingly contradictory feelings. Priests in Egypt, according to one Roman historian, avoided even the sight of beans as they were thought to be impure. The abstemious vegetarian philosopher, Pythagoras, is said by some to have eaten beans, while others claim that he found them so abhorrent that he was killed by his enemies rather than escaping across a field where beans were growing. The Greeks dedicated a temple to Kyanites, the God of Beans, on the sacred road to Elensis. The Kyampsia was a bean festival celebrated in Athens in honor of Apollo. The Romans held a feast, the *Fabaria,* when beans were offered to Carna, the wife of the god Janus. It was believed that the souls of the dead resided in beans and the pious refused to eat them because it was akin to cannibalism.

Today, some cultures still regard bean-eating as propitious. The person who finds the hidden bean in the French cake baked for Twelfth Night, which commemorates the visit of the three kings to the new born Christ child, is considered very lucky and is crowned for the night. In Italy, eating as many lentils as possible on New Year's Eve is said to ensure a prosperous year to come.

Beans and peas appear in several fairy tales. A real princess, who could feel a tiny pea secreted underneath a stack of mattresses, proved her sensitivity to be more acute than ordinary mortals. Enterprising Jack traded his mother's cow for a handful of beans for which he got a slap, but planted them and climbed up the giant beanstalk into a magical world.

RIGHT

If every bean grew into a magical stalk they would be worth their weight in gold.

Cuban Black Bean Soup

SERVES 6

1¼ cups/8 oz/225 g dried black beans,
   soaked in cold water to cover overnight
4 oz/115 g smoked bacon, diced
1 onion, minced
1 celery stalk, minced
1 tablespoon chopped fresh parsley
1 bay leaf
2 whole cloves
Salt and ground black pepper
¼ cup/2 fl oz/60 ml Madeira wine or dry
   sherry
1 hard-boiled egg, finely chopped
1 lemon, thinly sliced

Drain the beans. Put them into a large saucepan with the bacon, onion, celery, parsley, bay leaf, and salt and pepper to taste. Add 1½ quarts/ 2¾ pints/1.5 litres water and bring to a boil. Reduce the heat, cover, and leave the beans to simmer for about 3 hours, or until they are very tender.

Press the soup through a fine strainer, or strain the liquid and purée the solids in a blender or food processor. Return the thick purée to the pot, stir in the wine, and heat through over medium heat. To serve, top each bowl with a spoonful of chopped egg and a slice of lemon.

Black-eyed

WORLD OF PULSES

Pulses form a staple part of the diet all over the world, and each region is distinguished by its dependence on certain varieties, which are identified on the map and in the geographical keybox (below). A more detailed description of the pulses can be found in the numbered A-Z listing on this page.

AFRICA 2 *(black-eyed peas)* **BRITISH ISLES 5** *(broad beans)* **8** *(dried peas)* **CARIBBEAN 15** *(pigeon peas)* **FAR EAST 1** *(adzuki beans)* **13** *(mung beans)* **17** *(soy beans)* **FRANCE 5** *(broad beans)* **7** *(chick peas)* **10** *(haricot vert & blanc)* **12** *(lentils)* **INDIA 7** *(chick peas)* **12** *(lentils)* **18** *(split peas)* **ITALY 4** *(borlotti)* **6** *(cannelini)* **7** *(chick peas)* **12** *(lentils)* **MEXICO/SOUTHERN U.S.A. 3** *(black beans)* **11** *(kidney beans)* **16** *(pinto beans)* **MIDDLE EAST 5** *(broad beans)* **7** *(chick peas)* **9** *(ful mesdames)* **12** *(lentils)* **NORTHERN EUROPE 5** *(broad beans)* **8** *(dried peas)* **U.S.A. 2** *(black-eyed peas)* **11** *(kidney beans)* **14** *(navy beans)*

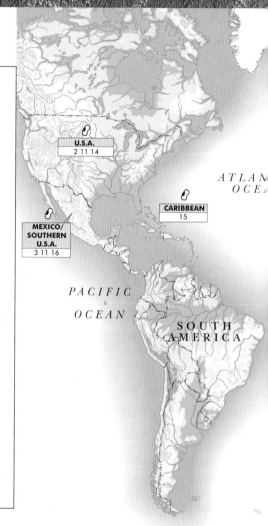

U.S.A.
2 11 14

CARIBBEAN
15

**MEXICO/
SOUTHERN
U.S.A.**
3 11 16

*ATLANTIC
OCEAN*

*PACIFIC
OCEAN*

SOUTH
AMERICA

AN A - Z OF PODS, PEAS & PULSES

ADZUKI
A sweet, small, red oriental bean, good for salads and sprouting. Made into a paste used in Chinese sweets.

BLACK BEAN
A sweet kidney bean, much used in Latin America; excellent for soup.

BLACK-EYE BEAN (BLACK-EYED PEA, COWPEA)
Used in southern U.S.A., India, Africa, and the Caribbean. An Old World bean known to the Romans and brought to America with the slave trade.

BORLOTTI
Italian variety of fava, used in soup and with pasta.

BROWN BEAN
A northern European variety, often cooked with pork for soups and stews.

RUSSIAN FEDERATION

NORTHERN EUROPE
5 8

BRITISH ISLES
5 8

FRANCE
5 7 10 12

ITALY
4 6 7 12

MEDITERRANEAN SEA

CASPIAN SEA

ASIA

MIDDLE EAST
5 7 9 12

FAR EAST
1 13 17

INDIA
7 12 18

AFRICA
2

SOUTHEAST
ASIA

*INDIAN
OCEAN*

cooked stews. Very good for purées.

LENTIL
Called *dahl* in India, these come in all colors and sizes; the tiny blue-gray French lentil from Puy is one of the best. Yellow and red lentils cook quickly and disintegrate; brown or dusty green lentils keep their shape better and have an earthy flavor. Lentils are often split or ground into flour. They do not require soaking before cooking.

LIMA BEAN
One of the most popular American beans; pale green and delicate, with a thinner skin than the fava bean.

MUNG BEAN
A tiny olive-green oriental, this is used for the most common bean sprouts. It is also ground into flour and made into noodles.

NAVY BEAN (YANKEE BEAN)
Used for baked beans, a good all-rounder.

PEA
Dried and split green or yellow varieties are excellent for soup and in English pease pudding. The whole dried pea is used for the dish called mushy peas.

PINTO BEAN (PAINTED BEAN)
A beautifully colored bean, which is popular in Mexico.

RED KIDNEY BEAN
The most popular American bean; robust and keeps its shape during cooking. Useful in salads and sometimes used in chili con carne.

SOYBEAN
The most nutritious bean, used in the orient for many flavoring sauces and pastes, bean curd, and miso. Soy milk and other dairy look-alikes made from soy are extremely valuable for vegetarians or the lactose-intolerant, since they are an excellent source of calcium and protein.

BUTTER BEAN
Soft and slightly sweet, good in salads and stews. Mostly available in the south and Europe.

CANNELLINI
The Italian haricot or white kidney bean, a good all-rounder.

FAVA BEAN
Pale-green when fresh, white when dried. One of the most common beans throughout Europe, where it is called broad bean.

FLAGEOLOT
The green haricot, very popular in France, especially served with roast lamb and garlic.

FUL MESDAMES
Also called foul and field bean, the pale brown bean needs long cooking to bring out its warm, nutty flavor.

GARBANZO BEAN
Nutty and golden, extremely versatile, popular in the Mediterranean, Middle East, and India. Also made into flour. It is also called a chickpea.

GUNGA (CONGO PEA, PIGEON OR JAMAICA PEA)
A brown-flecked, small pea much used in the Caribbean.

HARICOT
Small, white, bland bean used in Spain, Portugal, and South America in slow

A NEW WORLD CORNUCOPIA

*E*arly European settlers in the Americas found a group of vegetables which reminded them of European gourds and melons. They used the Native American names, squashes or squouterquashes, but sometimes still referred to them as gourds or melons.

BELOW

Pumpkins in New Hampshire. The autumn pumpkin harvest is just in time for Halloween jack-o'-lanterns and sweet, spicy Thanksgiving pies.

Squashes were probably among the earliest food plants cultivated by Native Americans and may even have been the first of the three important staple foods—squashes, beans, and corn—known as the Indian triad.

Gourds are still eaten in China and Africa, and hollow gourds were used as vessels in the ancient world. The main New World export eaten by Europeans is one of the smaller, green-skinned summer squashes, the zucchini, also called courgette in France and England. When it is allowed to keep on growing, often to a monstrous size, the English call it a marrow. Immature zucchini are often eaten with their flowers still attached.

Jack-o'-lantern

The earliest use of this term for a night watchman was in l663. A jack-o'-lantern is also a strange flickering light seen in marshy places which advances as approached but is always out of reach. It is an ominous phenomenon, said to be a soul from hell carrying demon coal as it wanders in the dark. A lantern carved from a pumpkin, with a grotesque grinning face and a candle inside, is associated in the north of England, Scotland, and the U.S.A. with Halloween or All Hallows Eve, the last day of October.

LEFT

Mixed squashes and pumpkins were among the earliest food plants grown by Native Americans.

Summer squashes, including yellow or orange crookneck, turban, and pattypan, generally have thinner skins and fairly bland flesh, and should be eaten fresh as they do not keep well. The winter varieties keep well because of their thicker skins and are usually larger with firmer flesh and a much stronger flavor. They also contain more protein, fat, carbohydrates, and vitamin A; the more vivid their color the more nutritious they are. They tend to lose flavor the larger they grow, so the smaller varieties are of more interest to the cook. These include the hubbard, winter crookneck, butternut, acorn, and the bright-orange pumpkin.

Although there are some delicious Spanish and Italian pumpkin dishes it is not very popular in France, except in the south. In North America excellent use is made of squashes, and even Europeans are occasionally won over to the delights of pumpkin pie.

As Cool as a Cucumber

The cucumber, which is a member of the same family as the squashes and gourds, is one of the most ancient cultivated plants in the world, and was brought to the Americas by the Spanish. When it was discovered that the Pueblo Indians of the American southwest ate it, it was wrongly assumed that it was native.

Used as both food and medicine by the Greeks and Romans, it is still valued as a diuretic and is high in potassium and the enzyme erepsin, which aids digestion. It has virtually no calories and is very refreshing because it contains mostly water.

It is very easy to grow and its flavor when freshly picked is incomparable. The tiny ridged cucumbers known as gherkins are used mainly for pickles. Cucumbers are sliced and made into the curiously named bread-and-butter pickles, and larger cucumbers are pickled with dill all over eastern and northern Europe. In the Levant, raw cucumbers are grated and mixed with mint and yogurt to make a dip or summer soup. In Britain, they are a classic accompaniment to fresh salmon, often thinly sliced and decorating the fish in imitation of scales, and in the eighteenth century, they were cooked in cream and served as a vegetable. The English are very fond of cucumber sandwiches made with buttered bread and served at tea time, and slice cucumbers for salads. In the Mediterranean, children snack on whole raw cucumbers in the summer, often in preference to ice cream or candy.

ABOVE

Cool, refreshing cucumber is one of the delights of summer meals in a warm climate.

FRUITS AS VEGETABLES

ABOVE

Making sun-ripened tomatoes into a thick sauce called catsup or ketchup is one of the most enduringly popular ways of enjoying their flavor all year round.

RIGHT

Tomatoes come in many shapes, sizes, and colors. These Sweet 100 and Golden Perfection varieties were grown in Alicante. Spain is one of Europe's major tomato producers.

The pulp surrounding the tomato, which is actually a berry, is eaten as a vegetable, as is the fleshy pulp of the avocado seed, botanically a drupe. Sweet and hot peppers, as well as the chayote, are also defined as fruits.

FROM GOLD TO RED: TOMATOES

The earliest tomatoes to arrive in Europe were yellow, and the Italians called them *pomodoro*, or "golden apples." From Naples, which was ruled by Spain, tomatoes traveled to Provence where they were known as "love apples," or *pomme d'amour*, and grown as ornamental plants for many years before the fruits were eaten. The English also called them love apples but were suspicious of new foods, especially if they were imported from Spain, with whom they were at war. The herbalist, John Gerard, noted that the Spanish ate tomatoes boiled, but that the little nourishment they had was "corrupt." In the eighteenth century, red tomatoes arrived in Europe with Italian Jesuits, and were finally eaten raw in Italy and Spain. But in America, the nineteenth-century food writer, Eliza Leslie, advised cooking tomatoes for three hours to get rid of their raw taste.

For the twentieth-century cook, raw and cooked tomatoes are now an essential ingredient, as are the commercial preparations of tomato paste and catsup, canned tomatoes, and a popular recent introduction, sun-dried tomatoes. Nutritionally, the most valuable part of the tomato is the pulp surrounding the seeds, which is rich in potassium and folic acid, while the whole tomato is very rich in fiber.

There are hundreds of different types but the best tomato, regardless of variety, is one that has been ripened by the sun. These are not easy to transport so most of the tomatoes now available all year round, even in cold countries, have little taste. Tomatoes which have been grown in the ground, warmed by the sun, and canned as soon as they are ripe are often a better choice for the cook than watery, pale tomatoes grown hydroponically and picked while they are still hard enough to withstand packing and shipping.

Even though the tomato is a tropical fruit, it has adapted to more northern climates and is one of the glories of the summer in temperate zones. Some of the older heirloom varieties have a much more robust flavor than the modern commercial tomatoes and are prized by gardeners, even though many are oddly shaped and not all of them are the bright red we associate with the classic supermarket tomato.

SWEET PEPPERS

The larger, milder members of the chili pepper family are eaten as vegetables. They are called bell or sweet peppers to distinguish them from both black pepper and chilies. These smooth-skinned peppers were accepted much more readily than either the tomato or the potato when the Spanish first took them to Europe. Perhaps their vivid colors—red, orange, yellow, purple, white, and green—made them more attractive. They grew well in southern Spain, Sicily, and southern Italy and spread very rapidly all around the Mediterranean. Sweet peppers are an essential ingredient for many Mediterranean dishes, such as ratatouille, where they are combined with eggplant and zucchini, and piperade made with tomatoes and scrambled eggs.

Sweet peppers are high in fiber, potassium, folic acid, and the vitamins B1, B2, and C. They can be eaten raw or cooked and are skinned for many recipes. This makes them more digestible, although the skin tastes pleasant if

Mediterranean Gazpacho

A favorite soup of Southern Europe, gazpacho can have more bread added to make it more substantial.

SERVES 4

1 lb/450 g large ripe tomatoes
1 large onion
2 cloves garlic
1 green bell pepper
1 red bell pepper
½ cucumber
2 slices whole-wheat bread, crusts removed
3 tablespoons olive oil
3 tablespoons wine vinegar
1¼ cups (10 fl oz/300 ml) tomato juice
1¼ cups (10 fl oz/300 ml) water
Salt and freshly ground black pepper

Skin the tomatoes, discard seeds and juice, and chop the flesh. Peel and mince the onion and garlic. Remove pith and seeds from the peppers; dice. Peel and dice the cucumber. Dice the bread.

Put the vegetables and bread in a large bowl, pour over the remaining ingredients, stir, and season. Chill well—overnight is best for a good tasty soup.

You can partly blend the soup if you wish, or blend all of it, in which case offer small bowls of chopped onions, tomatoes, peppers, cucumber, and croutons as a garnish.

Israeli Avocado Cream

SERVES 2

1 large avocado
½ cup (4 oz/115 g) cream cheese
½ small onion, minced
Dash of hot-pepper sauce
1 tablespoon lemon juice
Salt and ground black pepper

Halve the avocado, remove the seed, and scoop out the flesh. Mash the flesh, stirring in the remaining ingredients. Spoon the mixture into a serving dish. Serve at once, or cover with plastic wrap to prevent discoloration

LEFT

Avocados on the tree; it is clear from this photograph how this American native got its original Aztec name and also why it is sometimes called the avocado pear. The tough green skin of the ripe fruit protects the seductive richness of the flesh inside it.

very slightly bitter. If they are broiled or held over a flame for skinning, this softens the flavor and gives them an agreeable smoky taste.

CHAYOTE

Many parts of this central American native are edible. The large fleshy root is very similar to the yam, while the young shoots, leaves, and pear-shaped fruit with a single large seed are also eaten. This fruit ranges in color from green-tinged white to dark green and can be eaten raw or cooked. There are many West Indian and Mexican recipes for chayote, and it is often stuffed in the same ways as sweet peppers. In the Creole dishes of Louisiana, it is called *Mirlotin*.

AVOCADO

Although it is available throughout Europe, there is still something mysteriously alluring about the avocado, or alligator pear as it used to be called. Discovered in Mexico, the Aztec name for it is *ahuacatl*, translated as "testicle tree." It contains more protein than any other fruit and roughly a quarter of it is buttery fat. It is also rich in the B complex of vitamins and fat-soluble vitamin A. It was considered so sophisticated in England that in 1953, when Ian Fleming wrote his first Bond novel, he demonstrated how suave his hero was by describing his eating an avocado for dessert when dining with a female companion. Year-round availability has not dimmed the glamour of this extraordinary fruit.

TREASURES FROM THE SOIL

*A*ppearing as if by magic when summer wanes, wild mushrooms—
with their intense flavor and autumnal perfume—are found in
fields and woodlands until they vanish with the first frost. Some are
dried for use later; cultivated mushrooms are available all year.

The most widely cultivated mushroom is the white
Agaricus bisporus, called the button mushroom when
it is immature, and known as the closed cup slightly
later in its development. It has the strongest flavor
when it is fully mature and the cup opens up
revealing its pinky brown gills.

Button mushrooms are excellent for stuffing, and
they are good raw or cooked. The cremini chestnut
mushroom is a similar variety with a thicker stem
and pale beige to creamy white in color. Oyster
mushrooms are also extensively cultivated and said
to taste just as good as wild ones.

The most common oriental, cultivated mushroom is
the shiitake, which the Japanese domesticated more
than 2,000 years ago. It is available fresh or dried
and is the essential mushroom for Chinese cooking.
It is one of the most strongly flavored fungi of all.
Tiny, pale, delicate *enokitake,* or enoki mushrooms,
originally came from Japan but they are now
cultivated all around the world. They do not have a
great deal of taste but are very decorative. Another
Japanese mushroom, which is cultivated in Japan
but also gathered wild, is the tawny-brown *matsutake,*
or pine mushroom, which has a meaty flavor (one variety is actually native to
North America). It is available fresh, dried, canned, and pickled. The slippery
little Chinese straw or paddy-straw mushroom, which resembles a double
mushroom, is most commonly sold in cans but can sometimes be bought fresh.

Even though most people in America and Britain feel safer eating cultivated

Black Diamonds: Truffles

So far, in spite of many attempts, no one has successfully managed to cultivate the truffle, that most rare and costly member of the large family of fungi.

Canned and bottled truffles, or oil flavored with the mysterious tuber, give only the faintest suggestion of the extraordinary power they possess when fresh. Truffles can be found with the help of the admirable truffle-loving pig who can smell them, even though they may be buried as deep as a foot (30 cm) underground. Dogs and even goats can be trained to hunt truffles, and their presence is sometimes indicated by the proximity of swarms of several species of flies who like to lay their eggs in truffles. In France, truffles are hunted between November and March; the best come from the hills around the Massif Central, south from Périgord, and in the east on each side of the Rhône as far north as Burgundy.

The Italian white truffle has a strong smell but is not as intense in flavor as the black truffle. It is almost always eaten raw in thin slivers, shaved with a special razor-sharp truffle slicer. Truffles are found mainly in northern Italy, in the foothills of the Apennines on the south side of the Lombardy plain, and their short season begins in October and ends around Christmas.

A red or black tuber, somewhat similar to the genuine truffle, is found in North Africa. It is called the dessert truffle or *terfas*, and a white version exists in Morocco. The Roman historian Pliny, who did not know the French truffle, said that the best came from Africa but that they were not as good as the finest Roman mushroom.

LEFT
Wild mushrooms, from the forest of Takachiho on the Japanese island of Kyushu, spread out for drying. Dried funghi are used extensively in Japanese cooking.

mushrooms, they do not taste as exciting as wild ones. Fortunately for the cook, dried wild mushrooms are widely available and have an excellent flavor, as the process concentrates their earthy, autumnal taste of wood and field. One of the finest of all wild mushrooms is the *Boletus edulis*, *cèpe* in French, *porcini* in Italian, and penny bun in English. It has a fat round brown cap and a dark, velvety, meaty flavor. They should be rinsed, and it is advisable to keep the water after soaking, as it is also full of taste. The wild mushrooms which are most often commercially gathered and sold fresh or dried are the yellow *chanterelle*, grey *girolle*, the *morel* with its honeycomb conical cap, the fleshy *pied de mouton*, or wood hedgehog, and the dainty dark death trumpet which is said to taste like truffles.

LEFT
When searching for truffles with the help of a pig, the hunter must distract the animal when it has scented a truffle and then dig very carefully so that the tuber is not damaged.

FRUIT & NUTS

Expressions such as "the apple of my eye," and "a plum job," bear eloquent testimony to the esteem in which fruits are held in our society—at least in the last 400 years. Earlier in European history fruit had sometimes been thought dangerous to health. But by the 17th century, perhaps in response to the import of new fruits from the New World and elsewhere, all kinds of fruit dishes were in vogue. Fruit-based beverages like lemonade are traditional thirst quenchers, and orange juice has become a 20th-century symbol of health. But the premier product of pressed ripe fruit is wine, the natural accompaniment to good food and company.

THE LEGACY OF EDEN

*F*ruit makes a late entry into the story of cultivation. Unlike grain and vegetables, wild fruit seemed to be part of the bounty of nature—the trick was to be there when the fruit was ready to drop.

ABOVE

The "apple" shared by Adam and Eve was more than likely a quince, a fruit much valued by the people of Asia Minor. In this thirteenth-century Norwegian fresco, however, it resembles a date.

Armenia, northern Persia, and the Caucasus, where the quince, the pomegranate, and the fig grew in profusion, were the orchards of the ancient world. Today, all three fruits are anachronistic reminders of the tastes and fascinations of these long-gone cultures. In time, early gardeners realized fruit trees did, in fact, benefit from a well-chosen site and some care. The Etruscans, the Romans, and then the Gauls, improved upon the grafting skills of their predecessors; this was a necessity in establishing healthy orchards and creating new varieties.

In western Europe, the earliest attempts at some form of cultivation seem to have centered on the berry and near-berry fruits familiar to the women farmers of neolithic societies: bilberries, blackberries, strawberries, and sloes.

But fruits generally took longer to become an accepted part of Western diet. Even during the Renaissance, there was widespread belief fruits were actually poisonous. They were commonly held to be responsible for the many inexplicable ills that befell a poorly fed and ill-housed population.

MYTHICAL AND BIBLICAL FRUITS

The Greeks and Romans loved the elegant pomegranate (*Punica granatum*), with its translucent flowers and red hard-skinned fruit. The Greeks thought it the fruit of the Elysian fields, and gave it a pivotal role in the tale of Persephone and her exile to Hades—a metaphor for the pall of winter and the redemption of spring. The Romans grew some nine varieties of pomegranates for a range of uses, from eating to tanning leather.

Its air of exquisite luxury was based partly on its symbolic association with fertility (hence lushness and abundance) as well as on its innate beauty of form. It is crowned with a pendant coronet, and for this reason, it was appropriated as a decorative device by French and Austrian monarchs. Henry VIII planted the first pomegranate tree in Britain at Hampton Court.

In contemporary European and American gardens, however, the pomegranate is a rare commodity. The British retain an affection for the imported fruit as a decorative addition to a winter—and especially Christmas—centerpiece, a nostalgic reminder of the laden tables of Victorian times, when the pomegranate was a Burne-Jones, Pre-Raphaelite icon. It is still popular in Iran, Syria, India, and Pakistan, where its seeds are used as a condiment. The pomegranate's juice is a flavoring in Iran's national dish, *Faisinjan*.

THE FLOWER IN THE FRUIT

The ancient and mysterious fig (*Ficus carica*) is the only fruit to bear its flowers inside. This, together with its plump ripeness and white-and-pink flesh, has endowed it with an explicit erotic symbolism, reflected in the folklore, jokes, and insults of cultures as widely varied as Syria and Italy. Mentioned in Genesis, it is also recorded on Sumerian stone tablets of about 2500 BC. The Greeks believed this godly fruit was a gift of Demeter, and made it sacred to Dionysus. The twin founders of Rome, Romulus and Remus, were said to have been suckled by their she-wolf in the shade of a fig tree.

The fig is thought to be the sweetest fruit; delicious fresh, but also excellent cooked or dried. There are three main types of cultivated figs—red, purple, and green—and many varieties of each. The most prized is the Smyrna fig; a special breed of wasps, hatched in another species of fig, pollinate the Smyrna blossoms, and the fruit is noted for its pronounced flavor (especially when dried). Figs for eating fresh and for drying are grown commercially in Turkey, Greece, North Africa, France, and California (where nearly 100 percent of the crop is dried).

ABOVE

Prosperina (Greek Persephone) clutches her pomegranate in Rossetti's 1877 masterpiece.

THE EARLIEST FRUITS

The orchards of the ancient world lay in the Middle East and Asia. Certain fruits were first cultivated in these regions from as early as 7000 BC.

Dates, 7000–6000 BC
Quinces, 6000–5000 BC
Grapes, 4500 BC
Pomegranates 4000–3000 BC
Bananas, 3000–2500 BC
Apricots, 3000–2000 BC
Figs, 3000–2000 BC

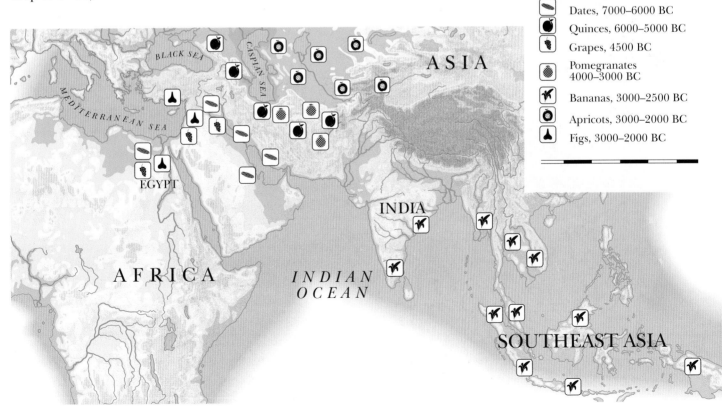

CLASSIC HARD & SOFT FRUITS

*T*raditionally, Western society has relied on the fruits of these six trees for many generations. They are grown in gardens, orchards, and greenhouses from the Mediterranean to Scandinavia.

A member of the huge and varied family *Rosaceae*, the apple was, indisputably, one of the earliest cultivated fruits, a highly bred lateral descendant of the lowly and sour crab apple, with a domesticated history of about 4,000 years.

The apple is native to both Asia and Europe. The Indo-European roots of the word "apple" are reflected in a multitude of languages, from German and English to Old French. Introduced to England by the Romans, where it thrived, the apple was in turn imported to the British colonies in America, becoming in both countries the main ingredient in a dessert staple. But the expression "as American as apple pie" shows Yankee annexation is now almost total.

Today, the apple is the most important temperate-zone fruit, with the U.S.A. providing one-quarter of the world crop. Over 10,000 varieties have been identified internationally; 2,000–3,000 varieties are suitable for commercial exploitation, but only 50 to 60 named varieties are marketed to any degree. Among the most popular and historic are: the autumn red Baldwin of New England; the Red Delicious, America's biggest apple crop; the Golden Delicious, an American variety that has conquered France; the green-skinned Granny Smith from Australia, now a worldwide best-seller; Britain's Cox's Orange Pippin; the McIntosh, one of the best all-rounders; and Reine des Reinettes, the French queen of the russet species.

The apple was once the only fresh fruit that could be reliably laid down to feed the family during winter. Improvements in transportation, as well as new methods of refrigeration and gas storage, mean that today there is always a year-long supply. The apple's iron, potassium, and vitamin content, as well as its versatility as both an "eater" and a "cooker," continue to make it a valued occupant of the household fruit bowl.

BELOW

Calvados from Normandy is a hard liqueur made from a hard fruit—the apple—with a reputation as one of France's finest liqueurs.

APRICOT—GOLDEN DROPS FROM CHINA

Apricots, which grew wild in China and Japan, probably originated in the Far East. From here, they spread gradually through northern India and the Caucasus.

It may have been the armies of Alexander the Great who brought back the sweet, slightly fuzzy fruits from Armenia to the shores of the eastern Mediterranean. The Romans named the fruit *Prunus armenicaca*. Apricots still appear in the savory cooked dishes of Iran and the Middle East, particularly with lamb. Their use in dumplings in Austria and in tarts in Provence and Italy are legacies of Turkish and Arab/Venetian influences respectively.

The fragrant, yellow-orange fruit thrived in the warm alluvial valleys of Iran, the Levant, and North Africa, but it could not adapt to hot, humid conditions, so it does not grow in the tropics, nor in colder areas except under glass. Today, large apricot farms exist in California, Australia, South Africa, and southern Spain.

Apricots do not travel well, becoming woolly if they reach their destination after ripening. Best served at room temperature, they are meltingly sweet with a concentrated flavor; there is not much juice. Luckily, apricots also make excellent jams and conserves, as well as luscious pastries.

Recent research implies that Vitamin A and carotene, in which apricots are rich, may help prevent many degenerative diseases common in the West—the peasants of Asia Minor are noted for both their long life and love of apricots.

ABOVE
A favorite Greek myth to inspire later European painters was that of the Judgment of Paris, here rendered by Niklaus Manuel, 1484–1530. By awarding the "apple of beauty" to Aphrodite, Paris earned the wrath of the other two contenders and launched the Trojan War.

THE NECTARINE AND CURIOUS PEACH

The peach (*Prunus persica*) originated in China, but made its way to Persia, and was discovered by the Greeks, who called it *periskin* (a catch-all word for fruit). It was a rare, expensive commodity until the sixteenth century. A perfect, ripe peach still has a voluptuous elegance, unmatched by any other fruit.

In Chinese myth and literature, the peach is the food of the gods; by consuming the golden peaches of immortality, which fruited once every 6,000 years, the gods escaped death. It was the Emperor's favored fruit, and laden baskets were transported from Samarkand to the Chinese court by camel train.

A millennium later, Louis XIV took a particular interest in the peaches of Montreuil, a suburb of Paris. Even today, the quality of French peaches, and their smooth-skinned sisters, nectarines, is unsurpassable. The white variety of both fruits is the more highly regarded, and usually more expensive. Another distinction is between "freestone" and "clingstone" varieties; the former is more commonly used in canning, the latter for preserves and cooked desserts.

The Spanish brought the fruit to North America in the late sixteenth century, where it was taken up with enthusiasm by southern Native American tribes. Cultivation spread to eastern tribes under British rule, who supplied the colonists with both fresh peaches and planting expertise. By the nineteenth century, large plantings in Virginia and Georgia, aided in the 1880s by the new canning technology, made peaches available nationwide, and even in Europe.

PEERLESS PEARS

Although there are more than 20 species of pear in the world, the vast majority of cultivated varieties derive from one species—*Pyrus communis*, the common pear. The ripe, juicy pear, with its thin, smooth skin and pale, faintly grainy flesh was considered second only to the apple in western Europe during the Middle Ages and Renaissance. Even in stony ground and with a modicum of water, the pear tree will bear well, although it cannot withstand extremes of climate. The fruit will also ripen after picking, and benefits from harvesting while firm—pears pose a temptation for wasps, and are at risk from bruising.

The pear is a native of southeastern Europe and the Middle East, and it spread west and north from Roman times. By 1629 there were 62 varieties cultivated in Britain alone and, by the beginning of the next century, more than 300 in France. Louis XIV's search for the perfect pear was insatiable, and boosted improvements in breeding, grafting, and cultivation. Nobles and gentlemen farmers vied for the chance to present the *Grand Gourmand* with a new variety, for Louis generously rewarded such initiative.

France has never lost her position as Kingdom of the Pear, where it is the third most cultivated fruit (after the apple and plum), with several yellow-, brown-, or green-skinned choices seasonally on sale. Some 30 varieties are widely cultivated. The Bon Chrétien (known as the Williams, or Bartlett, after the original distributors in the U.K. and U.S.A. respectively) and the Doyenne de Comice have become world famous. Other pear-growing countries include Italy, South Africa, Argentina, and Australia.

BELOW

Sorters and graders in a Georgia packing shed, c 1890. The state's peach industry overtook that of Virginia and Maryland which had enjoyed early success. The fruit became synonomous with the state's equally luscious girls.

PLUM PICKINGS

Until the Renaissance the medieval British only knew desiccated or cooked plums; "plum pudding" contained prunes brought from the Mediterranean and southern France. The most familiar fresh British plums were the wild sloe or blackthorn (*Prunus spinosa*), used in wines, liqueurs, and conserves, and the damson (*P. damascena*), a dark purple fruit from Syria, introduced by the Romans.

The continentals, on the other hand, welcomed the varieties brought back from Asia Minor by the Crusaders, and by the later part of the Renaissance enthusiastic cultivation and breeding of *Prunus domestica* had begun. In France, Queen Claude gave her name to an early and successful development imported from Italy, the Reine Claude. It took its English name (greengage) from William Gage who brought the plum to Bury St. Edmunds in 1724.

The Japanese plum (*P. salicina* and *P. triflora*) was introduced into the U.S.A. in 1870. Varieties of this species, among them the Santa Rosa and the Burbank, are among the most cultivated in California, the American capital of plum-growing, and are exported worldwide. In Europe, the little golden mirabelle and the purple quetch command respect, both fresh and in cooked tarts and preserves, and perhaps even more as excellent *eau-de-vies*.

CHERRIES RIPE

The cherry was a cherished medieval fruit, celebrated in song and folklore. In painting it became a symbol of the unattainable or of the passing of time and opportunity. This spirit invests the celebration of Japan's annual cherry blossom festival, when everyone picnics under the frothy white boughs in country orchards or in city parks.

The cherry begins its story in Euphrates and Tigris valleys. When the fruit was brought to Rome, the Mesopotamian name, *karsu*, became the Latin (*Prunus cerasus*), later to transmute into Old French *cherise*, and thus to English "cherry." The Mesopotamian "sour" cherry was the ancestor of the Montmorency, morello, amarello, and some 300 other cherries. These varieties are used for cherry pie, jams, and preserves, savory dishes with duck or game, to candy for pastries, or distilled for *kirsch*, the *eau-de-vie* from Alsace and Switzerland.

"Sweet" cherries (*Prunus avium*), ranging in color from pale yellow to dark red, are best eaten raw. The U.S.A. leads the world in sweet cherry production, most of which are canned for culinary use or sold fresh.

Hideg Meggyleves

HUNGARIAN COLD SOUR CHERRY SOUP

This is a traditional Hungarian summer soup, made when wild cherries are in season. Using cultivated cherries may not be as authentic, but it is still delicious.

SERVES 4

1 lb/450 g sour cherries or morellos
1 cup + 2 tablespoons (8 oz/225 g) superfine sugar
Large pinch ground cinnamon
Grated peel of 1 lemon
2 tablespoons lemon juice
1 tablespoon arrowroot
¾ cup (6 fl oz/175 g) dry red wine
3–4 tablespoons sour cream

Stone the cherries over a bowl so the juice is not wasted. Drop the cherries into the bowl and stones and stems into a large pan. Reserve the bowl of cherries.

Add the sugar and 3 cups (1½ pints/750 ml) cold water to the stones and stems in the pan. Bring to a boil and simmer for 5 minutes. Strain the liquid into another large pan. Add the cinnamon, lemon peel, and lemon juice. Bring to a boil, then add the cherries and juices. Partially cover and simmer for about 25 minutes, until the cherries soften.

Mix the arrowroot with 2 tablespoons cold water to form a paste; stir into the soup. Stir, bringing the soup just to a boil, then reduce the heat to low and simmer about 2 minutes, until thickened. Pour into a glass or earthenware bowl, cover and chill thoroughly. Just before serving stir in the red wine and swirl in the sour cream.

HARD AND SOFT FRUITS

These fruits have enriched the Western diet since the time of the Greeks and Romans, and are grown in both their original homelands and—as a result of importation by early colonists— in North America and Australia. A geographical key (below) lists the main countries of cultivation.

apples   apricots

cherries   peaches & nectarines

pears   plums

generic hard and soft fruit symbol

AFGHANISTAN *apricots* (**2**) **ARGENTINA** *pears* (**5**) **AUSTRALIA** *apples* (**1**); *apricots* (**2**); *pears* (**5**) **BRITISH ISLES** *apples* (**1**); *cherries* (**3**); *pears* (**5**); *plums* (**6**) **CANADA** (Ontario) *peaches & nectarines* (**4**) **CHINA** *apricots* (**2**) **FRANCE** *apples* (**1**); *cherries* (**3**); *peaches & nectarines* (**4**); *pears* (**5**); *plums* (**6**) **GERMANY** *cherries* (**3**); *plums* (**6**) **INDIA** *apricots* (**2**) **IRAN** *apricots* (**2**) **ITALY** *peaches & nectarines* (**4**); *pears* (**5**) **JAPAN** *apricots* (**2**) **NORTH AFRICA** *apricots* (**2**) **PORTUGAL** *peaches & nectarines* (**4**) **ROMANIA** *plums* (**6**) **SICILY** *plums* (**6**) **SOUTH AFRICA** *apples* (**1**); *apricots* (**2**); *pears* (**5**) **SPAIN** *peaches & nectarines* (**4**) **U.S.A.** (Alabama) *peaches & nectarines* (**4**) **U.S.A.** (Arkansas) *peaches & nectarines* (**4**) **U.S.A.** (California) *apples* (**1**); *apricots* (**2**); *cherries* (**3**); *peaches & nectarines* (**4**); *pears* (**5**); *plums* (**6**) **U.S.A.** (Carolina) *peaches & nectarines* (**4**) **U.S.A.** (Colorado) *peaches & nectarines* (**4**) **U.S.A.** (Georgia) *peaches & nectarines* (**4**) **U.S.A.** (Illinois) *pears* (**5**) **U.S.A.** (Michigan) *apples* (**1**); *cherries* (**3**); *peaches & nectarines* (**4**); *pears* (**5**) **U.S.A.** (New Jersey) *pears* (**5**) **U.S.A.** (New York) *apples* (**1**); *pears* (**5**) **U.S.A.** (Oregon) *cherries* (**3**); *pears* (**5**) **U.S.A.** (Pennsylvania) *apples* (**1**); *pears* (**5**) **U.S.A.** (Virginia) *apples* (**1**); *peaches & nectarines* (**4**) **U.S.A.** (Washington) *apples* (**1**); *cherries* (**3**) **YUGOSLAVIA** *plums* (**6**)

BELOW

Pears trained to grow flat against a wall or trellis are known as espalier. The fruit is more accessible to the sun and ripens faster.

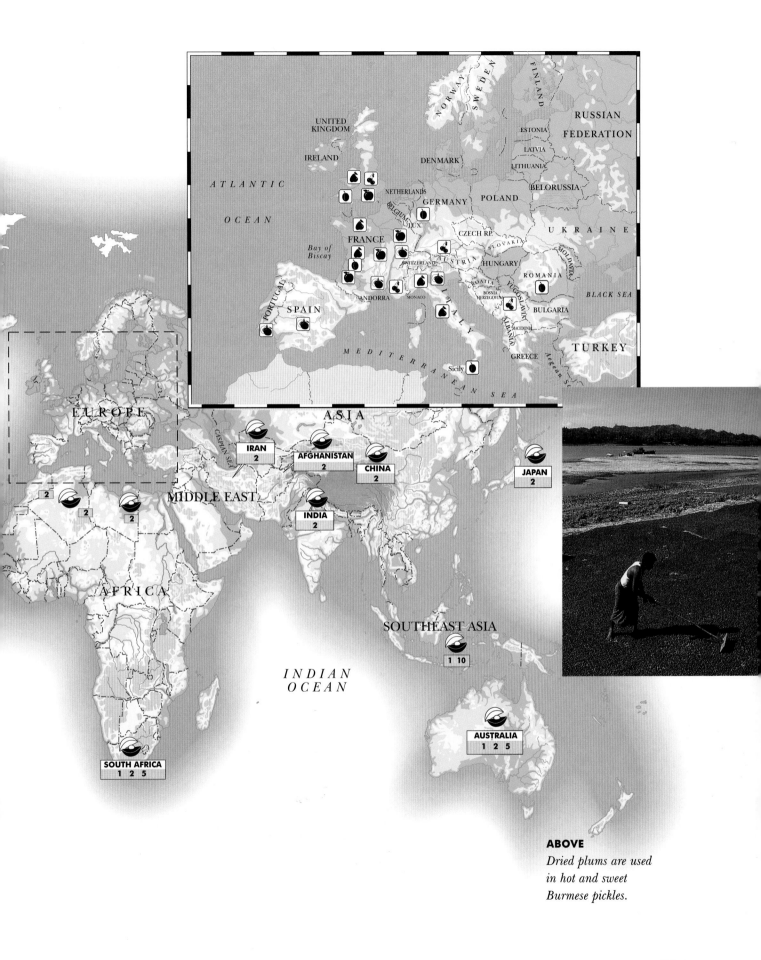

NORWAY
SWEDEN
FINLAND

UNITED
KINGDOM

RUSSIAN
FEDERATION

IRELAND

DENMARK

ESTONIA

LATVIA

LITHUANIA

BELORUSSIA

ATLANTIC

OCEAN

NETHERLANDS

GERMANY

POLAND

U K R A I N E

BELGIUM

LUX.

CZECH RP.

SLOVAKIA

MOLDAVIA

FRANCE

SWITZERLAND

AUSTRIA

HUNGARY

ROMANIA

*Bay of
Biscay*

ANDORRA

MONACO

CROATIA

BOSNIA
HERZEGOVINA

YUGOSLAVIA

BULGARIA

BLACK SEA

PORTUGAL

SPAIN

I
T
A
L
Y

ALBANIA

MACEDONIA

TURKEY

MEDITERRANEAN SEA

Sicily

GREECE

Aegean Se

EUROPE

ASIA

IRAN
2

CASPIAN SEA

AFGHANISTAN
2

CHINA
2

JAPAN
2

2

2

2

MIDDLE EAST

INDIA
2

AFRICA

*INDIAN
OCEAN*

SOUTHEAST ASIA
1 10

AUSTRALIA
1 2 5

SOUTH AFRICA
1 2 5

ABOVE
*Dried plums are used
in hot and sweet
Burmese pickles.*

FROM EXOTIC NEW WORLDS

T*he opening of sea routes to the east and the conquest of the New World brought to the Old an extraordinary abundance of delicious, nutritious fruits.*

Some fruits, like the tomato and avocado, were exploited as vegetables by their new "discoverers." The pineapple became the focus of fad and fashion, but the lip-puckering juiciness of the humble persimmon remained a more localized delight, restricted largely to the descendants of the English colonists in the eastern U.S.A. who had brought it into cultivation. Passion fruit, kiwi fruit, tomatillo, and prickly pears are some of the late developers, found in supermarkets across Europe and America only in the past 20 years, and there are more "new" fruits coming into circulation every season.

ABOVE
A collar protects ripening dates from fresh weather in the Indio, California.

RIGHT
On the Caribbean island of San Martin, local women form a de facto *banana market where boats discharge their cargo.*

AN A - Z OF EXOTIC FRUITS

BANANAS
(Musa sapientum)

The banana originally came from India, where Hindus believe its leaves were used by the first man and woman to cover their nakedness. It made its way as far as the Persian borders by about 1000 BC, but was not heard of again, except as a curiosity presented in the Roman court, before about AD 650–700, when the Arabs brought it to Palestine and North Africa.

By the fifteenth century, the banana had traveled as far as the west coast of Africa. Both the fruit and plants were packed on Portuguese slave ships going from Africa to the West Indies and Brazil. The fruits provided food for the voyage, while the plants supplied a source of fodder for the unfortunate cargo once planted at their tropical destination, where they thrived. They spread across the Gulf of Mexico to Central America, a region which later become a major supplier to the U.S.A., giving rise to the pejorative nickname "Banana Republic."

The names given to the banana in French, English, Italian, and German are almost identical, and are held to come from the Arabic for "finger." Each large bunch is a "hand," holding between 50 to 200 fruits, depending on the variety. There are usually about a dozen "hands" on a 30-foot (9 m) tree. There are 400 varieties, ranging greatly in size and taste. The plantains, the largest of all, are fried, stewed, or mashed and eaten with curries or other spicy Indian, Caribbean, or African foods. They are also dried into chips or ground into flour.

In European cuisine the banana is almost always eaten raw unless served in a dessert; nutritionally, this is the best way to enjoy it. Its high potassium content makes it particularly valuable to sufferers of heart disease.

DATES
(Phoenix dactylifera)

Though fresh dates have been known in the eastern and southern Mediterranean since ancient times, until recently Westerners mainly consumed the dried fruit. Today, several varieties of fresh dates from Israel are available on the European market, while southern California supplies almost 100 percent of American dates, both fresh and dried, from a small desert town called Indio.

Like "banana," "date" means finger or toe, though this time the word is of Greek derivation. The oval or oblong fruits are brown and fleshy, with a skin which slides off when fresh.

Originating in the Persian Gulf, the date was spread by Arab traders through North Africa and south into Saudi Arabia where it is cultivated primarily for local consumption. Despite the commercial dominance of Israeli produce, Iraq still claims preeminence for the quality of its harvest.

GUAVA
(Psidium guajava)

Originating in Central America and Haiti, the guava is from the same family as the eucalyptus and allspice, though its tree is much smaller. First described to a European readership in a mid-sixteenth century chronicle of New World flora, it spread into South America and was transplanted to India and Southeast Asia, Cuba, and Hawaii.

There are several varieties; the fruit can be either round or pear-shaped, the skin greenish-yellow or creamy, and the flesh salmon or ivory colored. The entire fruit is edible, including the seeds; it is sweet with an acid tang. The imported fruit is difficult to obtain at the correct ripeness. It is best eaten raw, or pulped and sieved to make preserves and drinks.

KIWI FRUIT
(Actinidia chinensis)

The kiwi's alternative name, Chinese Gooseberry, recalls its place of origin, though little is known about its Chinese background. Its recorded history began when a few plants were imported to New Zealand and were grown in Wanganuwi. Success only came in 1937 with larger plantings around the Bay of Plenty, and the area remains the biggest exporter. It is a key ingredient in the Antipodean meringue creation, the Pavlova.

First exported to London in 1953, the explosion of nouvelle cuisine in the 1970s launched its international stardom as the movement's signature garnish.

The ovoid Kiwi fruit has a light brown, hairy carapace over a bright green, slightly gelatinous interior with a central circle of edible black seeds. Since it has ten times the vitamin C content of an orange, products are being developed to further exploit its health potential.

LITCHI
(Litchi chinensis)

These sweet, slightly cloying fruits have become a much anticipated winter luxury in Europe and America. They are native to the subtropical regions of China and Southeast Asia, where they may have been grown 2,000 years ago, and were introduced as an export crop into South Africa and the West Indies in modern times. The advent of canning in the twentieth century made the fruit available for general consumption.

Kiwi fruit

A – Z OF EXOTIC FRUITS

Lychees are round, walnut-sized fruits with warty, bright pink, tough skins, which peel away exposing translucent juicy white flesh, which encloses a single large brown seed. Other luscious options from the same family are the longan (*Euphoria longena*) and the rambutan (*Nephelium mutabile*).

MANGO
(Mangifera indica)

Britons were familiar with the existence of mangoes long before most other Europeans ever saw or tasted one. Seventeenth-century English recipes instructed housewives how to "mango" vegetables and fruits, a term taken from Indian mango pickles. The British colonists of the Raj actually experienced fresh mangoes and real mango pickles and chutneys, and brought samples back with them. But Europeans were only able to enjoy the succculence of a fresh mango with the era of refrigeration.

Mango trees have been cultivated in India and Malaysia for some 4,000 years; the name itself has Tamil-Malay roots. There are three main varieties of the fruit, two of which, the summer and the Alfonso, are sweet and are the most frequently encountered in the West. Both should be eaten fresh, so their orange succulence can be appreciated. The Indians use the small green mango for chutneys and pickles, in fruity curries, or as a marinating agent. Today, mangoes are also grown commercially in Australia, Israel, Kenya, and tropical U.S.A.

MELON
(Cucumis melo)

The melon is a quintessentially Middle Eastern fruit. The sand, blazing sun, and dry summer heat of the region, from Israel east to the steppes of Uzbekistan and Kazakstan, bring out its inherent sweetness. More than 1,000 varieties of melon are grown in Uzbekistan alone.

Muskmelons, with their heady perfume, were probably among the earliest type of melon to be cultivated. Chief among them, with flesh varying from pink to salmon to deep orange, are the Persian melon and the American cantaloupe. Another group of melons includes the smooth-skinned or lightly-netted melons with pale white-to-green flesh: the large casaba, the creased, yellow-skinned honeydew, and the ogen and galia, two melons developed in Israel. The true cantaloupe also has pink or orange flesh, but the greenish skin is smooth or warty, and sometimes striped. Examples include the Charentais and the Cavaillon, both French varieties also grown elsewhere.

Melons were probably brought to Italy in the fourteenth century by the Venetian-Arab trading connection. In the late fifteenth century, Charles VIII of France planted a specimen from

TRAVELS WITH A BANANA

The banana has made a long journey from its southern Asian roots, as the map and chronology (right) demonstrate. Today, the banana export trade is dominated by the Caribbean islands and Central America—the fruit was first exported to these regions by European colonists in the sixteenth century.

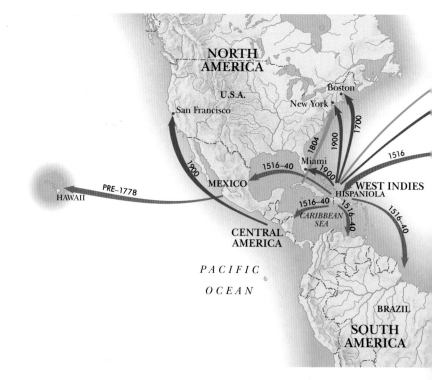

bananas growing pre–1500 BC

bananas growing 1000 BC

← spread of banana cultivation

← first samples exported

← mass transportation in refrigerated ships

Cantaloupo, Italy. By the sixteenth century, greenhouse melons were the pride of English gardeners. Today, melons are an important export fruit in Spain, France, Israel, and California.

PAPAYA

(Carica papaya)

The large, pear-shaped papaya has a smooth yellow skin, orange flesh and black seeds, and grows in clusters around the slim trunk of an 8-foot (2.4 m) tree. Described as a "tree melon," it was noted by Columbus and later explorers to be one of the staples of the Carib Indian diet. The Spanish planted specimens in the Philippines, from where it spread to Nepal and Southeast Asia, reaching India by 1600. Today, there are also commercial plantings in parts of South America, Africa, and the U.S.A., particularly in Hawaii.

The papaya is appreciated most when served fresh. Its ripe, fragrant flesh is the quintessential breakfast of the tropical traveler and makes an exotic addition to fruit salad. Native peoples,

however, also use unripe papaya in stews, fried as a vegetable, or pickled as a condiment. It is high in vitamins B and C, and one of its enzymes, papain, is said to slow the ageing process.

PASSION FRUIT OR PURPLE GRANADILLA

(Passiflora edulis)

The reputation of this small, round, brown-purple, wizened exotic rests on its evocative name and its heavenly fragrance. A perennial climber, the passion fruit was discovered by a Jesuit missionary who first noticed its flowers in the jungles of Brazil. The stamens and pistils called to mind the instruments of Christ's passion.

An alternative name, granadilla, literally means "little pomegranate." This is explained by the interior, which is full of small black seeds. The best way to enjoy the fruit is to cut off the top and use a spoon to scoop out the flesh, crunchy seeds and all. The flesh can also be pulped and strained, and the juice used for ice creams, sorbets, drinks,

Chronological Chart:

🛫	PRE-1500 BC	Bananas growing in coastal India and Southeast Asia
🛫	1000 BC	Bananas growing in Assyria and Mesopotamia
🛫	AD 650	Arab traders bring bananas from India to Egypt
🛫	1100–1400	Bananas transported by Arab traders along trans-Saharan trade routes to West Africa
🛫	1480s	In 1482, bananas discovered in West Africa by Portuguese, who plant them on Canary Islands
🛫	1516	First banana planted on the island of Hispaniola
🛫	1516–40	Banana trees spread throughout West Indies, Central America, and northern and western South America
🛫	1633	First banana brought to Britain, and exhibited in the store of herbalist, Thomas Johnson
🛫	1778	Bananas are discovered growing in Hawaii by Captain James Cook
🛫	1804	First banana brought from Cuba to New York by Captain John Chester
🛫	1882	First banana shipment from Canaries to London
🛫	1900	Introduction of refrigerated banana boats allows the United Fruit Company to export large shipments to San Francisco, Miami, New York, and Boston
🛫	1901	Refrigerated banana boats of Imperial Direct Line (U.K.) begin operations from British West Indies to London

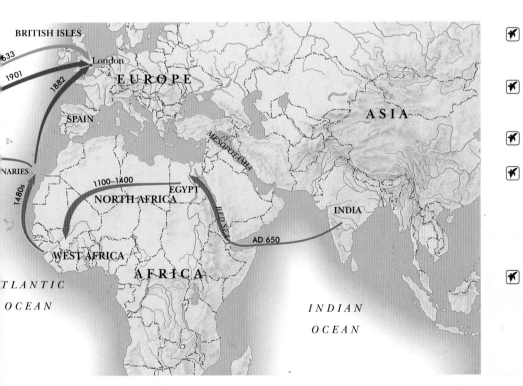

EXOTIC FRUITS

Long credited with life-enhancing qualities, from staving off the effects of ageing to stimulating sexual appetite, these fruits are grown commercially in many parts of the world, as the map and geographical keybox (below) indicates. More detailed descriptions can be found in the numbered A-Z listing, which starts on the preceding page.

Exotic fruits key

AUSTRALIA *banana* (**1**); *mango* (**6**); *passion fruit* (**9**) **AZORES** *pineapple* (**12**) **BELIZE** *mango* (**6**) **BRAZIL** *guava* (**3**); *mango* (**6**); *passion fruit* (**9**) **CANARIES** *banana* (**1**); *mango* (**6**); *pineapple* (**12**) **CENTRAL AMERICA** *guava* (**3**); *passion fruit* (**9**) **EGYPT** *mango* (**6**) **FRANCE** (south) *melon* (**7**); *Physalis/Cape gooseberry* (**11**) **GREECE** *fig* (**2**) **INDIA** *banana* (**1**); *guava* (**3**); *mango* (**6**); *papaya* (**8**); *prickly pear* (**13**); *tomatillo* (**14**) **IRAN** *melon* (**7**) **ISRAEL** *mango* (**6**); *melon* (**7**); *Sharon fruit* (**10**) **JAPAN** *persimmon* (**10**) **KENYA** *mango* (**6**); *passion fruit* (**9**); *pineapple* (**12**) **MALAYSIA** *guava* (**3**); *passion fruit* (**9**) **MEXICO** *bananas* (**1**); *mango* (**6**); *passion fruit* (**9**); *pineapple* (**12**); *prickly pear* (**13**); *tomatillo* (**14**) **MIDDLE EAST** *melon* (**7**); *watermelon* (**15**) **NEW ZEALAND** *kiwi fruit* (**4**) **NORTH AFRICA** *fig* (**2**); *melon* (**7**); *watermelon* (**15**) **PHILIPPINES** *papaya* (**8**) **SOUTH AFRICA** *lychee* (**5**); *Physalis/Cape gooseberry* (**11**); *pineapple* (**12**) **SOUTH AMERICA** *banana* (**1**); *papaya* (**8**) **SOUTHEAST ASIA** *banana* (**1**); *papaya* (**80**); *watermelon* (**15**) **SPAIN** *melon* (**7**) **TANZANIA** *passion fruit* (**9**) **TURKEY** *fig* (**2**) **THAILAND** *guava* (**3**); *lychee* (**5**) **U.S.A.** (Arizona) *melon* (**7**); *tomatillo* (**14**) **U.S.A.** (California) *fig* (**2**); *melon* (**7**); *papaya* (**8**); *prickly pear* (**13**); *watermelon* (**15**) **U.S.A.** (Florida) *mango* (**6**); *papaya* (**8**); *pineapple* (**12**) **U.S.A.** (Hawaii) *guava* (**3**); *papaya* (**8**); *passion fruit* (**9**); *pineapple* (**12**) **U.S.A.** (Indiana) *watermelon* (**15**) **U.S.A.** (Puerto Rico) *pineapple* (**12**) **U.S.A.** (Texas) *melon* (**7**); *prickly pear* (**13**); *tomatillo* (**14**); *watermelon* (**15**) **U.S.A.** (Virginia) *persimmon* (**10**) **WEST AFRICA** *banana* (**1**) **WEST INDIES** *banana* (**1**); *guava* (**3**); *lychee* (**5**); *papaya* (**8**); *passion fruit* (**9**); *pineapple* (**12**)

A – Z OF EXOTIC FRUITS

frappés, and cooked desserts. Today, the fruit is grown commercially in Central and South America, as well as in the West Indies, Australia, Southeast Asia, tropical Africa, Hawaii, and Florida. There is also a less well-known yellow variety (*P. edulis flavicorpa*).

PERSIMMON AND SHARON FRUIT
(*Diospyros virginiana*)

When Americans talk of persimmon, they are referring to the plump fruit discovered by the European colonists. They put the pulpy fruit into persimmon pudding and bread, to this day classic east coast recipes. Unripe, the fruit is mouth-puckeringly tannic.

The Europeans call a variety of oriental persimmon, bred in the rich earth between Tel Aviv and Haifa, Sharon fruit. The Oriental persimmon (*Diospyros kaki*) can be eaten uncooked, and slightly unripe; it is used in fruit salads and other light desserts.

PHYSALIS OR CAPE GOOSEBERRY
(*Physalis peruviana*)

Also called "Love-in-a-Cage," this orange-yellow, smooth berry, with the pointed ends of its papery calyx folded back toward the stem end, is a native of South America. It was introduced to South Africa in the nineteenth century, becoming an important export with the introduction of canning. Today, the swiftness of food transport, and the excellent storage quality of the berries, means that they are available fresh, adorning cakes and pastries or dipped in fondant or chocolate for petit fours.

PINEAPPLE
(*Ananas comosus*)

The pineapple came originally from South America, but was already being cultivated by the natives when Columbus arrived on the island of Guadalupe in the Caribbean in 1493. Its Brazilian name was *nana*. The Spanish named it *pina de Indes*, because of its resemblance to a pine cone. By 1555, the Spanish

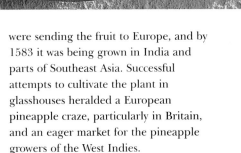

were sending the fruit to Europe, and by 1583 it was being grown in India and parts of Southeast Asia. Successful attempts to cultivate the plant in glasshouses heralded a European pineapple craze, particularly in Britain, and an eager market for the pineapple growers of the West Indies.

The British introduced the pineapple to the Hawaiian Islands in 1790. When James Dole opened his pineapple canning factory there in the 1920s, it became the biggest business in the islands for the next forty years. Today Hawaii's share has shrunk, and pineapples are also grown in the West Indies, the Canaries and Azores, Central America, Mexico, Puerto Rico, and the west coast of Africa.

The pineapple plant produces a single "armored" fruit, crowning a central stem. When ripe, it should smell wonderful, be brown and slightly tender, and a leaf should pull easily from its top. At the peak of growth, a huge surge of fruit sugars suffuses the fruit, enriching the flavor.

PRICKLY PEAR
(*Opuntia megacantha*)
A New World fruit, the prickly pear has only recently reached a wider market, mainly because of Hispanic immigration and settlement in the western U.S.A. It is known by other names, including cactus pear and Barbary or Indian fig.

The large green spiny pads of the mother plants are a familiar sight in Hollywood movies. Baby pads (*nopales*) are sold spined, to be cut into small pieces and eaten raw in salads or cooked in soups and other Mexican dishes. The oval fruits (*nopalites*), usually yellow or red, are also spiny and ripen along the edges of the pads from fall to December. They can be bought spined, cooked, and bottled, but are also available fresh, still attached to a small part of the pad to help conserve flavor. The delicate flesh can be eaten raw in salads, braised, made into preserves, or pickled.

TOMATILLO
(*Physalis ixocarpa*)
The tomatillo, or Mexican tomato, is a near relative of the Cape gooseberry. It

is much larger than the latter, with the fruit filling the papery calyx or husk, which must be removed before cooking. The tomatillo is harvested and used when unripe and green. It can be used raw, and is an essential ingredient in a true guacamole, but heat brings out the flavor, best appreciated in hot salsa verde and in conserves.

WATERMELON
(*Citrullus vulgaris*)
Originally from Africa, the watermelon was brought by African slaves to the U.S.A. It has always had associations with the culture of the Southern states, the sure sign that summer has come. It is a commercial crop in Texas, Indiana, and California. It is also grown in India, Africa, and Southeast Asia.

Sharon fruit

SWEET & TANGY: CITRUS FRUITS

The most widely available internationally, citrus fruits are important to health, particularly as a ready, rich source of vitamin C, and as a flavoring agent in many ethnic cuisines.

ABOVE

Lemonade enjoyed its American heyday from 1850–1950 as the beverage of genteel—especially Southern—ladies.

Though all the citrus fuits are indigenous to Asia, rapid transportation, cultivation in both hemispheres, and the continuous appearance of new varieties and hybrids, mean that the major species are available all year-round.

CITRONS: A LOST TASTE

The large, knobby citron (*Citrus medica*) no longer boasts the importance of its sixteenth-century heyday. The answer to its erstwhile popularity and subsequent decline lies in its skin, which was once grated to flavor a variety of sweet and savory dishes and candied for sweetmeats. Its extracted oil was used in perfumery. The conquering Greeks found the fruit in the land of their adversaries, the Medes; this pedigree is remembered in the Latin name, though it probably came from farther afield—India or China. Today cultivation is restricted to the south coast of France, where the thick skin is still rendered into fine candied peel for use in cakes and pastries, and to Corsica and the Greek Islands, where it is distilled into local liqueurs.

SEA-SICKNESS AND LEMON-AID

Though in its prime the citron surpassed the lemon in the estimation of Western diners, the lemon (*Citrus limon*) was soon to take its place. Like its sister fruits, the lemon probably originated in the East; its name is from the Persian, and it has been a local fruit of the eastern Mediterranean for at least 2,000 years. It is probable the fruit passed with Arab invaders into Spain in the seventh century, but it was the Crusades which led to its conquest of Europe. The knights were seduced by its sour accents in the savory dishes of the Arabs, and upon their return to Britain it gained status as a rare and coveted luxury. Subsequently, small orchards began to dot the shores of the Mediterranean.

By the turn of the fourteenth century, the lemon was gaining acceptance in the Christian kitchen. Its peel, juice, and oil extract were used in cakes, pastries, and candies from Britain (when they could be had) to the Balkans, but its sour flavor in meat, poultry, fish, and grain dishes was more to the liking of the Italians and Spaniards. Today, the lemon continues to be grown all over the Mediterranean and in Portugal, with major commercial concentrations in Spain, North Africa, and Italy. In the U.S.A., California is the main grower, with some help from Texas and Arizona. The majority grown in the U.S.A. are thick-skinned varieties, which keep better; in Europe both thin- and thick-skinned varieties are cultivated; in the Middle East thin-skinned varieties are preferred, especially for Morocco's famous salted, preserved lemons.

OLD EASTERN FRUIT, NEW WESTERN ROLE

The lime (*Citrus aurantifolia*) shares the Persian root of its name, *limah* ("citrus fruit") with the lemon. Its origins can be traced with more certainty to the Far East, where it is a fixture of southeast Asian cuisine. It needs tropical heat to survive, explaining its unenthusiastic welcome when it was introduced into Italian and Spanish gardens, probably through Venetian-Arab trade. However, its potential must have been appreciated, since Columbus planted seeds from the Canary Islands in Haiti's receptive soil.

The trees spread throughout the West Indies, across the Gulf of Mexico, and into Mexico. These "Caribbean" limes are an important ingredient in both West Indian and Mexican cooking, and are also combined with many drinks

War Against Scurvy

Caused by a deficiency of vitamin C, which man cannot synthesize himself, scurvy was the scourge of both seaman and voyager on long-haul journeys across the Atlantic and Pacific oceans during the centuries of exploration and settlement. On land it was not such a problem—fresh vegetables and fruit were more available. But at sea, garden produce did not survive long. Those making their way over the ocean were likely to fall ill with bleeding gums, loose teeth, general hemorrhaging, and a terrible aching weakness. In 1536, nine-tenths of a crew on an icebound ship succumbed to the disease, but were rescued by drinking an Indian concoction made from the bark of the Arbor Vitae tree. Not for nothing was it named "the tree of life."

As early as 1600, the sailors of the East India Company were aware of the connection between eating citrus fruit and avoiding scurvy, and several informed captains provisioned their ships accordingly, but only through individual initiative. It was not until 1753 that the Scottish surgeon, James Lind, published *A Treatise on Scurvy*, and not until 1795 that the Lords of the Admiralty made the issue of limes (and lime juice) official government policy, leading to the famous soubriquet "Limeys" for British sailors, though lemons soon replaced limes.

LEFT
Lemons, limes, oranges, and watermelons are the sole products on offer at this London stall c 1850.

such as tequila, beer, and rum. In both North America and Europe, the Tahiti lime, a large, green, and sweet variety, is the most common, but other varieties are appearing as Europeans and Americans become ever-more enamored of Mexican, South American and Southeast Asian cuisines.

THE ORANGE FAMILY

The word "orange" ultimately derives from a Dravidian Indian term, meaning "perfume from within." There are three main branches of the family: bitter oranges (*Citrus aurantium*), the oldest in terms of chronicled history and today the most restricted in cultivation; sweet oranges (*C. sinensis*), commonly encountered as breakfast orange juice, or weighing down school lunch boxes; and the popular, if more recherché, loose-skinned oranges (*C. reticula*), with their foreign-sounding names and associations with Victorian opulence and Christmas stockings.

All oranges originated in the Far East, but no two culinary historians agree on what happened next. The bitter orange seems to have made its way to Italy in the second century AD, introduced by Roman spice dealers who traded with Arab caravans on the desert sands east of Palmyra. Absentee Roman landlords planted great groves of bitter oranges along the North African coast. But there is no evidence of farther European penetration, until the arrival of the Arabs in Spain, bringing the small, thin-skinned fruit with them. It thrived in the southern hills near Seville.

The flesh of the fruit was of little consequence; what won admiration was the incredible perfume of the flowering tree, whose blossoms were harvested for orange water; the powerful flavor of the skin when used in cooking or sweetmeats, or distilled in alcohol; and even the pungent oil, called petitgrain, contained in the leaves, which was used to infuse pastries and comfits with a spicy orange tang. Though all orange flowers smell wonderfully, nothing quite matches the perfume of the Seville orange. The trees were grown to scent the air around palaces in Spain, then in Italy and eventually France; the distilled orange water perfumed baths, pomades, and food. The French town of Orange on the river Rhône was to become the center of the orange import trade; the name was an approximation of the Spanish *naranja*. By the Renaissance, the whole of western Europe was besotted with oranges.

The stage was set for the usurper, in the form of the sweet orange (*C. sinensis*). This probably appeared at the same time as the lime (*sinensis* actually means "from China," though most evidence points to a Malaysian origin). After Vasco de Gama's epic voyage around the Cape of Good Hope, more specimens became available for planting in royal gardens; the sweet golden globes inspired Louis XVI to build the first orangerie at Versailles, while the British king's appetite for oranges, among other indulgences, made a royal mistress of fruit-seller Nell Gwyn.

HOME OF THE ORANGE BOWL

Hernando de Soto is credited with bringing oranges to Florida in 1539; the first plantation was set up in 1579; in 1776 a large grower recorded sending 65,000 oranges to London; by 1820 the Sunshine State was America's prime commercial grower. Though the California missions were cultivating trees as early as 1707, their progress was restricted by distance and a hacienda mentality. By the mid-nineteenth century, when groves were finally beginning to run as a business, gold pushed everything else from the Californian agenda. Only the appearance of refrigerated ships in the 1880s gave the state the impetus to compete with its eastern rival. The introduction of the navel orange from Brazil into California's orchards also changed the balance between the two states; today 90 percent of Florida's crop goes into the juicer; California grows the vast majority of eating oranges. Together, the two states grow about 16 percent of the world crop, most of it destined for American consumption. Spain, North Africa, Israel, and South Africa supply European needs, with Italy providing a small percentage of coveted blood oranges.

Finally, there are the fruits of the *C. reticula* family, which includes the mandarin, tangerine, and satsuma. The mandarin was the first to arrive in Western countries, described in an English translation of a Dutch chronicle in 1771. Its Cochin origins, together with its brilliant color, led to its being christened in honor of the gaudily attired mandarins of the Chinese court. Now it is mainly encountered canned, its tiny segments used to decorate pastries and in fruit salads. The slightly squashed-looking tangerine and satsuma, in contrast, are well distributed; the former was introduced to Western markets via Tangier in the 1840s, hence its name; the latter is a relatively recent newcomer from Japan. The satsuma's many strengths have made it a welcome addition to the company of commercially successful citrus fruits: its tough skin makes it hardy; it is easy to peel, because of puffy detachment of that skin from the meat; it is full-flavored and lacks seeds.

POMELOS AND GRAPEFRUIT

While most people who see a pomelo in a supermarket think it a rather neglected offshoot of the grapefruit, in fact the opposite is true: the pomelo (*C. glandis*) predated the grapefruit in European knowledge and appreciation. It was the original French "pamplemousse" (now the word for grapefruit in that country), and the name contracted to "pomelous" and then "pomelo" in English. The fruit was first encountered by the seventeenth-century Dutch in Indonesia and Malaysia, who named it "apple-lemon" (*pompelimoes*); it was rapidly taken up by French planters in the Indian Ocean and in the Caribbean. British planters in the West Indies called it a shaddock.

French Spiced-and-Soused Sweet Clementines

This is a traditional treatment for clementines, popular since the fruit's introduction in France at the turn of the century.

FILLS 5 X 2¼ CUP (17 FL OZ/½ LITER) JARS

4 lb (1.75 kg) whole clementines
Strained juice and pared peel of 2 lemons
2 sticks cinnamon
2¼ cups (1 lb/450 g) superfine sugar
⅔ cup (5 fl oz/150 ml) brandy

Put the clementines in a large steamer basket or in a deep-fat fryer basket. Place over boiling water and steam, covered, for 15 minutes. Meanwhile, wash the jars and sterilize in a hot oven with the lids open and rubber seals off for about 15 minutes.

Remove the clementines in their basket; pour the steaming water, now also containing juices, into a smaller saucepan. Spoon the clementines into the larger saucepan, cover, and reserve.

Add the lemon juice, peel, and cinnamon sticks to the smaller pan. Bring to a boil and continue to boil for about 2 minutes. Slowly stir in the sugar, stirring all the time. When the sugar is dissolved, return the liquid to a boil, and keep at a low roll for about 5 minutes, or until it is thickened and syrupy. Remove the cinnamon sticks.

Remove the jars from the oven. Use metal skewers to pierce the clementines and pack them in the jars. Pour the syrup over the clementines, covering the fruit completely. Add 2 tablespoons of brandy to each jar. Cover and seal. Leave for at least 2 months; the clementines will keep in a dark, cool place indefinitely.

The pomelo was only accorded the status of a separate species in 1880, but by that time its popularity was already being overtaken by that of the grapefruit (*C. paradisi*). This is easy to understand, since the grapefruit is juicier and more versatile than its precursor, though without the thick, easily-peeled skin. The grapefruit is most probably an offshoot of the West Indian pomelo, or may be a hybrid of that and the sweet orange. It was introduced into Florida by the innovative French grower, Count Philippe Odet, in 1823. By 1830, it was identified as a species (incorporating, at the time, the pomelo), but it would take several decades before the grapefruit would attract commercial investment.

Now, just over 100 years since large-scale cultivation began in Florida, it is the second most important citrus fruit internationally after the orange, with several popular pink, seedless and pigmy varieties, as well as the standard large yellow. Although Florida continues to supply 80 percent of world trade, additional producers ship from Texas, California, Arizona, the West Indies, South Africa, and South America. More than half the tonnage is squeezed into juice.

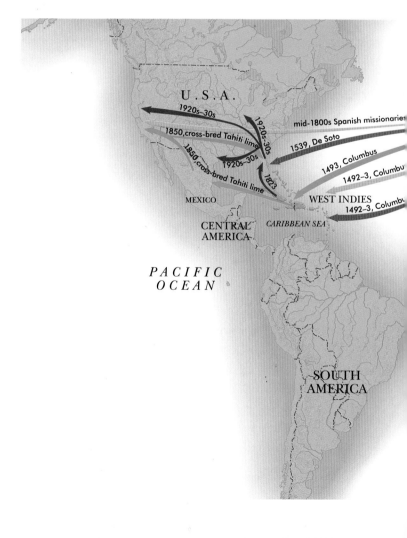

THREE CITRUS HYBRIDS

Here are three fruits often encountered by shoppers. Two—the ugli and the tangelo—are hybrids of grapefruit crossed with tangerine, but the results are quite different. While the tangelo (*C. spp*) is attractively orange colored and smooth-skinned, with a pleasing, slightly elongated shape, the ugli is just plain ugly (hence its name). The tangelo is the result of a controlled double-cross of two different grapefruit trees then grafted to a tangerine. It is sometimes also called a mineola, after the town in Florida where this grafting was accomplished in 1931. The tangelo is also sweeter and juicier than its ugly sister—though less so than an orange. The ugli is native to India, where it is sometimes cooked in hot ashes to intensify its flavor and juiciness. It is recognizable by its rough, muddy colored orange-green skin, worn over its meat like an ill-fitting overcoat. It peels easily, however, and can be eaten raw or cooked, just like grapefruit.

Finally, there is the small, juicy, and almost seedless clementine. It is a cross between a tangerine and an orange, whether a sweet or Seville orange is now a matter of controversy, and was the creation of a priest, Père Clement, in Algeria in 1902. Clementines began to appeal to Anglo–Saxons in the late 1920s-30s. And as well as being eaten fresh, they are excellent pickled in spices or preserved in brandy. Today, they are raised mainly in Spain, Morocco, and Italy, as well as Algeria; and the seedless, full-flavored Corsican variety is the *ne plus ultra* of the species.

CITRUS FRUITS

The four main citrus fruits have traveled great distances from their areas of original cultivation, transported by traders, colonists, explorers, and missionaries.

LEMONS
area of original cultivation
← subsequent spread

LIMES
area of original cultivation
← subsequent spread

ORANGES
area of original cultivation
← subsequent spread

GRAPEFRUITS
area of original cultivation
← subsequent spread

Chronological Chart:

LEMONS

AD 600	Asian lemons go to Levant.
900–1100	Lemons brought by Arab traders from Levant to Africa, Spain, and France.
1492–93	Lemon seeds introduced to West Indies by Columbus.
MID-1800s	Spanish missionaries bring lemons to California.

LIMES

AD 700	Limes from Southeast Asia are taken to Spain.
1493	Columbus brings limes from Spain to Haiti and Mexico.
1850	The Haitian lime moves from California to Florida.

ORANGES

1000 BC	Oranges were brought from India to China.
AD 100	Roman traders carried oranges from India to Italy.
1492–93	Columbus brought the first oranges to the Caribbean.
1500s	Oranges taken from China to Asia and to the Canaries.
1539	Oranges brought from Spain to the Caribbean.

GRAPEFRUITS

1823	Brought from the West Indies to Florida.
1920s–30s	Introduced to the U.S.A.

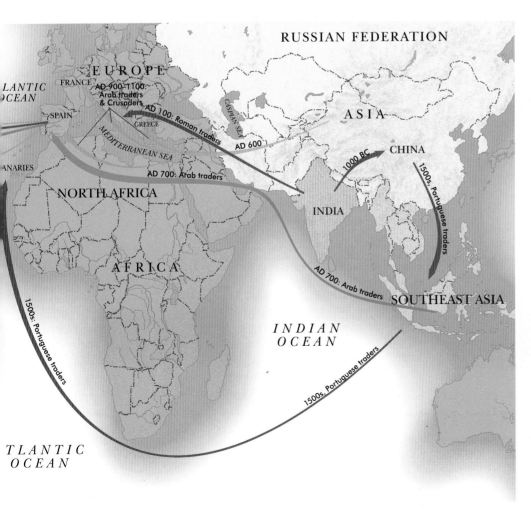

RUSSIAN FEDERATION

EUROPE

FRANCE

AD 900-1100: Arab traders & Crusaders

ATLANTIC OCEAN

SPAIN

AD 100: Roman traders

GREECE

MEDITERRANEAN SEA

CASPIAN SEA

ASIA

AD 600

CHINA

1000 BC

1500s: Portuguese traders

CANARIES

AD 700: Arab traders

NORTH AFRICA

INDIA

AFRICA

1500s: Portuguese traders

AD 700: Arab traders

SOUTHEAST ASIA

INDIAN OCEAN

1500s: Portuguese traders

ATLANTIC OCEAN

SUMMER'S JEWELS: BERRIES

*B*erries are among the most ephemeral of fruits and, if picked in the wild, a delight to be savored immediately.

Berries divide into two main types: those which bear single, rounded fruits—either several along a length of stalk (red and black currants, bilberries) or one fruit at the end of it (strawberries); and those composed of a number of drupes united into an aggregate fruit (blackberries, raspberries, mulberries, etc.). The strawberry also has a special distinction, being the only fruit to have its many seeds exposed on the surface of its skin, rather than inside it. Despite its lack of apparent similarity to the raspberry and blackberry, it is also a member of the rose (*Rosaceae*) family. Cranberries, bilberries, and blueberries are members of the heather (*Ericaceae*) family, sharing the characteristic low, shrubby growth and liking for the acid soils of heath and moorland displayed by their bell and ling cousins.

The best way to enjoy these delights crosses genus and variety. Preserves and conserves apart, there are broad guidelines suggested by centuries of picking and preparation. Strawberries are never cooked; they are added after pastry is baked, or stirred, mashed, and strained into prepared custards. Fresh raspberries deserve to be treated the same way for the sake of their exquisite flavor, but they can be cooked. Blackberries, boysenberries, loganberries, and bilberries can be served either fresh or cooked; but blueberries, cranberries, currants (all colors), and gooseberries generally need cooking, with sugar, to bring out their true strength of flavor. All berries are low in calories and high in vitamins and several trace minerals.

ABOVE

California's Knott's Berry Farm is best known for its boysenberries.

RIGHT

Picken' for packin'—harvest time in Cape Cod's cranberry bogs, 1890s.

A PUNNET OF BERRIES

BILBERRY OR WHORTLEBERRY
(Vaccinium myrtillus)

A tiny, round, purple-blue wild berry harvested by hand in northern Europe and North America using special combs. Late summer; makes superb preserves, liqueurs, and tarts; particularly rich in vitamins B and C.

BLUEBERRY
(Vaccinium spp)

A larger, cultivated species of the above, with rich, full flavor, though not as wonderful as the wild version. It is raised mainly in northern U.S.A. and Australia. Mid to late summer; used in pastries, desserts, and syrups.

BLACKBERRY
(Rubus fruticosus)

There are more than 400 varieties worldwide. Often called "bramble," the wild varieties are less juicy than the cultivated, but the strained juice of the wild berry is superior in flavor. Late summer; used in jams, jellies, liqueurs, syrups, desserts, and pastries; medicinal use for sore throat and mouth ulcers.

BLACK CURRANT
(Ribes nigrum)

The juicy, round black berries grow wild in northern Europe, but are also widely cultivated. High in vitamin C, they have long been used in children's drinks and health drinks. The main growers are France, Belgium, Germany, and the Netherlands. Renowned as base of *cassis*, the French liqueur, also used in syrups, jams, and jellies and used cooked in pastries and desserts.

BOYSENBERRY
(Rubus spp)

A California hybrid, the result of double-crossing: a loganberry with a blackberry and a raspberry. This was the original product of the famous Knott's Berry Farm, though also grown elsewhere for jams, jellies, and pastries.

CRANBERRY
(Vaccinium oxycoccus and V. macrocarpem)

The *oxycoccus* is the common European cranberry or lingonberry, which grows wild on most continents. The *macrocarpem* gets its name from its meaty interior, and is the traditional accompaniment to Thanksgiving turkey. It is cultivated on the U.S.A.'s east coast (Cape Cod) and in Oregon. It is also a popular health drink due to its high vitamin C content.

GOOSEBERRY
(Ribes grossularia)

A large ovoid, slightly "hairy-skinned" berry, light- or yellow-green in color, grown mainly by the British and Dutch, and cooked in desserts or pastries.

HUCKLEBERRY
(Gaylussacia baccata)

A North American berry, easily confused with the wild blueberry or bilberry, though it is smaller, blacker, and even more acidic. It was a favorite of the Native American tribes, and can be used with added sugar, like the bilberry.

LOGANBERRY
(Rubus loganbaccus)

An American cross between a raspberry and blackberry, this elongated, dark red aggregate is used for desserts and pies. A Scottish hybrid is called the Tayberry.

MULBERRY
(Morus nigra)

The black mulberry is a traditional fruit introduced into Europe from Asia Minor, used in preserves and puddings since roman times. Eaten only when ripe, it is unsuitable for commercial cultivation.

RASPBERRY
(Rubus idaeus)

Gathered wild since prehistoric times and cultivated since medieval times, this bright to deep-red, sweet, juicy berry shares honors with the strawberry as king and queen of dessert fruits. A midsummer fruit; excellent fresh and in jams, preserves, liqueurs, syrups, cooked desserts, ice cream, and pastries.

RED CURRANT
(Ribes rubrum)

Particularly appreciated in Britain, Scandinavia, and Germany where this glowing red fruit with its sweet-sour flavor is both partnered in a sauce or as a jelly with savory dishes (hare, pheasant, venison), and incorporated into desserts. The rarer white currant is a cultivated offshoot of the red currant, with a delicate flavor. Considered at one time to make wonderful fruit wine, it is now used mostly for garnishes.

STRAWBERRY
(Fragaria spp)

Even in Europe, cultivated strawberries are hybrids of species and varieties imported from North and South America during the eighteenth and nineteenth centuries; these superseded low-yield, smaller European varieties. There are several hundred strawberry varieties worldwide, with enormous range in color, size, and flavor; they are also available year-round from some sources. They are delicious fresh, but are also made into jams, liqueurs, ice creams, tarts, and (uncooked) desserts.

WILD STRAWBERRIES

Fragaria vesca and **alpine strawberries** (a cultivated variety of *F. vesca*) are tiny descendants of original European strawberries. They have a superb flavor, but are correspondingly rarer and more expensive.

GRAPES: THE FESTIVE FRUIT

The vine is a beneficent plant. Its leaves and seeds have many culinary uses, but it is for the fruit—white, red, or black grapes—that it has won its reputation as a valued foodstuff.

A great variety of wild grapes grow worldwide, from the Himalayas to the tip of Tierra del Fuego, but only a bare selection of species are considered worthy of cultivation. Of these, over 90 percent belong to *Vitis vinifera*, "the vine that bears wine," commonly known as the European wine grape.

There are more than 5,000 varieties of *V. vinifera* alone, and table wines are also made from some of the species indigenous to the Americas and elsewhere. Indeed, both the great and lesser vintages of Europe owe a resounding vote of thanks to the native rootstock of the U.S.A. The phylloxera plague, which ravaged the European vintages in the mid-nineteenth century, was eradicated by grafting new, unaffected growth onto disease-resistant midwestern American *V. lambrusca*, which was imported for the purpose. (The fact that the epidemic was itself caused by the importation of infested American vines into France for experimental cultivation in the early 1850s usually escapes comment!)

THE BEVERAGE OF THE GODS

Almost every culture has its elaborate myth explaining the invention and spread of wine. The best known are the Greek and Roman versions which credit the gods Dionysus and Bacchus with the invention. Their names now grace wine labels, drinking societies, wine bars, liquor stores, gourmet shops, and many other vinous outlets. In Judeo-Christian tradition, the hero is Noah, who "began to be a husbandman, and he planted a vineyard, and he drank of the wine and was drunken," the first of many. Noah's disrespectful son reacted to his inebriation with disapproval, a foreshadowing of Western Christian intolerance. Other early cultures—the Assyrians, Babylonians, Greeks, Egyptians, and Romans—cherished their festivals of intoxication, where license was permitted to revel, something frowned upon the rest of the year. The word "enthusiasm" (Greek: *enthousiasmos*) originates from these times of ritual overindulgence, and means "possessed by the god (of wine)."

Wild grapes formed part of the very earliest human and fossils incorporating grape leaf impressions have been found dating from the Miocene epoch (23 to 5 million years ago). But the cultivation of grapes, and the pressing and storing of the juice in an approximation of something like wine, seems only to have begun in the region between the Black Sea and the coast of Persia in the sixth millennium BC.

Even with the advent of the Greeks and Romans, the wine drunk at table and at *symposia* (parties devoted to drink and conversation) was unpalatable by our standards. It was cooked and, in the case of Greek wines, blended, then aged in earthenware amphorae whose insides were sealed with pine pitch. This taste for resinous wine persists in the retsina of modern Greece. When decanted into the traditional huge serving bowl, it was a thick, cloying syrup, which had to be cut with water. Roman women were never allowed at such gatherings, nor were they permitted wine.

Both the Greeks and Romans appreciated the exceptional climate of southern Gaul for grape-growing and, by the latter days of Imperial Rome, the vintners of Provence and the lower Rhône Valley were competing with domestic suppliers in Italy. It was actually the clever Gauls who changed the character of both the wine itself and the way it was consumed. Because their initial beverage of choice had been barley beer, they had developed the accompanying skills of barrel-making which they transferred to wine, dispensing with the need for porous amphorae and pitch sealant. As a direct result, they preferred to drink their wine free of water; the unadulterated taste of the grape now became important. *V. vinifera* now grew all over France and new strains, particularly frost-resistant ones, proliferated. The Gauls were democratic in their pleasures; wine could be bought across the counter at wayside open-fronted stores, to be taken home and enjoyed in the bosom of the family.

ABOVE
Wine ages in cellars cut into the stony terrain where vines flourish.

WINES OF IMPERIAL ROME
The Romans were supplied with wine from several regions of their extensive empire— southern France, Spain, northern Italy, the Rhineland, and the Aegean. Today, these are still among the main wine-producing areas of Europe.

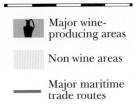

Major wine-producing areas	
Non wine areas	
Major maritime trade routes	

Table Grapes

It was not until the Renaissance that raising grapes to be eaten, rather than to serve as the raw material of wine, gained some support. But even though estate owners and aristocratic gardeners experimented with table grapes, dessert grapes only became an accepted social custom in the eighteenth century. Today, a greater distinction is made between table grapes and grapes for wine-making, although some, like America's northeastern native, the black, foxy-flavored Concord, continue to be used for both, as well as for jello and grape juice.

Generally speaking, table grapes should be more thin-skinned than wine grapes, the juice not as sweet, nor the tannic bite of the skin as marked. Seedless varieties, such as Thompson, are now gaining ground, but more challenging favorites include large black and green hothouse grapes from Belgium, the golden-green Muscatel, the verdant Almeria, and the deep-red Cardinal and Napoleon. Notable table grape-growing countries include Belgium (but only exclusive hothouse varieties), Israel, Spain, Turkey, the U.S.A., South Africa, and Australia.

RIGHT

The vendage—*or grape harvest— takes place at the end of the summer. To reward the workers for their labor, all are treated to a gargantuan meal—with copious amounts of wine.*

A MONASTIC TRADITION

When the curtain of the Dark Ages descended, monks became both the guardians of wine-making traditions and the innovators (as was fitting with a drink which was transformed into the blood of Christ). St. Martin of Tours is dubbed the Father of Monastical Wine-Making, and the monasteries he established still make wine to this day. He is credited with devising the classic pruning methods still pursued today in the majority of French (and many other) vineyards, as well as with developing the art of grafting, one result of which was the Chenin Blanc grape. The Benedictines held sway along the Rhine in Germany, the Danube in Austria, and in northern Italy; the Cistercians on the Moselle and the Loire, and in Burgundy, Provence, and Languedoc. Monastic discoveries were numerous: it was the monks who realized storing wine in cold cellars, rather than above ground, benefited its keeping qualities; in the late seventeenth century a blind monk, Dom Perignon, created champagne, the unsurpassed wine of secular celebration; and it was missionary monks who brought the skills both of growing grapes and turning them into wine to California, Lebanon, and South America. In California, Junipero Serra, founder of nine missions extending from San Diego to San Francisco, planted the first vineyards of *V. vinifera* to thrive in North

America. The 800 or so wineries which flourish there today, supplying more than 90 percent of American wine and a large export market, can trace their heritage, if not their rootstock, to his first vintage of 1783 at Mission San Juan Capistrano.

France led the way in the export of wines. By the thirteenth century, her best markets were the Hanséatic and Flemish towns, where white "hock" was much appreciated, and England, where the claret of Bordeaux was preferred, a liking which persists today. But by the end of the Middle Ages, Spanish and Portuguese wines were gaining ground, to be followed by wines from the north of Italy, and the sweet (eventually fortified) wines of Crete, Malaga, and Madeira.

The fashion among Anglo-Saxons for sherry (from Jerez in Spain) and port (from the high banks of the River Douro, in northern Portugal) was a result of eighteenth-century wars and embargos, when French wine was unobtainable. Port was wine that had been fortified to endure the delays of voyage and distribution, and this preventative measure was gradually refined to become part of the fermentation process. Today, of the notable fortified wines, only sherry is still enhanced with the addition of alcohol at the end of its maturation process.

The Grape Is Mother to the Wine

The variety (or varieties) of grapes used to make a wine are the primary determining factor in its style and flavor. Traditionally, most European wines have been identified by region rather than by grape variety, but these regional products are, nevertheless, associated with particular grapes. Thus, in France, the Chenin Blanc is the choice for the light, feminine wines of Vouvray and Saumur, and for the more honeyed Coteaux du Layon and Savennières. Cabernet Sauvignon is the signature grape of Bordeaux reds. The key grape of sweet, rich Sauternes wines is the golden Sémillon, married to Sauvignon Blanc to improve aroma and balance in these and other Bordeaux whites. Sauvignon is an important grape in the production of Pouilly Fumé and Sancerre, while Pinot Blanc and Noir varieties define Champagne, Chardonnay, and the wines of Burgundy.

In Italy, the Nebbiolo grape is responsible for the greatest of the Italian red vintages, Barolo and Barbaresco. Furmint is the most important contributor to Hungary's fabled Tokaji, and Grenache to all the Spanish red wines, most notably when blended with Tempranillo to produce Rioja.

This deference to regional nomenclature is not universal, even in France. In Alsace, the variety of grape—Gewurztraminer, Riesling, —is emblazoned proudly on the wine label, a practice followed in the New World wines of the U.S.A., South America, New Zealand, and Australia, as well as in Bulgaria, northern Italy, and South Africa. The New World wineries have contributed to the industry, introducing indigenous strains, such as California's Zinfandel; improving and experimenting with varietals, as with Shiraz (Syrah) in Australia and Merlot in California; and creating new technology to provide as little interference from "spoilers" as possible.

WORLD OF WINE

Wine production has spread far from its historical roots, in the classical civilizations of Greece and Rome. This map clearly indicates that the 'new worlds' of the Americas, South Africa, and Australia are now, like much of Europe, major wine-producing regions, equally distinguished for their own specialist vintages.

Major wine-producing areas
Specialist wine-growing regions
Table grape-producing areas

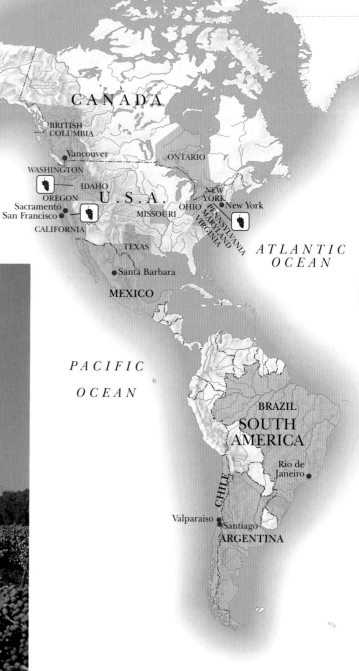

LEFT
Gathering the grape harvest in a Chilean vineyard.

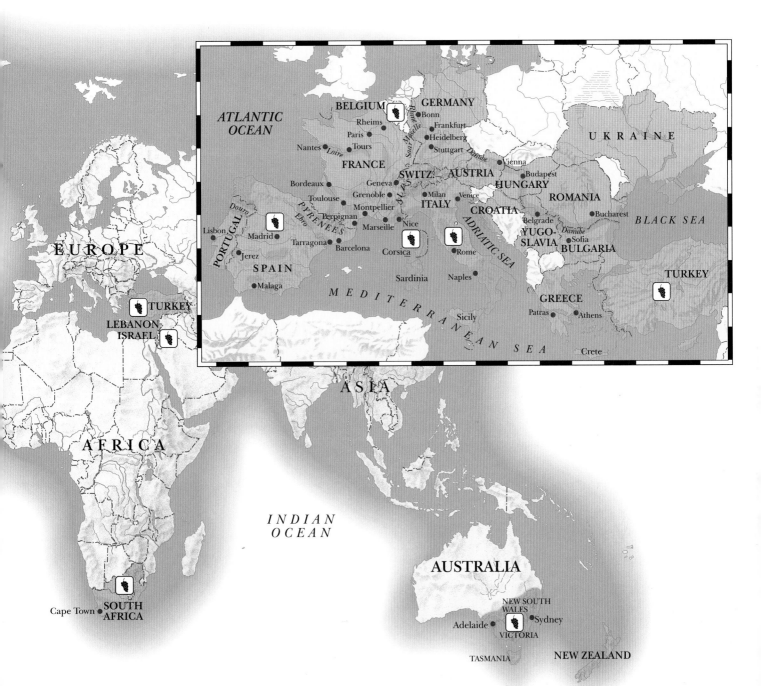

LEFT

A vineyard in the Barossa Valley in southern Australia. This area is Australia's largest quality wine-producing region.

CRACKING THE CODE: NUTS

*N**uts, like berries, were among mankind's earliest forage food. Cultivated by the Persians, Greeks, and Romans, they contributed taste and texture in cooking, as well as crunchy satisfaction straight from the shell.*

Nuts are defined as single-seeded, hard-shelled dry fruits, or as any seed or fruit which contains an edible kernel in a woody shell. Such a broad categorization allows the term "nut" to include the sweet chestnut, almond, and hazelnut (which conform to the first description) and the cashew, coconut, and Brazil nut (which conform to the last). The peanut is neither, it is a legume; however, it conforms enough to the second definition to traditionally qualify as a nut.

What all these share is a high calorific content and a brittle-textured "meat" always rich in fats and protein, with varying amounts of carbohydrate, minerals, and vitamins B and D. Most nuts are bought dried, which increases the concentration of these constituents. Generally speaking, they are a good source of nutrients, and are particularly recommended for those on a vegetarian diet.

The Western use of nuts in cooking—in everything from stuffing to charcuterie, from marzipan to nougat, from green salad with walnut oil to trout with almonds—is the result of recipes and combinations which have their origins in the courts of the Persian caliphs, and which were subsequently passed through a succession of Romans, Arabs, Crusaders, and Italian merchants. Moorish influence in Spain also had direct repercussions on the cuisines of Mexico and Central America, where almonds and walnuts were added to the native ingredients of pine nuts and pecans. In other parts of the world, nuts have also played an important role: peanuts, coconut, and almonds in southeast Asia; almonds, cashews, and gingko nuts in the Far East; coconuts and peanuts in Africa.

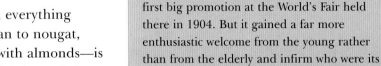

The All-American Butter

Tooth-sticking peanut butter was actually invented as a health food, a protein replacement for people whose bad teeth prevented them from chewing meat. Patented in 1890 by a St. Louis doctor, it received its first big promotion at the World's Fair held there in 1904. But it gained a far more enthusiastic welcome from the young rather than from the elderly and infirm who were its target market.

By 1922, the Rosefield Packing Company in Alameda, California, had developed a process to prevent separation and spoilage. Ten years later, their product, Skippy Peanut Butter, became the first name brand on the grocery store shelf. Soon peanut butter-and-jelly sandwiches, Reese Peanut Butter Cups (patented 1923), peanut butter-filled Ritz crackers, and peanut butter pie were fixtures of American food culture.

LEFT

A veritable hill of peanuts expectorated mechanically on a single-crop farm in Senegal. Such peanuts may be used for peanut butter, but it is more likely they will be crushed to make oil.

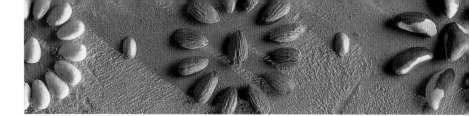

BEYOND BRAZIL

Nuts are produced commercially in many different parts of the world, as the map and geographical key indicate. A more detailed description of the world's major nut crops can be found in the A–Z listing on page 146.

Nuts of the world

AFGHANISTAN *almond* (**1**); *pistachio* (**11**
AUSTRALIA *almond* (**1**); *macadamia* (**7**); *walnut* (**12**) **BRAZIL** *brazil nut* (**2**); *cashew* (**3**); *peanut* (**8**) **CHINA** *hazelnut* (**6**) **FRANCE** *almond* (**1**); *chestnut* (**4**); *hazelnut* (**6**); *pine nut* (**10**); *pistachio* (**11**); *walnut* (**12**) **GREECE** *almond* (**1**); *hazelnut* (**6**); *pine nuts* (**10**); *pistachio* (**11**)
INDIA *cashew* (**3**); *coconut* (**5**); *peanut* (**8**); *pine nut* (**10**) **IRAN** *almond* (**1**); *pistachio* (**11**)
ITALY *almond* (**1**); *chestnut* (**4**); *hazelnut* (**6**); *pine nut* (**10**); *pistachio* (**11**); *walnut* (**12**)
JAPAN *hazelnut* (**6**) **JAVA** *peanut* (**8**)
KASHMIR *almond* (**1**) **MALAYSIA** *cashew* (**3**)
MEXICO *pecan* (**9**) **NIGERIA** *peanut* (**8**)
NORTH AFRICA *hazelnut* (**6**); *pine nut* (**10**); *pistachio* (**11**) **PACIFIC ISLANDS** *coconut* (**5**)
PARAGUAY *brazil nut* (**2**) **PHILIPPINES** *coconut* (**5**) **PORTUGAL** *almond* (**1**); *hazelnut* (**6**)
SOUTH AFRICA *almond* (**1**); *macadamia* (**7**); *pecan* (**9**); *walnut* (**12**) **SPAIN** *almond* (**1**); *chestnut* (**4**); *hazelnut* (**6**); *peanut* (**8**); *pine nut* (**10**); *pistachio* (**11**) **TURKEY** *almond* (**1**); *hazelnut* (**6**); *pine nut* (**10**) **TIBET** *hazelnut* (**6**)
U.S.A. (Alabama) *peanut* (**8**) **U.S.A.** (Arizona) *pistachio* (**11**) **U.S.A.** (California) *almond* (**1**); *pistachio* (**11**); *walnut* (**12**) **U.S.A.** (Carolina) *peanut* (**8**) **U.S.A.** (Florida) *pecan* (**9**) **U.S.A.** (Georgia) *peanut* (**8**); *pecan* (**9**)
U.S.A. (Illinois) *pecan* (**9**) **U.S.A.** (Mississippi) *pecan* (**9**) **U.S.A.** (New York) *chestnut* (**4**) **U.S.A.** (Oklahoma) *pecan* (**9**)
U.S.A. (Oregon) *hazelnut* (**6**); *walnut* (**12**
U.S.A. (Tennessee) *peanut* (**8**) **U.S.A.** (Texas) *peanut* (**8**) **U.S.A.** (Virginia) *peanut* (**8**)
WEST AFRICA *cashew* (**3**); *peanut* (**8**)
WEST INDIES *cashew* (**3**); *coconut* (**5**)

BELOW
Ripening cashews growing in the West Indies.

LEFT
*Coconut palms
growing on an
island in the South
China sea.*

EUROPE

ASIA

FRANCE
1 4 6 10 11 12

SPAIN
1 4 6 8 10 11

GREECE
1 6 10 11

ITALY
1 4 6 10 11 12

TURKEY
3 6 10

AFGHANISTAN
1 11

JAPAN
6

PORTUGAL
1 6

IRAN
1 11

TIBET
6

CHINA
6

KASHMIR
1

NORTH AFRICA
6 10 11

INDIA
3 5 8 10

PHILIPPINES
5

WEST AFRICA
3 8

MALAYSIA
3

NIGERIA
8

SOUTHEAST ASIA

*INDIAN
OCEAN*

JAVA
8

5

5

AUSTRALIA
1 7 12

SOUTH AFRICA
1 7 9 12

A MODERN NUTTERY

ALMOND
(Prunus amygdalus)

There are two types: bitter (proscribed in many places) and sweet. Native to Asia, it was introduced to Europe by the Greeks. An ingredient in savory and sweet dishes of the Far and Middle East, and mainly in desserts, pastries, and confectionery in Europe and America.

BRAZIL
(Bertholettia excelsa)

The seed of the Amazonian hardwood tree; each seed (nut) is a segment packed into woody spherical fruit .Whole nuts are traditonal Christmas fare. The best specimens are harvested in the wild from the Upper Amazon, but nuts are also cultivated in Brazil and Paraguay.

CASHEW
(Anacardium occidentale)

A South American fruit brought to India from Brazil by the Portuguese in the sixteenth century, the cashew is now widely cultivated in the tropics. The nut, uniquely, sprouts from the bottom of the tart, fibrous fruit. Roasted in its shell, the smooth, kidney-shaped kernel has a rich, sweet flavor. In the West it is most often served salted; in India, notably Kerala, it is added to meat curries, vegetables, rice, and desserts. In southeast Asia and China, it is a favorite stir-fry ingredient.

Pecan

Almond

Hazelnut

CHESTNUT
(Castanea sativa)

The chestnut must be roasted or boiled before the kernel inside the shell can be eaten. Used in soups, in stuffing for poultry and game, in sweet desserts, patisserie, and *marrons glacés*.

COCONUT
(Cocos nucifera)

Known by Egyptians in the sixth century AD; recorded by Marco Polo in the Far East; and named "coconut" by Spanish and Portuguese in southeast Asia. It was referred to in print by this name in 1555. It is eaten fresh or used dried in baking and confectionery in the West, as a condiment, and in meat and fish curries and rice dishes, in marinades and soups in the East.

HAZELNUT/FILBERT
(Corylus avellena/C. maxima)

Varieties within species are not always clear-cut: the Kentish cob nut, with milky, tender meat, is actually a filbert, though the rest of the "cob" nuts qualify as hazelnuts. Widespread, with varieties in Europe, Asia, and North America. Eaten fresh and dried, hazelnuts are used in savory European dishes and confectionery, and filberts in American candies.

MACADAMIA
(Macadamia ternifolia, M. integrifolia)

Originating in Queensland, and named for the Australian chemist who promoted its cultivation in 1904. The hard-shelled round nut contains an oily, sweet, kernel which can be roasted and salted, used as a plain ingredient in cakes, pastries, and candies in the West, and curries and stews in Indian and Indonesia.

PEANUT
(Arachis hypogaea)

The peanut probably originated in South America, was imported to Africa on slave ships, and later returned across the Atlantic to take root in the southern U.S.A. Peanuts are used raw or roasted and salted as snacks; for cooking, in savory dishes and in candies; and for peanut butter. Most are processed for groundnut oil.

PECAN
(Carya illinoensis)

The nut of the native American hickory tree, whose heartland is the Mississippi Valley. From its first mention in 1773, it has become America's second most popular nut. Its smooth, light brown carapace, dyed and polished for sale, contains a high proportion of meat. It is the main ingredient of the eponymous pie, a southern trademark.

PINE NUT
(Pinus pinea)

The tree bearing the pine cone grows wild along the Mediterranean shore, from Portugal to the Black Sea, and was planted centuries ago in North Africa. The dried seeds of the cone are common to the sweet and savory cooking of all the Mediterranean countries. Usually toasted, but can also be salted.

PISTACHIO
(Pistacia vera)

The seed of a small, hardy deciduous tree native to Asia Minor. After the nuts are harvested, they are left to dry in hot sun for a week; the shells open to expose the pale green kernel with its reddish skin.The sweet nuts are good salted or used in stuffing for poultry and white meats, in sauces, rice dishes, and in charcuterie, ice creams, and nougat.

WALNUT
(Juglans regia)

The fruit of a tall deciduous tree native to southeastern Europe and the Caspian Sea, whose range extends into China. Several varieties cultivated commercially; mostly for desserts and confectionery. In France and Italy, some is used for oil.

MEAT
& POULTRY

*D*omesticated herd animals, fowl amd wild game are man's principle source of protein in societies which do not have a bias against meat on religious or cultural grounds. Raising animals for food was a development of civilization; in prehistoric times all meat was the product of hunting.

Today in the United States and much of Europe, ecological concerns and the march of urban values has meant that game has become an expensive and, ironically, an exclusive commodity.

$\mathcal{T}$AMING THE WILD: EARLY FARMERS

$\mathcal{T}$*he importance of meat, poultry, and game in the human diet dates back to our early ancestor,* Homo erectus, *who hunted for survival.*

The diet of *Homo erectus* contained a high proportion of meat. The flesh was cooked over the heat of a fire, while the animal bones were split to obtain the nutrient-rich marrow. As human beings evolved, hunting skills improved. Neanderthal man, who devoted most of his time to hunting and gathering, developed into a skilled hunter of large mammals such as the saber-toothed tiger, all of them now extinct. His successor, *Homo sapiens*, controlled the use of fire, and developed both his weaponry and intelligence, allowing him to both obtain food and keep it.

Climatic changes greatly increased forest cover, introducing the nomadic hunter-gatherer to new mammals. Reindeer moved north and wild cattle, red deer, and wild pigs began to populate the European continent. For more than a million years early humans roamed the globe, adapting to varied conditions and settling in organized groups. The spread of ice sheets during the last ice age, which ended 10,000 years ago, forced early humans into new hunting grounds, and the Americas, Australia, and New Zealand were finally colonized. This was a golden age of nutrition; low-fat game meat was eaten each day in conjunction with vegetables, berries, nuts, and fish.

As humans settled to a more sedentary existence, large areas of forest were cleared for growing food and domesticating animals. Small farming communities formed, and, with the age of the wheel, markets and trading between the small towns and villages began. Forests shrank as settlements grew, although hunting remained a necessity. Different species of animal were domesticated across the world and, with increased mobility as well as growing knowledge of crossbreeding, new breeds developed. Some animals were bred for specialized uses, solely as a food source or traction animals. The commercialization of foods and animals, however, did not greatly influence diet until the Middle Ages.

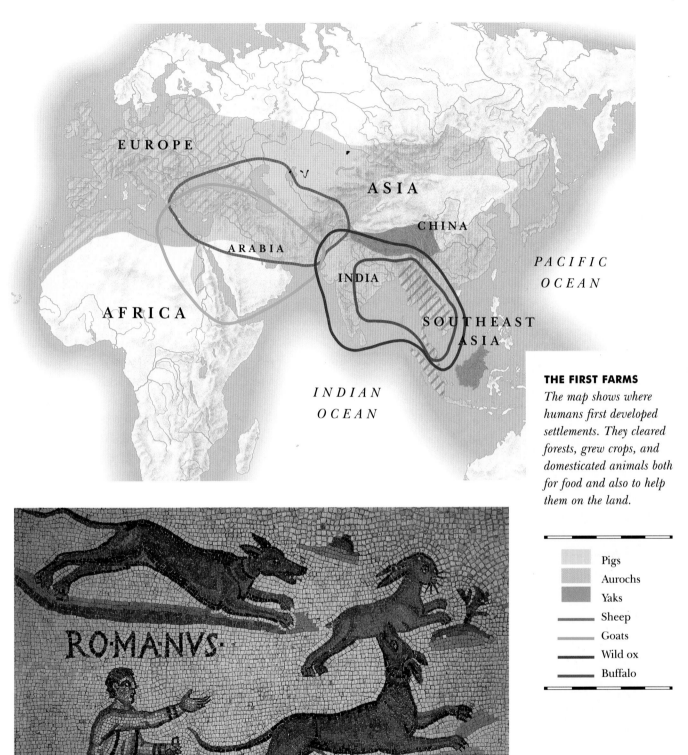

THE FIRST FARMS

The map shows where humans first developed settlements. They cleared forests, grew crops, and domesticated animals both for food and also to help them on the land.

	Pigs
	Aurochs
	Yaks
	Sheep
	Goats
	Wild ox
	Buffalo

LEFT

This Roman mosaic dates from the first century AD. It shows how dogs were used for hunting hares.

BEEF & VEAL

*T*oday's specialized breeds of cattle have developed a long way from their early ancestors, the aurochs or wild oxen, the last major food source to be tamed for milk, meat, power, and leather.

Settled existence in the Near East and Europe dates back to about 6000 BC, and from this point oxen were used for plowing, as farmers began to replace food-gathering tribes. By 5000 BC, there were domesticated cattle in the valleys of the Tigris and Euphrates rivers. By 4000 BC, cattle were bred for meat in the Indus valley, as were buffalo. Throughout Europe, the Near East, and India, cattle were raised for meat and milk. They were also domesticated in China.

Cattle-breeding spread southward from ancient Egypt throughout the continent of Africa. To this day, cattle are still held in great respect throughout Africa, and in parts of the continent the marriage dowry is still calculated in terms of head of cattle. Agricultural departments of new African republics still have difficulty persuading pastoral tribes not to hoard cattle in a country where protein deficiency is endemic.

In 1521, Ponce de León, the Spanish explorer, introduced cattle to the west coast of Florida, and in 1524, the Spanish conquistador, Pedro de Alvarado, brought cows and other animals to the central American highlands. Cattle were introduced to southwestern America in 1540 by Francisco Vásquez de Coronado, who is credited with turning the Pueblo natives from hunters to raisers of domestic livestock, and ultimately for founding the American beef industry.

ABOVE

An Ayrshire cow which was originally bred in Scotland. A sturdy dairy cow, it was bred mainly for its milk yield.

RIGHT

Texas Longhorns were the backbone of the early American cattle industry. In the spring, calves were branded in preparation for the cattle drives to market in the fall.

INTENSIVE BREEDING

In the early eighteenth century, the British learned a lesson from their Dutch neighbors; cattle could be kept all year round if they were fed a subsistence diet of turnips during the winter months. Cattle consequently became larger, and beef was available throughout the year. By 1732,

London's beef was coming from as far afield as Ireland, Scotland, and Wales, but the meat was both tough and expensive. Experiments began to improve beef cattle and, in 1760, deeper, wider-bodied breeds were developed in Leicestershire, England, with shorter, thicker necks and with more flesh on the hind, ribs, and loins. Cattle continued to grow in size and, by 1795, those sold at London's Smithfield Market were twice the weight of those sold in 1710.

AMERICAN RANCHES AND THE CATTLE TRADE

Throughout the eighteenth century, British beef was exported to the Americas and, from 1777, cattle ranches began to flourish in Argentina, now known for its fine beef. In 1817, Hereford cattle were imported into the American state of Virginia for the first time. This English breed was to become dominant on the western plains and, by 1840, the first significant breeding herd of quick-fattening Hereford cattle had been established.

Some cattle were bred solely for their meat, while others, such as the Jersey cow, imported in 1850, were raised as a dairy breed. The Texas Longhorns are descendants of the Andalusian cattle brought to America by the Spaniards. By 1850, open-ranging longhorn cattle herds on the American western plains numbered 50 million head, and cattle ranches were developing. In

The American Cattle Trails

By the 1820s, Texas had become established as the land of the longhorn steer, and, by 1830, Chicago had become the national meat-packing center.

On September 5, 1867, the first cattle were shipped by railroad from Abilene, Kansas, a town purchased by livestock-trader Joe McCoy to establish a central depot for cattle movement out of Texas. He offered a good price for cattle, encouraging ranchers to use his depot. This was the beginning of the era of the great cattle drives, and the "cowboy" became an increasingly central figure in the myths and romance which surrounded the old west.

There were three main cattle drives: from Texas to Abilene, Kansas (known as the Chisolm Trail); from San Antonio, Texas, to Baxter Springs, Kansas (the Shawnee Trail); and from Bandera, Texas, to Ogallala, Nebraska (the Western Trail). It is estimated a total of six million head of cattle were driven from Texas to Kansas City between 1866 and 1885, with a peak of 600,000 in 1871 alone.

In 1875, barbed wire was introduced and this, coupled with the movement of more farming families into western territories, meant an end to the free access to land.

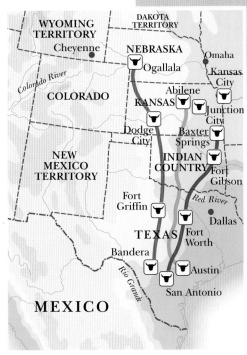

CATTLE TRAILS
The three main cattle routes are shown on this map.

🐂	Cow town
▨▨▨	Western trail
────	Chisholm trail
────	Shawnee trail

Sacred Cows

The Aryans were warriors whose source of wealth and food was cattle. They came to the Indian subcontinent from Afghanistan and Persia in the first millennium BC. Aryan beliefs originally demanded blood sacrifices, after which the meat was eaten. The people eventually began to revolt against this, and dough effigies were offered in place of the sacrificial animal. As increased population exerted pressure on land and resources, the value of the cow increased. It was considered far too valuable to be killed for meat, as when alive it provided milk, calves, and dung. In the sixth century BC, a ban was placed on killing cows for food. Hindus later declared the cow a sacred animal, and it was not permitted to kill a cow for sacrifice or food.

The first letter of the alphabet, A, began life in the Cretan, Greek, and Latin alphabets as a representation of the head of the ox, the foremost source of wealth. This is taken as proof that the cattle were deeply respected for the services they rendered. This respect is still shown in India and there is farther evidence of the reverence with which certain societies have viewed cattle in the winged bulls of Assyria and Babylon, the zoomorphic Egyptian gods, Apis and Osiris, the sacred cow of the Chinese, and other gods which were depicted as bulls. Ancient Germanic tribes thought so highly of their cattle, according to Tacitus, a girl's dowry was paid in cattle rather than gold.

1852, the Holstein cow arrived in the U.S.A. aboard a Dutch vessel, and became a significant addition to the American dairy trade.

In 1863, the cattle trade in both the U.S.A. and Britain faced difficulties. A bad winter meant cattle-rustling was an endemic problem in the U.S.A., while in Britain, cattle disease struck – Dutch cattle were also affected. Meat prices rose and Australian canned meats threatened the fresh meat trade.

The rise in American population in the years following the Civil War led to an increased demand for beef. As the frontier of settlement moved west, less and less land east of the Mississippi was available for foraging, which also increased demand. The never-ending quest for the ultimate cattle breed led to many experiments in interbreeding and, in 1940, a new breed of cattle, the Santa Gertrudis, was recognized in America. The American beef trade, boosted by the consumption of 50

LEFT

A Hindu man parades a sacred cow. In India, it is forbidden by Hindu law to slaughter cattle for food or leather, their value as "work horses" being too great.

WORLD

CATTLE-REARING

The main species of beef and dairy cattle, and the main areas in which they are reared, are identified on this map. Some breeds, such as the Hereford, were exported to the New World; some, such as the Sancta Gertrudis, were the result of experimental cross-breeding.

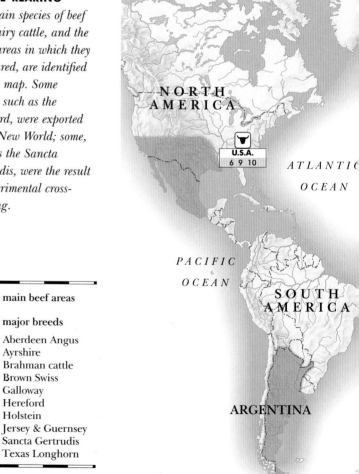

main beef areas

major breeds

1 Aberdeen Angus
2 Ayrshire
3 Brahman cattle
4 Brown Swiss
5 Galloway
6 Hereford
7 Holstein
8 Jersey & Guernsey
9 Sancta Gertrudis
10 Texas Longhorn

billion burgers a year, continued to grow. Beef consumption reached an extraordinary 128.5 pounds per capita by 1976.

THE FATTENED CALF

Veal had always been a popular meat, although reserved in latter times for the rich. The fattened calf which marked the return of the Prodigal Son, has always been considered one of the choicest dishes on a festive table. From the thirteenth to the sixteenth centuries, calves' eyes were considered the most exquisite delicacy of all. Veal represented annual income rather than capital, and could be slaughtered as soon as the problem of weaning arose.

Veal has been an important part of the Italian diet since Roman times. The French are also enthusiastic veal-eaters, particularly when the calves are reared on raw eggs. Today, however, controversy surrounds the veal trade: veal calves are reared in very different circumstances to their ancestors, and are fed hormones to enhance their color.

Russian Beef Stroganov

SERVES 4

1¼ lb/600 g sirloin or filet mignon, trimmed of excess fat and thinly sliced
3 tablespoons all-purpose flour
Salt and ground black pepper
4 tablespoons (2 oz/60 g) butter or vegetable oil
1 onion, sliced
3 cups (7 oz/200 g) peeled and sliced open-cap mushrooms
1 cup (8 fl oz/225 ml) sour cream

Coat the beef in flour and season with salt and pepper. Heat half the butter or oil in a large skillet and cook the beef for 5 to 6 minutes, or until browned on both sides. Remove the beef from the pan and add the remaining butter or oil. Cook the onion and mushrooms for 3 to 4 minutes, then return the beef to the pan. Stir in the sour cream and warm through. Serve.

LAMB & MUTTON

Sheep were first domesticated in Mesopotamia, where their meat in the form of mutton or lamb was preferred. Sheep-rearing eventually spread across the world to Australia, New Zealand, China, and Britain.

BELOW

Mutton and lamb from varying breeds of sheep are popular across the world. The spread of lamb and its successful breeding was aided by the animals' ability to survive in many climates. Kept for both their meat and fleece, they are widely farmed in many countries.

Mutton and lamb were, and remain, the preferred meats of the people of the Middle East and North Africa. Sheep ancestry dates back to about 9000 BC to Mesopotamia, where the long-haired mouflon sheep (*Ovis orientalis*) were kept for their fleece before eventually being slaughtered for their meat. In about the seventh century AD, extravagant Persian tables were laden with the finest foods, including mutton.

In 7200 BC, sheep were domesticated in Greece. Goats, however, adapted more successfully to the arid, mountainous terrain, and remain a more popular source of meat and milk. The first sheep were introduced to the Indian subcontinent in about 1500 BC by Aryan nomads from Afghanistan and Persia. The Israelites who migrated from Egypt to the Holy Land brought sheep with them. By the seventh century AD, the northern Chinese were eating mutton, which was, however, scorned by the people of the south. Nevertheless, by AD 1271, mutton had also become a staple in China, particularly in the imperial kitchens where special vats for boiling whole sheep were installed. This trend spread over the country, and boiled lamb or mutton became some of the most popular Chinese dishes.

Mutton, which is obtained from sheep more than two years old in the U.S.A. and more than one year old in Europe, was eaten throughout Europe, where lamb was considered a luxury for centuries. Large cuts of mutton were roasted over an open fire. Mutton has an unjustified reputation for being tough and overpowering, but if hung properly it has a delicious flavor, although it tends to be fatty.

REGIONAL DISHES

Once flocks of sheep were colonized around the world, their importance as a food source was increasingly recognized.

Sheep and lambs are fattened for sale at local markets, a common sight across Europe.

Lamb is now enjoyed in many countries and regions, including Ireland, Britain, Spain, Japan, Sweden, the Middle East, the U.S.A., New Zealand, and Australia. New Zealand and Australia are the main producers of lamb today, exporting to Britain, Russia, and the Middle East, as well as having a strong market with Japan.

Over the centuries, many specialist regional recipes have developed. In Britain, "spring lamb" was favored and is still often served at Easter when it is first ready for eating. It is not neccessarily the best lamb available because it is slaughtered at a mere four months old when it has not yet developed a great deal of flavor. It is commonly agreed the best lamb is worth waiting for, and at approximately eight months old it will have reached the correct balance of flavor and tenderness.

In France, where lamb is very popular, the animals at market fall into three categories. The milk lamb, known in France as *agnelet*, is killed before being weaned at the age of 30 to 40 days, and its meat is consequently very tender and delicate. The second category is the *agneau blanc* or *laiton*, which is available from Christmas to June and comprises 70 percent of French lamb consumed. Slaughtered at the age of 70 to 150 days, its rich, milk-based diet produces dark pink meat which becomes tender during cooking. Lastly, there is the grazing lamb, known as *broutart* because it has grazed on grass. It is killed between six and nine months. Its grass diet causes the fat to lose its whiteness, and for this reason it is named "gray lamb." The flesh is firm with a strong flavor, which is not dissimilar to mutton. It was once very popular but, as with mutton, demand for it has decreased.

Lamb as a Religious Symbol

Roast sheep were among the first sacrifices made to the gods. There are many accounts in ancient literatures of sacrifices, where meat was roasted over fire, its odor rising to heaven to please the gods and its fat used for annointing altars. Leviticus 7 states "...And the Lord spake unto Moses, saying, Speak unto the children of Israel, saying, Ye shall eat no manner of fat, of ox, or of sheep, or of goat. And the fat of the beast that dieth of itself, and the fat of that which is torn with beasts, may be used in any other use: but ye shall in no wise eat of it."

The religious symbolism of lamb is derived from the sacrifice of lambs at the Jewish Passover, a celebration of the liberation of Jews from Egypt. It is said when a census was ordered by Cyrenius in Palestine during the period in which Jesus was born, the Jewish people used sacrificial Passover lambs to obtain the information required. Each lamb was said to feed ten people, so the number of lambs sacrificed was multiplied by ten to obtain a census figure.

Lamb is eaten at many religious festivals and carnivals across the world. At Easter, in villages throughout Greece, for example, the figure of Christ is paraded through the streets and a whole lamb is spit-roasted to mark the end of fasting. Whole suckling lambs are also popular at spring festivals in Italy and the Middle East where they are flavored with local delicacies such as spices.

SHEEP-REARING AREAS

As this map shows, sheep are reared in many varied conditions and terrains.

Main sheep-rearing areas

English Lancashire Hotpot

SERVES 6

3 lb 5 oz/1.5 kg shoulder chops, separated into chops
Salt and ground black pepper
3 large onions, halved, and sliced
3½ cups (1½ pints/750 ml) lamb stock
3½ cups (8 oz/225 g) mushrooms, wiped
8 large potatoes, peeled and sliced
2 tablespoons (1 oz/25 g) butter

Heat the oven to 350°F/180°C/Gas mark 4. Place half the chops in the base of a large Dutch oven or casserole. Season and cover with a layer of onions. Season again and repeat the layers. Pour in the stock, add the mushrooms and cover completely with a layer of overlapping potato slices. Dot with half the butter. Cover and cook in the oven for 2 hours. Remove the cover and dot with the remaining butter. Return the Dutch oven to the oven for 1 hour longer until the potatoes are golden brown and the meat cooked through.

BREEDS ACROSS THE WORLD

Sheep are reared in many different climatic conditions and terrains, their pasture affecting the final flavor of the meat. In France, for instance, salt-marsh, or *pre-sale*, lamb is rated highly, whether it be "home-reared" or from the salt marshes of Wales or Romney Marsh in eastern England. The salty grazing is said to add a distinct quality to the flavor, making it sweet and tender. The Texel, which originated in the Frisian Islands of northern Europe, is now found in Britain, France, South America, and South Africa. In Spain, Merinos are raised on arid slopes dotted with herbs for grazing, which delicately flavor the meat.

The earliest domesticated sheep were the long-haired mouflon sheep, a handful of which remain in Corsica and Sardinia. Direct descendants of these ancient breeds are the Soay of Scotland, the Spanish Merino, the Daton Drente, and the British Norfolk Blackface. Over the years, selective breeding has changed sheep from long-haired

Kleftiko *or "robbers
lamb" named after
the gangs of robbers
hiding in the Greek
mountains, who
cooked their meat in
a tightly closed oven
or* klefti *as above.*

animals with thick, woolly fleeces to shorter-haired
breeds, such as the Wiltshire Horn.

A WORLD OF LAMB

Lamb can be cooked with a variety of flavorings: mint and
capers in Britain; prunes and almonds in Algeria; lemons
and olives in Morocco; and dill in Sweden. Herbs, most
commonly cilantro and rosemary, are also used to flavor
the meat. In Middle Eastern countries and North Africa,
lamb features as a whole spit-roasted carcass, or *mechoui*,
or is grilled on skewers, as *shish kebab*. It is cut into slices
and packed onto a rotating spit for *doner kebab* and eaten
ground as *kibbi nayya*. The French roast the leg; their *gigot*
can be stuffed, wrapped in pastry, or casseroled with
beans. Mutton is served in a variety of stews: in Tunisia it
is cooked with spices and fruit, in Britain it features in
popular recipes such as Irish Stew and Lancashire Hotpot
—that are made from inexpensive cuts that are cooked
slowly.

Halal Meat

In southern Arabia in the seventh century AD,
the prophet Muhammad, a bedouin
tribesman, was changing the religious balance
of the world. Some of his teaching related to
food, which was considered a gift from God.
The eating of pork, any animal found dead,
blood, animals killed for sacrifice, fish without
scales, and alcohol were all forbidden, or
"halam." Animals killed for food were to be
slaughtered in the correct manner. The
butcher should say, "In the name of God,
God is most great," and the animal's throat
should be cut so the blood could drain. These
food regulations are followed to this day by
many Muslims.

LAMB DISHES OF THE WORLD

A universally popular meat, lamb has been enhanced and flavored in many distinctive ways by different national cuisines. This map shows the main countries with specialty lamb dishes, which are listed in the numbered key (below).

⑮ ▦ Countries with famous lamb dishes

① **ARAB STATES** *Sfeeha* ② **ARMENIA** *Lamb shanks & lentils* ③ **AUSTRALIA** *Barbecued lamb* ④ **BELGIUM** *Casserole d'agneau Brugeoise* ⑤ **CARIBBEAN** *Port Royal lamb; Guisodo de Carnero* ⑥ **CHINA** *Tung-yang-jour; Peking lamb hot pot; Chop suey* ⑦ **FRANCE** *Roast saddle of lamb; Noisettes; Haricot of mutton* ⑧ **GREECE** *Moussaka; Souvlakia; Koftah* ⑨ **INDIA** *Roghan Gosh; Biryani; Kheema kebabs; Parsi dhansak* ⑩ **IRAN** *Khoresh Bademjan Dizh* ⑪ **ITALY** *Agnello all'Arrabbiata; Spezzatoni di mantone* ⑫ **MALAYSIA** *Giema curry; Saté; Lamb dhal* ⑬ **MOROCCO** *Kibbi; Khauzi; Tagine* ⑭ **OMAN** *Kigmeh Mashut Omani* ⑮ **RUSSIA** *Shashlyk; Livlia kebab* ⑯ **SOUTH AFRICA** *Sosasties* ⑰ **SOUTH AMERICA** *Cazuela de cordero; El seco de chivo* ⑱ **SPAIN & PORTUGAL** *Lamb with lemon & garlic; Chafana a moda de coimbra; Lamb stew with red peppers; Roast fricassee of lamb* ⑲ **TURKEY** *Sis kebab* ⑳ **UNITED KINGDOM & IRELAND** *Irish stew; Lancashire hot pot; Shepherd's pie; Crown roast; Haggis* ㉑ **U.S.A.** *Miners' camp pie; Hunters' leg of lamb; Marinated grilled lamb*

U.S.A.

ATLANTIC OCEAN

WEST INDIES

CENTRAL AMERICA

PACIFIC OCEAN

SOUTH AMERICA

RIGHT

Souvlakia is a favorite, traditional Greek dish. Pieces of lamb, and bay leaves for flavoring, are cooked on skewers over an open heat.

SCANDINAVIA

UNITED
KINGDOM

RUSSIAN FEDERATION

15

20

4

BEL

FRANCE

EUROPE

7

ITALY

11

8

SPAIN

18

GREECE

TURKEY

19

ASIA

6

CHINA

2

TUGAL

MEDITERRANEAN SEA

1

IRAN

10

CASPIAN SEA

13

MOROCCO

1

EGYPT

SAUDI
ARABIA

INDIA

9

AFRICA

1

YEMEN

OMAN

14

SOUTHEAST
ASIA

MALAYSIA

12

INDIAN
OCEAN

AUSTRALIA

3

SOUTH
AFRICA

16

NEW
ZEALAND

RIGHT

*Slices of leg of lamb
served with rice and
salad.*

ABOVE

*This Chinese dish is
made from shredded
lamb and a mixture
of vegetables, and
stir-fried to seal in
all the flavors.*

PORK: PRESERVED & FRESH MEAT

The ancestor of the domesticated pig is the wild boar which roamed the temperate forests, rooting for acorns. The pig was first domesticated in Japan, and plays a large part in the world's gastronomy today.

BELOW
Chinese pigs, shorter-legged and plumper than other breeds, were used for crossbreeding. In 1760 they were crossed with the slimmer, longer-legged English pig and later the White China Hog. Pig farming and breeding remains popular in China today.

As nomadic hunters settled in temperate forests, pigs were drawn to the area to forage for food. Although they were easily caught, they were considered by many to carry disease. The Egyptians credited the pig with carrying leprosy, and the animal never appeared in Egyptian wall paintings as it was considered unworthy. Despite these strictures, by 1800 BC, the pig had been domesticated by farmers all over the world, since it was the one reliable source of affordable meat for the poor. It was fattened on kitchen slops and was left to roam around

the woodland or a backyard. Pigs were a popular breeding animal as each sow could mother up to twelve piglets from each pregnancy.

The *sus*, a mammal similar to the pig, was found in ancient Spain, France, Italy, Greece, North Africa, and Persia. It was longer in the leg and smaller in body than today's pigs. The warthog covered almost the whole of Africa and Europe, up to the shores of the Indian and Pacific oceans, but never reaching America or the West Indies, where the domesticated pig was later introduced by Western conquerers.

In 1539, the Spanish landed in Florida with thirteen hogs, the first to be seen in this area. Crossbreeding began in 1760 when English pigs were bred with Chinese pigs to produce a cross between the slim, long-headed English pig and the plump, short-legged Chinese pig. In 1784, the Shakers developed the Poland China Hog by crossing backwood hogs with the Big White China hog. This breed later became the backbone of the American pork industry and remained so for many generations.

Today, the main consumers of pork are central and eastern Europeans, and the Spanish-, French-, and English-speaking countries. Up to the middle of this century, the majority of peasant families from these

Chinese Sweet-and-Sour Pork

SERVES 4

2 teaspoons rice wine
1 egg, beaten
1 lb/450 g pork belly, trimmed and cubed
1 cup/4 oz/115 g cornstarch
2½ cups/1 pint/600 ml peanut oil
1 red pepper, cored, seeded, and thinly sliced
1 green pepper, cored, seeded, and thinly sliced
1 carrot, halved and sliced
3 cloves garlic, crushed
1 teaspoon sesame oil

FOR THE SAUCE

2 tablespoons dark brown sugar
1 tablespoon peanut oil
5 teaspoons rice wine vinegar
1 teaspoon cornstarch

Mix the rice wine and egg together. Add the pork and stir to coat. Remove the pork from the mixture and roll in the cornstarch. Heat the peanut oil in a wok or large skillet until smoking. Add the pork and cook for about 5 minutes until crisp and cooked through. Remove the pork from the oil with a slotted drainer; reserve.

Pour the oil from the wok, leaving about 2 tablespoons in the base. Add the peppers, carrot and garlic and stir-fry for 2 to 3 minutes. Return the pork to the wok. Blend the sauce ingredients together and stir into the wok, stirring until thickened. Sprinkle with sesame oil and serve with rice.

LEFT
Peasant families used to keep pigs in the back yard which were fattened to feed the family during the winter months, a practice which persists today in rural Europe..

Hawaiian Pit-Roasting

The traditional feast of Hawaii, known as the *luau*, dates back 2,000 years, and today utilizes food introduced by European explorers. A roasted pig forms its centerpiece. Hot lava rocks from the presiding volcano are stuffed into the belly of the pig, and a pit is lined with lava rocks and wood. Once the wood has burned and the rocks are red hot, a layer of banana tree stumps is placed in the pit to create steam and to protect the food. The pig is wrapped in banana leaves and layers of canvas and earth are placed on top to allow the pig to cook all day. This practice was developed in the absence of fireproof cooking pots. The pig is served with other local specialties, such as salmon, bananas, coconut, and pineapple.

American Barbecued Spareribs

SERVES 4

3–4 lb/1.3–1.8 kg pork belly, including ribs
4 tablespoons soy sauce
3 tablespoons honey
2 tablespoons cider vinegar
1¼ cups/½ pint/300 ml beef stock
2 tablespoons soft dark brown sugar
2 cloves garlic, crushed
½ teaspoon chili powder
½ teaspoon ground ginger
1 tablespoon chopped fresh thyme

Trim any skin and excess fat from the pork. Place in a nonreactive bowl. Mix all the remaining ingredients together and pour over the meat. Cover and leave to marinate overnight, or for 3 to 4 hours, turning the meat. Heat the oven to 350°F/180°C/Gas mark 4. Roast the meat in a roasting pan for 1½ hours, basting frequently with the marinade.

LEFT
Many pigs are now intensively farmed. They are reared in cramped sheds, which prevents the formation of the muscle and flavor. which characterizes "free range" pigs.

countries kept a pig, which they fattened and killed to provide meat. The meat was salted or pickled for preserving, and all of the pig was utilized for sausages and preserved meats. Many peasants existed on little else. Navies fed salt pork to their seamen who grew to hate it, as did the aristocracy who considered it a food of the poor.

As palates changed, the stout breeds became unpopular, and new leaner breeds emerged to meet modern demands. Today, pigs are generally intensively reared to be lean and "healthy," but they lack the flavor of their ancestors. In Britain, many of the older breeds, such as the Saddleback, Gloucester Old Spot, and Tamworth, which had been replaced by more productive, leaner animals, are now making a welcome comeback.

RELIGIOUS DIETARY LAWS AND THE PIG

With a reputation of a scavenger of refuse and a carrier of parasites and disease, the pig was considered by many to be unclean. This aversion may have some bearing on the fact that some religions proscribe pork. Another theory for this is that pork has certain similarities to human flesh—cannibals have referred to man as "long pig" when discussing their preferences for the cooking pot. Another possibility is that, being omnivorous like man, the pig succumbed to similar diseases and became associated with the ritual of human sacrifice, and therefore became a condemned food. In ancient Turkey, pigs were associated with death. Jews and Muslims are forbidden to eat pork; Moses declared the pig too unclean to even be touched.

CURED MEATS & SAUSAGES

Cured meats and sausages evolved from the discovery meat could be stored and preserved for longer if the moisture content was reduced by drying, salting, or smoking, providing a year-round supply.

Once the discovery that meat could be preserved by drying had been made, it became a universal practice. In hot climates, meat was pounded to release the juices and dried in strips in the sun—South African biltong is an example of this process, along with "jerked" beef, or buffalo strips dried in the sun, originated in Mexico and Central America. In Britain and continental Europe, salting and smoking were more common methods.

Although beef is easily preserved, it is doubtlessly around pork much of the preserving tradition lies. The word sausage originates from the Latin word *salsus*, meaning salted. The first sausages were made by filling the paunch of an animal with other meats, which were then cooked over fires. The Romans passed the art of sausage-making on to the Germans and French. Today, France, Germany, and Italy are the main producers of hams and sausages, although some type of salami or ham is produced in most European countries. These traditions were exported to America where, in the nineteenth century, the diet was dominated by salt pork. When a pig was slaughtered, some of the meat was salted or smoked to produce bacon and ham as a source of winter meat; the remainder was made into sausages.

ADAPTABLE PORK

A ham is a leg of pork which has been cured in one of a variety of ways. The salting and smoking of pork is of French origin, the Gauls being renowned for their hams. Hams were originally named according to the region where they were produced and hence the method of curing, the breed of pig, and its diet. Today, many of these names still indicate a regional ham, but others are attributed to

Polish Bigos

SERVES 6

1lb 10 oz/750 g sauerkraut, chopped
½ oz /15 g dried mushrooms, reconstituted and drained
Salt
6 oz/175 g pork tenderloin
6 oz/175 g lean veal piece
4 oz/115 g smoked bacon piece
2 tablespoons lard or dripping
1 large onion, chopped
1 oz/25 g pork fat or bacon rind
2 tablespoons all-purpose flour
9 oz/250 g Polish kielbasa sausage, skinned and sliced
⅔ cup (5 oz/150 g) chopped tomatoes

Simmer the sauerkraut in a pan with a little water and the mushrooms for 1 hour. Salt the pork and veal and cook with the bacon in the dripping or lard until browned all over. Add the meat to the sauerkraut. Cover and cook for 40 minutes longer until tender. Remove the meats from the pan and cube; set aside.

Meanwhile, sauté the onion with the pork fat. Stir in the flour to make a roux and cook for 2 minutes. Add to the sauerkraut with the sliced sausage and tomatoes. Heat well and serve.

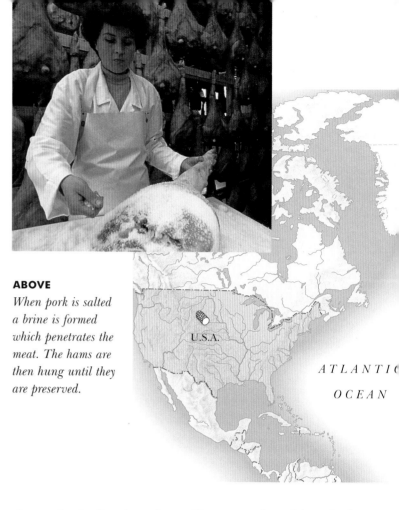

ABOVE
When pork is salted a brine is formed which penetrates the meat. The hams are then hung until they are preserved.

U.S.A.

ATLANTIC

OCEAN

the method of curing alone. Hams may be sold cooked, or raw and pickled in brine, dried, or smoked. The difference between British gammon and ham is that ham is cut from the leg and then brined, whereas gammon is cut from the carcass after brining and either sold in this form or smoked. Hams should appear plump with a good layer of fat under the rind.

A sausage, such as a pink sausage, is a mixture of minced, seasoned meat, enclosed in a tube casing. The French refer to a *saucisse* when describing a small fresh or lightly smoked sausage, and a *saucisson* for a larger, smoked, dried, or preserved and sliced sausage. *Saucisses* generally contain pork meat and fat, but may contain other meats. The ingredients are funneled into a casing, made either from a pig's or sheep's intestines, or a synthetic casing made from reconstituted collagen. Some sausages are cooked from fresh, and others are boiled or poached after curing—the German frankfurter is the most famous example.

PRESERVING PROCESSES

Curing meat involves removing, or "healing" its natural process of putrefying. The most popular early methods of

Cured meats and sausage

CHINA *lap cheong* (chopped pork, soy sauce, and paprika) **DENMARK** *Danish salami* (pork, veal, garlic, and spices) **GERMANY** *bratwurst* (minced, spiced pork or veal) *teewurst* (minced pork or pork and beef, spiced and smoked) *frankfurter* (minced pork and bacon, lightly smoked) *metwurst* (spreading sausage of pork, beef, and paprika) *bierwurst* (pork, or pork and beef with fat, smoked) *knackwurst* (pork, beef, and pork fat, with parsley and cumin) *cervelat* (pork and garlic, or beef and spices) *netz salami* (pork salami, bound with string) *Westphalian ham* (rich, dark ham) **GREECE** *Greek spiced sausage* (dark short sausage, heavily spiced) **HUNGARY** *salami* (spiced fat pork) **ITALY** *luganeghe* (pure pork sausage) *salsiccie* (pork sausage with garlic and peppercorns) *pepperoni* (pork and beef sausage with red peppers and spices) *toscana* (pork with lean meat and fat) *felinetti* (white wine, peppercorns, and garlic) *bresaola* (dried salt beef) *Parma ham* (raw ham with pepper and spices) *Milano salami* (lean and fat pork, beef, garlic, pepper, and white wine) **POLAND** *kabanos* (a spicy minced pork sausage) *kielbasa* (spiced sausage made with beef or pork) **PORTUGAL** *linguic* (cured pork sausage, with garlic and spices) **SPAIN** *butifara* (pork sausage with garlic and spices, pre-boiled and air-dried) *morcilla* (black pudding) *chorizo* (pimiento and pork) **SWITZERLAND** *alpenluber* (air-dried pork, beef, and pork fat) **U.K.** *black pudding* (pig's blood, groats, fat, oatmeal, and seasonings) *haggis* (Scottish, a sheep's stomach filled with liver, lungs, and heart of a sheep, flavored with oatmeal, onions, and parsley) *saveloy* (pork and lights; UK cervelat) *salt beef* (brisket soaked in brine) *bradenham* (ham soaked in molasses) **U.S.A.** *frankfurter* (*see Germany*) *corned beef* (cooked, cured beef, preserved in brine and jelly)

---

curing meat were dry salting, or using sugar. Sugar softened the meat, but was very costly.

Today, several methods are used, and each region of the world imparts its own variations and flavors:

Dry curing Salt is rubbed into the meat especially around the bone. The salt absorbs the juices from the meat to form a brine, which in turn penetrates the meat.

Smoking Thought to originate from drying meat over a fire. Wood smoke contains tar products which preserve the meat, and flavors can be imparted by the use of different woods. The duration of the process can vary from several hours to several days, and the most commonly used woods are beech, hickory, oak, and chestnut. Smoking is most commonly used for hams and bacon, sausages, poultry, and game.

Corning In the sixteenth century, this method acquired its name from the similarity between grains of corn and grains of salt. Salt was rubbed into the meat to preserve it, although there were regional variations here, too. Corned beef is the most widely recognized "corned" meat, and is popular in America and Britain.

Air drying In warm climates hanging meat in warm dry air will remove the moisture and preserve the meat. The same technique is applied in China where meats such as duck are imbued with a special flavor by wind-drying.

DOMESTIC FOWL

*T*he wide range of domestic birds that now grace our tables,
including chicken, turkey, goose, duck, and guinea fowl, is
reflected in varied festive traditions in both Europe and America.

ABOVE

Chicken remains one of the most popular poultry meats around the world. Battery farming made chickens economical to breed, but free-range farming, as above, produces chickens with more flavor, although they are a little more expensive to buy.

The chicken is descended from the Asian red jungle fowl, the *Gallus gallus*, which belongs to the pheasant family. In 4000 BC, Chinese diets were rich in poultry, which were boiled, roasted, or steamed, while jungle fowl were domesticated as early as 2500 BC in the Indus valley. The Egyptians preserved chicken meat in the sun as early as 2600 BC. The Romans were also partial to chicken and, in the first century AD, gelded cocks to produce the larger capon. The chicken's adaptability and versatility was to make it one of the world's most popular foods.

By 1934, poultry farmers on the Delmarva Peninsula, off America's east coast, began raising the broiler chicken. Chicken was to remain an expensive and a seasonal food, however, until the battery-raised bird eventually replaced the "spring chicken." By the mid-1940s, Tyson Foods, in Kansas, were experimenting with vertical integration, a concept which revolutionized poultry farming: once farmers were able to combat the diseases that had prevented large concentrations of poultry being raised together, three-floor poultry houses could be built with up to 30,000 birds on each floor. Mature birds could be produced for market in just 42 days. Today, the trend is to return to "free-range" birds, which are favored for their better flavor than the mass-produced chickens.

COMMON BREEDS, TYPES, AND COOKERY METHODS

There are hundreds of varieties of chicken, which are also sold under different names according to their age and weight. The most common varieties are:

Capon Neutered male chickens that are bred for their good flavored meat. They are especially fattened and have a larger proportion of white meat to dark than other types. They weigh around 6–10 lb/2.7–4.5 kg and are usually roasted.

Poussin Young chickens weighing from 1–2 lb/450–900 g. They should be old enough to have good firm flesh and a good flavor. Their delicate flesh can be roasted, broiled, and casseroled. The whole bird is served as one portion.

Roasting chicken Usually a young cockerel or hen of about twelve weeks, weighing about 5 lb/2.2 kg. They may also be fried and barbecued.

Stewing or boiling chicken/hen/fowl These are mature birds which require long and gentle cooking to tenderize the tougher flesh. The age of the bird is determined by its breastbone—the older the bird the more rigid the breastbone. Stewing fowl weigh from 2½–6 lb/1.1–2.7 kg. They are most commonly used in pies, fricassées, galantines, and soups.

TURKEY: THE FESTIVE BIRD

The turkey has a disputed history, there being several schools of thought to its origin and spread. One theory is that it was discovered by the Spanish adventurer, Hernán Cortés, when he sailed from Cuba to conquer New Spain in 1519. The wild turkeys of Yucatán could not be domesticated, but a different variety known as gallopavo were brought back to Europe in 1523, and became known as peacock. When they arrived in England they obtained their name in confusion with Guinea fowl, which had been introduced by the turkey merchants or "turks" from the eastern Mediterranean. Some food historians are of the opinion that Jewish traders expelled from Spain may have taken the bird to England, the Hebrew name for peacock being "tukki." Turkey soon replaced the peacock, swan, and goose on many tables across Europe.

Eventually, the turkey replaced the Christmas goose in England, a tradition that persists to this day, and roast turkey is also the traditional fare in America on Thanksgiving Day. Today, turkey is a popular meat, both for specific festivals, such as Thanksgiving, Easter, and Christmas, as well as for more everyday eating. It is now more affordable and is sold in smaller cuts appropriate for ordinary meals. Its health values are an important factor when considering its increased use.

Turkey is available all year round. It is sold as a whole bird in varying weights, according to its type and breeding—some birds are bred with heavy breasts and a small bone structure to speed the cooking process and produce a moist meat. The male is larger than the female, but the latter is usually more tender. The younger birds are suitable for roasting, while older birds are best used in soups and stews. It is now possible to buy turkey breast joints for those preferring white meat only, and large turkey drumsticks for roasting. Lean turkey meat is also sold for stir-frying and casseroles, and in scallops for broiling and frying.

A Traditional Thanksgiving

In the U.S.A., turkey is the traditional meal for Thanksgiving—an annual festival which commemorates the first successful harvest for the European colonists, who were saved from starvation by the wild turkey in 1621. It is celebrated on the Thursday before the last Friday in November. Family members gather together for the traditional meal consisting of roasted turkey stuffed with cornbread, which is served with chestnuts and orange-and-cranberry sauce. Mashed and roasted potatoes, squashes, and pickles are served as side dishes. This is all followed by a selection of all-American desserts, such as pumpkin pie or apple pie and ice cream.

ABOVE

Freedom from Want. *Norman Rockwell's painting captures a traditional Thanksgiving family gathering.*

DUCK AND GOOSE-REARING AREAS

The main areas of France where duck and goose are reared intensively, mainly for France's famous liver pâtés, are indicated on this map. Regional specialist breeds are identified.

🦆 Duck rearing

🦢 Goose rearing

ABOVE

Geese, once eaten at celebratory meals such as Michaelmas and Christmas in the U.K. and Scandinavia, have now largely been replaced by the turkey. Geese are mainly bred for roasting and goose-liver pâté.

COOKED GOOSE

The migratory goose, originally a game bird, was a popular domestic fowl in Germany by 1000 BC. The goose also found favor with the Romans who developed the technique of force-feeding their birds, to fatten them up in preparation for making goose-liver pâté. The French were to use these methods to make their own pâté, or foie gras. Goose was traditionally the meat of the poor, served in Scandinavia, and in England on Michaelmas (September 29) and at Christmas. Today, it remains the traditional fare in Scandinavia and Germany, but has been supplanted by the turkey in England.

Many of the recipes used for turkey and chicken can be applied to goose, although it is generally roasted and served with stuffing. It has always been cooked in winter months, the first goose being eaten at Michaelmas, when it had just reached maturity. If properly cooked, goose is a truly celebrational fall meal, especially when served with seasonal fruits. There are many varieties of goose, some of the most popular being the Emden from Germany, the Roman, and the Brecon Buff. White geese remain expensive and generally have less meat on them than a turkey. They have a gamy flavor and, although they are very fatty, are still considered to be the best poultry by many. Generally, a goose weighs 6–12 lb/2.7–5.4 kg, and is sold fresh or frozen.

DEPENDABLE DUCK

Records show that the first ducks were bred in Mesopotamia, (1000s of years ago). Duck is thought to have been domesticated in China more than 2,000 years ago. It is generally believed all of our domesticated ducks have descended from the Wild Mallard, or *Anas platyrhyncha*, except for the South American Muscovy.

Most of the ducks now consumed are domesticated. They have a large frame and high fat content, supplying a small quantity of meat in relation to their weight. Many breeds of duck are eaten, and France is a particularly good source of special breeds such as the Rouen, Nantes, Mulard, and Barbary ducks. Generally, ducks are roasted or cooked on the spit if tender, but older, tougher birds may be braised or used in pâtés. Some wild ducks, such as the shoveler, gadwall, baldpate, and pintail, are still consumed and are much sought after. Generally, only the legs and breast fillets of wild duck are eaten. They are not hung before cooking and are usually roasted.

THE "STUPID" GUINEA FOWL

These birds are native to the Guinea coast of West Africa. All the domesticated varieties are descended from the African bird, known as the Numidian or Carthage hen. Related to the pheasant, it was once considered a game bird, and much enjoyed by the Romans. It has the dubious reputation of being the stupidest of all birds.

Today, guinea fowl is bred for the table, and has been domesticated for centuries in many parts of the world, in particular France. Artificial insemination now allows the birds to be bred all year round. The term *fermier* applies to the free-range birds as opposed to the factory-reared fowl. Guinea fowl is regarded as poultry, although it is hung, like game.

Guinea fowl are cooked in the same way as a pheasant or chicken. They are either covered in bacon, or larded before roasting to produce a moist meat, or casseroled, poached, or braised. Their tender flesh has a gamy flavor.

French Duck Confit

SERVES 6

10 lb/4.5 kg goose (choose a very fat goose)
2 lb/900 g salt
¼ oz/7 g saltpeter
5 cloves, crushed
3 bay leaves, crushed
1 teaspoon thyme or parsley
4 lb 8 oz/2 kg goose fat
1 lb/450 g lard

Quarter the goose. Mix together the salt, saltpeter, cloves, and herbs. Rub some of this mixture over the goose quarters. Transfer the goose to an earthenware baking pot and add the remaining salt mixture. Cover and leave for 24 hours.

Melt the goose fat in a large skillet. Remove the goose pieces from the salt mixture and rub clean. Cook the goose in the fat over a low heat for 3 hours until cooked through. Remove the goose from the skillet. Bone the goose, discarding the bones. Pour a thick layer of fat through a fine strainer into a large eathenware pot and leave to solidify. Once solidified, place the goose meat on top of the fat and cover with more liquid goose fat. Leave to stand for 2 days.

Melt the lard. Pour a ½-inch/1 cm layer over the top of the pot; leave to set completely. Cover with waxed paper, excluding any air, then cover with another double thickness of paper and tie with string. Keep in a cool place until required.

LEFT
Ducks were first domesticated in China over 2,000 years ago. Almost all the ducks eaten in China today are domesticated, the rarer wild ducks are much sought after.

GAME: FURRED & FEATHERED

The word "game" is used to describe all birds and animals hunted for food. Hunting continues to be enjoyed as a sport in some areas, particularly the Americas and Europe, where strict "seasons" are enforced to preserve stocks.

ABOVE
Although some wild pheasant remain, most are bred in captivity and released into the wild before the shooting season begins.

FURRED AND FEATHERED GAME
Although wild birds and animals are still hunted in certain parts of the world, some of these species are now domestically reared.

Game hunting areas

AUSTRALIA *Rabbit* (**13**) **CANADA** *Snipe* (**8**); *Deer* (**10**); *Moose* (**12**); *Reindeer* (**15**) **EGYPT** *Quail* (**7**); *Deer* (**10**) **FRANCE** *Grouse* (**1**); *Partridge* (**3**); *Pigeon* (**5**); *Thrush* (**9**); *Hare* (**11**); *Rabbit* (**13**) **GREECE** *Deer* (**10**); *Rabbit* (**13**) **HUNGARY** *Hare* (**11**); *Rabbit* (**13**) **ITALY** *Ortolan* (**2**) **MEXICO** *Pheasant* (**4**) **NORTH AFRICA** *Pigeon* (**5**) **NORTHERN EUROPE** *Pheasant* (**4**); *Ptarmigan* (**6**); *Quail* (**7**); *Reindeer* (**15**); *Wild boar* (**16**); *Wild turkey* (**17**) **SOUTHEAST ASIA** *Pheasant* (**4**); *Wild boar* (**16**) **U.K.** *Grouse* (**1**); *Partridge* (**3**); *Pheasant* (**4**); *Pigeon* (**5**); *Deer* (**10**); *Hare* (**11**); *Rabbit* (**13**) **U.S.A.** *Grouse* (**1**); *Deer* (**10**); *Moose* (**12**); *Racoon* (**14**); *Reindeer* (**15**); *Wild turkey* (**17**)

CANADA
8 10 12 15

NORTH AMERICA

U.S.A.
1 10 12
14 15 17

MEXICO
4

ATLANTIC OCEAN

PACIFIC OCEAN

Animals regarded as game vary from country to country. Some, such as racoon, Canadian snipe, squirrel, moose, and the Mexican pheasant, are unique to the Americas, while others, such as reindeer and wild turkey, are also hunted and eaten all over the northern hemisphere.

Game is distinguished from other poultry or farmyard animals by its characteristic dark meat and strong flavor. Feathered (or winged) game is a term which covers all birds (including waterfowl), while furred (or ground) game accounts for all other hunted animals, including hare, rabbit, deer, and boar.

Today, strict laws control game hunting and most of the so-called "game" which we see displayed in supermarkets, where it has become increasingly popular, is, in fact, domestically reared.

ABOVE

Once a necessity for survival, hunting is now a pleasurable pastime and sport in Europe and the Americas. The sporting horseback hunters seen above are chasing and tracking their animals across country with a pack of hunting dogs.

U.K.
1 3 4 5
10 11 13

SCANDINAVIA

RUSSIAN FEDERATION

NORTHERN EUROPE
4 6 7 15 16 17

ITALY
2

HUNGARY
11 13

FRANCE
1 3 5 9
11 13

EUROPE

GREECE
10 13

CASPIAN SEA

ASIA

CHINA

MEDITERRANEAN SEA

EGYPT
7 10

NORTH
AFRICA
5

INDIA

SOUTHEAST ASIA
4 16

AFRICA

INDIAN
OCEAN

AUSTRALIA
13

NEW
ZEALAND

AN A - Z OF GAME

Feathered:

GROUSE (1)
There are several types of grouse hunted. British species include the red grouse of Scotland, black grouse, and the capercaillie. The most common French species are the hazel grouse and the pintailed grouse, found in southern France. Although they are not true grouse, the sage grouse, ruffed grouse, and blue grouse of America are also hunted.

ORTOLAN (2)
This small migratory bird was once considered the finest small bird in culinary terms. It is now officially protected.

PARTRIDGE (3)
This highly prized game bird is hunted in France and Britain. The main species of France are the red-legged partridge, and the more common, smaller gray-legged partridge. The American partridge, also found in France, is also highly prized. Young partridges are cooked in pâtés, roasted, or casseroled; the older birds are most commonly used for long, slow-cooking braises.

PHEASANT (4)
Wild pheasant may be found worldwide and remain one of the most popular game birds. Farm-reared birds are sold fresh or frozen in supermarkets but the wild bird is best after hanging. Roasting is the most successful cooking method.

PIGEON (5)
The pigeon can be domesticated or wild. The wood pigeon, also known as the ring dove, is the most common wild pigeon in France. The pigeon is best casseroled, in pâtés and ragouts, or stewed. Younger birds may be roasted or broiled.

PTARMIGAN (6)
A member of the grouse family, ptarmigan are found in northern Britain and northern Europe. Changing color from brown to white in winter, they are hunted and cooked as grouse.

QUAIL (7)
Quail varieties include the Californian and European quail, which are reared on farms. Wild quail is found in Europe from April to October but is rapidly becoming scarce. Its flavor is superior to the farmed varieties. Weighing only 5–7 oz/ 150–200 g, the bird is usually roasted, broiled, or sautéed, often stuffed.

SNIPE (8)
Snipe are hunted from August to April, their prime season being in the fall. Snipe are best roasted, usually cooked with the entrails, which are considered a delicacy.

THRUSH (9)
A dozen species of this small bird are found in France. They are hunted in the fall and winter for their delicate flesh. Their flavor is influenced by the berries on which they feed.

Furred:

DEER (10)
Venison is the meat of any kind of deer, but the term is also applied to the meat of other large game such as wild boar, derived from the Latin word *venari*, meaning to hunt. Venison requires both hanging and marinating, unless the animal is very young. Young venison are broiled or larded with pork fat and roasted.

HARE (11)
The hare belongs to the same family as the rabbit, but is larger and has darker flesh. The most sought after French hares are found in Beauce, Champagne, Normandy, Gascony and Perigord (the *a la royale* hare dish originates from there). All hare meat is considered highly flavored, but the mountain hare is thought to have a more delicate flavor. Hares are usually roasted or sautéed.

MOOSE (12)
These are the largest members of the deer family, weighing up to half a ton. Moose are hunted for both their meat and fur. The meat is generally roasted or casseroled.

RABBIT (13)
Rabbit is often served as pie or stew. Wild rabbit has a better flavor and is roasted or broiled, rather than being cooked in a pie or casserole. Domestic rabbits are raised for their fur as well as for the table.

RACOON (14)
Found in America and weighing around 10 lbs/4½ kg, the racoon ranges from southern Canada to Panama. They are trapped for their valuable fur and for their meat.

REINDEER (15)
These are found in the arctic regions of Europe and western Asia. Reindeer are not well domesticated, but are broken in to pull sleds. They are hunted for their milk, meat, fur, and leather.

WILD BOAR (16)
This animal still roams parts of France, Italy, Germany, and other European countries. It is a fully flavored dark meat, which is now farmed either from foreign breeds, or by cross-breeding with domesticated pigs. Best roasted.

WILD TURKEY (17)
Wild turkeys are native to America, Mexico, and Guatemala. While they are fairly plentiful in Mexico, overhunting has made them scarce in the U.S.A. They are cooked by the same methods as meatier domesticated turkeys.

Numbers on this page key to the map on the previous page.

DAIRY PRODUCTS

*I*n parts of Asia cheese is regarded as "rotten milk," and oil, rather than butter, is the cooking fat of choice. In Spain, southern Italy, and southern France, olive oil is preferred for frying and basting. But for most westerners, milk, butter, and cheese, whether

full fat or low fat, are a major element in the diet. Britain is famed for rich Jersey cream, France for slightly sour crème fraîche, and central and eastern Europe has given us sour cream and yogurt, now a fashionable supermarket product.

MILK: THE GOOD DRINK

ilk is a rich and perfectly balanced food, so emblematic of plenty that in the Bible "a land of milk and honey" represents the ultimate in abundance.

BELOW

Milk from cows is more widely used than that from sheep, goats, or buffalo. These contented cows, sitting peacefully in a green field, show the most agreeable face of the dairy industry.

Milk is designed to feed baby mammals, but is also a favorite of both adult and baby humans. Not all humans, however, consume the milk of other species. In fact, roughly 80 percent of non-whites around the world are lactose-intolerant because they do not drink milk after weaning. Instead, they consume milky substances derived from plants such as soybeans, coconut, or other nuts. Native Americans made milk from hickory nuts, for example, and in Europe from the Middle Ages until the eighteenth century, liquid extracted from almonds and sometimes walnuts was used as a substitute for milk and cream, especially on fast days when dairy products, called white meats, were forbidden.

It is not certain whether it was sheep or goats which were first domesticated, but milk from both these animals is still used extensively for making cheese and yogurt, as it was in ancient times. Although the cow was domesticated later, it has now become the greatest producer of milk and dairy products in the Western world. Milk from other herbivores, the horse, camel, yak, and buffalo, is still made into butter and cheese in some parts of the world, as it has been for millennia.

The omnivorous pig, which can be fed on household scraps and does not need to be grazed or fed on special winter fodder, is the only major animal commonly used for food which does not also provide milk. Pigs were indispensable in land-poor and densely populated China, as they can be kept in a small area and are easily fed and fattened. To this day, there is no significant dairy farming in the Far East, and most Asians dislike milk because it is difficult for them to digest.

117

LEFT
*A statue of the
Hindu god Krishna
with a cow. The cow
is regarded as sacred
in India because it
is the great provider.*

Fresh milk needs to be consumed rapidly because it does not keep well and quickly turns sour. To maximize its usefulness, it was imperative to find ways to preserve milk. Cheese was eaten in Pharaonic Egypt, Greece, and Rome, and was smoked in Gaul, as it is today. Curds, whey, and sour milk drinks were also known. In areas where vines did not grow, milk was fermented into alcohol—the Celts made a curdled milk beer for special feasts, and milky alcoholic mixtures such as egg nog and syllabubs are still festive drinks.

Central Asian nomads of the first millennium AD, who ate very little fruit or vegetables, relied heavily on mare's milk, which contains twice as much vitamin C as human milk and four times more than cow's milk. Nomads also turned mare's milk into a fermented drink, called *kumiss*. They probably also made curds, simple cheese, and yogurt. Centuries later, Marco Polo reported that the Mongols he had encountered on his travels dried milk after skimming off the cream to make butter. The dried milk was mixed with liquid, and carried in a gourd attached to their horses so the vigorous motion dissolved it as they rode.

Intensive Dairy Farming

The Netherlands is a very small country and was one of the first to develop an intensive dairy industry. By 1750, the Dutch were exporting butter and cheese. Manure from cattle was a valuable byproduct which was used to enrich the land used for market gardening. Until a mechanical cooler was invented in 1860, milk in cities was supplied by local cowmen and was often of dubious quality. The customers' demand for milk warm from the cow was sometimes satisfied by diluting it with hot water, and water was not always safe to drink. By the end of the nineteenth century, quickly cooled milk which stayed cold in metal containers could be brought into urban areas by rail.

A glance at any Victorian menu or cookbook proves that the use of cream and butter was lavish at this time. Although most people could not afford to keep their own dairy herds to guarantee a constant supply of fresh produce, butter and cream were now much more widely available. Cream soups were considered the height of elegance, while meats and vegetables were cooked in butter and then smothered in dense creamy sauces, and the dessert course was awash with thick cream. The British still expect most desserts to be served with a pitcher of cream, and an outing for afternoon tea to Ye Olde Tea Shoppe in an historic town or grand hotel is considered a poor experience without lashings of cream and butter.

FROM CHURN & CULTURE

*W*here dairy products are abundant, rich golden butter is the preferred cooking fat. It is used less lavishly where the olive grows, and in one area of France goose fat takes its place.

The olive reigns supreme around the Mediterranean, so cheese and yogurt, most often made with sheep, goat, or buffalo's milk, are the main dairy products. The terrain and climate of northern Europe is better suited for raising cattle, and most dairy produce made from cow's milk. Cattle were introduced to the Americas and the Antipodes by early European settlers, and both regions are now major consumers and exporters of dairy products. Denmark and the Netherlands are also important exporters of dairy products, especially butter.

ABOVE

An illumination in the Louterell Psalter *of 1340 showing milk being churned in medieval England.*

RIGHT

The image of the dairy maid in art has associations with purity and rural contentment— although in fact it is very hard work carrying pails of milk hanging from a wooden yoke.

MODERN MILK

Most of the milk in the world comes from temperate zones. The U.S.A. produces the most, far more than it consumes, mainly from Holstein-Fresian crossbreed cows whose milk is one of the lowest in fat and nonfat milk solids. Wisconsin is the leading dairy state, producing more than 18 percent of the U.S.A. milk total and half the cheese. Russia is second to the U.S.A. in world production, followed by India, France, Germany, Ukraine, the U.K., and Poland.

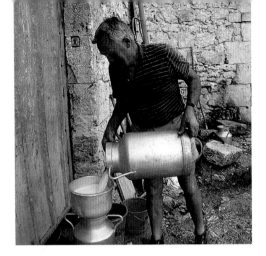

LEFT
In southwestern France, milk which has been heated and cooled is poured into a churn, and then made into yogurt or cheese.

Pasteurized milk is heated to 161°F (72°C) for 15 seconds and then quickly cooled down to 50°F (10°C), which makes it safe to drink but also destroys some of the vitamins, calcium, and antibodies. Milk is often then homogenized by forcing it through a small valve under pressure, which breaks up the clusters of fat and distributes them uniformly throughout the milk.

Milk can be heated to an even higher temperature, 270°F (132°C), for one second, and then packed in sterile cartons which will keep without refrigeration. This Ultra Heat Treatment (or UHT) destroys even more nutrients. Sterilized milk is homogenized and poured into bottles, which are sealed and then heated to 230°F (110°C). It will then keep indefinitely at room temperature.

Buttermilk can either be the milk strained off during butter-making, or skim milk with a culture added to it, known as "cultured buttermilk." It is useful for cooking—acting, for example, as a rising agent with flour. It has ten times more protein proportionately than ordinary milk and very little fat.

In the U.S.A. the fat is removed from bulk milk by a mechanical cream separator which uses centrifugal force. In the U.K. the richest cream is thick, yellow, clotted cream produced in Devon, Cornwall, and Somerset, which is thickened by gentle heating. Crème fraîche is a slightly soured French cream, treated with a culture. Sour or soured cream is treated with a souring culture, which gives it an agreeable tart taste, stronger than crème fraîche. Other useful milk products are canned evaporated milk, with half the water evaporated, and condensed milk with 40 percent added sugar, which helps to preserve it.

BUTTER: THE SACRED SPREAD

If milk is left undisturbed, the oil-rich cream rises to the top. When this is skimmed off, chilled, and then agitated or churned, the protective membranes of some fat

Yogurt—Elixir of Life

The widespread consumption of yogurt in Europe and America is a fairly recent phenomenon, but yogurt is, in fact, an ancient food. When the king of France, Francois I (r. 1515–47), was suffering from depression, it is said that he was given a drink of fermented sheep's milk by a Jewish doctor in Constantinople that cured him. But yogurt did not make serious inroads on the dietary habits of the West until this century, when a biologist from the Pasteur Institute in Paris, with a theory that toxins in the intestine were responsible for most ills, was impressed by the longevity of peoples in the Balkans, Eastern Europe, and the Caucasian mountains. He studied their diet and discovered that one of the constants was yogurt.

Yogurt is made with a combination of two strains of bacilli, which act in tandem when added to milk warmed to blood heat. Within hours they change the lactose, or milk sugar, into lactic acid which results in a coagulation of the casein solids. The bacteria which cause putrefaction in the form of gas, active in intestinal infection, cannot live in lactic acid. The beneficial bacteria in yogurt can also make the whole range of the B complex vitamins in the gut—critical for anyone who has taken one of the many modern drugs which kill off all intestinal flora, good and bad. Adding sugar to yogurt kills off the valuable bacteria which will continue to live in the yogurt if it is left alone.

Yogurt made from sheep's milk is thought to have the finest flavor and is very popular in the Middle East. Cow milk yogurt may be more digestible, although goat milk yogurt is recommended for very young babies. The flavor of yogurt varies according to the culture, and the milk used to make it. Those made with whole milk and a mild culture are creamy and firm, while others have a strong, acidic taste. The longer yogurt is left to work the fuller the development of the healthy micro-organisms will be—it can take six to seven hours to reach the desired consistency.

Greek Yogurt, Cucumber, and Garlic Dip

This dip should always be served well chilled, and can be eaten with fresh pita bread or as an accompaniment to fritters and other fried foods.

SERVES 4 TO 6

1 lb/450 g natural yogurt
½ cucumber
3 cloves garlic, crushed
2 tablespoons chopped fresh mint
2 tablespoons olive oil
1 tablespoon white wine vinegar
Salt, to taste
Chopped fresh mint, to garnish

Place the yogurt in a medium-sized bowl. Peel and grate the cucumber, squeezing a little at a time in the palm of your hand to remove the excess water. Stir the cucumber into the yogurt.

Stir in the garlic, fresh mint, olive oil, and vinegar and season with salt, to taste. Cover and chill until required. Garnish with chopped mint.

RIGHT

Making butter by traditional methods is a labor of love but for many people, butter made in this way has no equal. There are still dairy farmers who make fine butter with pride.

globules break, and liquid fat is released, which helps to cement other globules together. These, together with other free fats, become granules which lump together to form a semisolid mass, held in the liquid called buttermilk which is then drained away.

This miraculous substance was used as holy ointment and called "sacred" or "magical" food in the Celtic languages; *imb* in Irish, *ammanh* in Breton. In Tibet, yak butter is not only a holy drink but an offering which devotees rub on religious images. Indians of the highest caste will only eat food which has been ritually purified by being cooked in the clarified butter called ghee.

In the fourteenth century, the Church prohibited butter-eating on fast days, a decision which did not please the butter-eating nations of northern Europe. They felt they were being forced to eat inferior oil, and many were even prepared, grudgingly, to pay for dispensations that allowed them to eat butter on fast days, providing revenue for the Church of Rome in the oil-eating south. The traffic in butter dispensations was one of the many practices which so outraged Martin Luther in 1520 when he wrote furiously that "Eating butter they say is a greater sin than to lie, blaspheme, or indulge in impurity." It is no coincidence that it was those countries where butter was preferred exclusively to oil, that broke away from the Church during the Protestant Reformation—the hated premium charged for eating butter was one of the many abuses which the reformers were protesting against.

CURDS & CHEESE

The discovery that the protein in milk will coagulate into curds when combined with acid, rennet, alum, or plant extracts, was made at least 6,000 years ago.

Many of the cheeses we eat today have venerable origins: gorgonzola, the Italian blue cheese, was made before AD 879. In the twelfth century, very large cheeses, such as Parmesan, Emmenthal, Comte, Gruyère, and Beaufort, made from as much as 220 gallons of milk, were the collective effort of a village or region. Reblochon takes its name from the second milking, the *rebloche*, which was not declared for taxation by farmers and shepherds in Savoy. Others were made by monks, such as those of the abbeys Port-Salut and Maroilles.

Cheese has long taken pride of place at the most venerable tables. In *c.* 1570, at a banquet devised by Bartolomeo Scappi for Pope Pius V, the fourth and final course, called "Delicacies from the Sideboard," included Parmesan and Riviera cheese and milk curds with sugar sprinkled over. One other dish in the previous course contained cheese, sprinkled with sugar and cinnamon over stuffed fat geese, boiled Lombard style and covered with sliced almonds.

The Spanish introduced cheese-making to the New World, and the U.S.A. is now the largest producer of hard cheese. France is the second largest producer, followed by Germany, the Netherlands, Mexico, Argentina, Denmark, Russia, and Canada. The French still eat the most cheese. Italy is the second largest cheese-consuming country, followed by Denmark, the Netherlands, Sweden, Belgium, and the United States.

CHEESE-MAKING TECHNIQUES

The kind of milk used to make cheese, and the percentage of fat it contains, will affect the flavor. Firstly, the milk must be warmed, which sours or acidifies it, then a starter culture is introduced. When the desired acidity is reached, a coagulating agent—rennet or a plant-derived equivalent—is added. The milk then separates into curds and whey. The curd now has to be broken up; how finely it is cut up at this stage determines the amount of whey which will be left in the cheese, and this in turn affects its character. The curd for very hard cheese is very finely cut, while the curd for fresh soft cheese is hardly broken up. To produce an extra hard cheese, the curd is heated to shrink it, enabling

Mexican Quesadillas

Quesadillas are a very simple, very economical, and surprisingly filling and delicious snack. They consist of nothing more than tortillas with a melted cheese filling. The cheese is Oexaca, but Jack and mozarella are fine, and cheddar will do.

The usual way to make them is to fry a tortilla in an almost dry pan (or on a griddle) until it is soft; flip it over; put a lump or a handful of grated (shredded) cheese in the middle; fold it in half; and continue to cook it, turning it over occasionally, until the cheese melts.

Quesadillas Sincronizadas, or "synchronized quesadillas," are made as shown, with two quesadillas stuck together with melted cheese; they are quartered for serving.

If you are making quesadillas with uncooked tortillas, you can pinch together the edges of a basic turnover quesadilla and fry the whole thing in deep fat.

LEFT

Cheese-making requires enormous skill and, even with modern production methods, there are many variables which can affect the flavor, texture, and keeping quality.

even more moisture to be extracted. The curds are put into molds and left to drain; some are pressed.

The flavor of a cheese is also determined by the micro-organisms added. The final factor affecting taste is the ripening conditions; temperature, humidity, and length of time. The rind develops during this process; it can form naturally, or the cheese may be wrapped in leaves, waxed, or rolled in ashes. Soft cheeses, such as Camembert, develop a bloomy white, orange, or yellow mold, while mold inside produces blue-veined cheeses. The curd can be treated with hot water and molded as Provolone is, salted like Cheshire, or, like St. Paulin, soaked in brine.

Cheese can be divided into three categories: soft, semi-hard, and hard. Soft cheeses can be unripened, as well as mold- or bacteria-ripened. Some typical unripened soft cheeses are Neufchâtel, Primost, ricotta, and feta. Camembert, Brie and Pont l'Évêque are mold-ripened. Limberger and Liederkranz are bacteria-ripened.

Semi-hard cheeses which are often aged for 60–90 days include the mold-ripened Stilton, Gorgonzola and bacteria-ripened Munster, Bel Paese, Fontina, Gouda, and Jack cheese.

Aged hard cheeses are excellent for cooking. Bacteria-ripened, some well-known examples are Asiago, Cantal, Caccio Cavallo, Cheddar, Edam, Gjetost, Gruyère, Provolone, Sapsago, Sbrinz, Swiss, Cheshire, Parmesan, Romano, and Sardo.

A WORLD OF CHEESE

FRANCE

France produces more than 300 kinds of cheese and has three types of land forms, four types of climate, as well as an Atlantic and Mediterranean coastline.

Beaufort and Beaumont (1) Cow's milk, semi-hard, from the Savoie region.

Bleue d'Auvergne (2) Cow's milk, semi-soft, from Savoie.

Boulette d'Avesnes (3) Buttermilk, soft, with parsley, tarragon, and paprika. Originating in Flanders and northern France.

Boursault and Boursin (4) Soft, triple-cream cow's milk, from the Ile de France, and Normandy.

Brie (5) Pasteurized and unpasteurized cow's milk, soft, from the Ile de France.

Brillat-Savarin (6) Triple-cream cow's milk, soft, from Normandy.

Camembert (7) Pasteurized or unpasteurized cow's milk, soft, from Normandy.

Cantal (8) Unpasteurized cow's milk from the Auvergne region, semi-hard, summer only.

Cantal laitier (9) Pasteurized, year-round cheese from Auvergne.

Carre de l'Est (10) Pasteurized cow's milk, soft, square, from northeastern France.

Chèvre (11) Soft goat's milk.

Comte (12) Cow's milk, Gruyère type, from the Jura mountains.

Coulommiers (13) Cow's milk, soft, from the Ile de France.

Fourme d'Ambert (14) Cow's milk, soft, blue-veined, from Auvergne.

Gaperon (15) Low-fat skimmed cow's milk, semi-soft, with garlic, from Auvergne.

Livarot (16) Cow's milk, semi-soft, from Normandy.

Maroilles (17) Cow's milk, soft, square, from the area around Lille.

Montrachet (18) Goat's milk, wrapped in vine or chestnut leaves, from Burgundy.

Morbier (19) Cow's milk, semi-hard, band of soot or charcoal through middle. Made in the Jura mountains.

Munster (20) Unpasteurized cow's milk, soft, sometimes with caraway seed, from the Voges mountains, Alsace.

Neufchâtel (21) Cow's milk, soft, fresh, or ripened, from Normandy.

Pont l'Évêque (22) Cow's milk, soft, square, from Normandy.

Reblochon (23) Cow's milk, semi-soft, from the Haute-Savoie.

Rigotte (24) Cow or goat's milk, soft, sometimes packed in wine or oil, and made all over France.

Roquefort (25) Ewe's milk, soft, blue-veined, from the Les Causses region.

Saint-Marcellin (26) Goat or cow's milk, soft, from the Isère Valley, Dauphine.

Sainte-Maure (27) Goat's milk, soft, from the Touraine region.

Sainte-Nectaire (28) Cow's milk, semi-hard, from Auvergne.

Saint-Paulin Cow's milk, semi-soft.

Tomme de Savoie (29) Whole or semi-skimmed cow's milk, semi-hard.

Valençay (30) Goat's milk, soft.

CHEESES OF FRANCE

This map indicates, by numbered symbols, the main areas of production of France's most famous cheeses. More detailed descriptions can be found in the numbered A–Z listing on this page.

① Major cheeses of France

① *Beaufort & Beaumont* ② *Bleue d'Auvergne*
③ *Boulette d'Avesnes* ④ *Boursault & Boursin*
⑤ *Brie* ⑥ *Brillat-Savarin* ⑦ *Camembert*
⑧ *Cantal* ⑨ *Cantal laitier* ⑩ *Carre de l'Est* ⑪
Chèvre ⑫ *Comte* ⑬ *Coulommiers* ⑭ *Fourme
d'Ambert* ⑮ *Gaperon* ⑯ *Livarot* ⑰ *Maroilles*
⑱ *Montrachet* ⑲ *Morbier* ⑳ *Munster* ㉑
Neufchâtel ㉒ *Pont l'Évêque* ㉓ *Reblochon* ㉔
Rigotte ㉕ *Roquefort* ㉖ *Saint-Marcellin* ㉗
Saint-Maure ㉘ *Sainte-Nectaire* ㉙ *Tomme de
Savoie* ㉚ *Valençay*

A WORLD OF CHEESE

ITALY

Parmesan is Italy's best-known and best-loved cheese. Named for the city of Parma, it is one of the type called *grana*, which are aged so that their distinctive flavor develops. These hard cheeses are grated and used almost daily in cooking.

Bel Paese *Cow's milk, semi-soft, made all over Italy.*

Cacietto *Cow's milk, semi-hard, from southern Italy.*

Cacio cavallo *Cow's milk, semi-hard, pear-shaped, from southern Italy.*

Caciotta *Cow, ewe, or goat's milk, semi-soft, farmhouse. Made all over Italy.*

Fontina *Cow's milk, semi-hard, from the Valle d'Aosta region.*

Gorgonzola *Cow's milk, semi-soft, blue-veined. From a village near Milan.*

Grana Padano *Cow's milk, hard, from the Po Valley region.*

Mascarpone *Fresh, soft cream cheese, from Lombardy.*

Mozzarella *Cow or buffalo's milk, soft. Originally from the Latium-Campania region in the south.*

Parmesan *Semi-skimmed unpasteurized cow's milk, hard, from the region around the Po and Reno rivers.*

Pecorino *Ewe's milk, semi-soft when fresh, hard when matured. From central and southern Italy.*

Provolone *Unpasteurized cow's milk, semi-soft, hand-molded, from the Po Valley region.*

Ricotta *Ewe or cow's milk whey, soft. Made all over Italy.*

Taleggio *Cow's milk, semi-soft, from northern Italy.*

SWITZERLAND

Agriculture in Switzerland is very intensive, but most farms are still small. Milk, cheese, butter, and meat account for half of the agricultural output of this small land-locked country. The best known cheese is Emmenthal from the mountains in the center of the country.

Appenzellar *Cow's milk, semi-hard, made in northeast Switzerland.*

Emmenthal *Unpasteurized cow's milk, ripened four months, semi-hard.*

Gruyère *Unpasteurized cow's milk, semi-hard.*

Raclette *Unpasteurized cow's milk, semi-hard, from the southwestern canton, Valais.*

Sapsago *Skimmed cow's milk or whey, mixed with melilot, a pale green clover.*

Sbrinz *Unpasteurized cow's milk, cured for two to three years.*

Tête-de-Moine *Cow's milk, semi-hard, originally from Bellelay Abbey, now made all over the Jura mountains near Bern.*

Tilsit or **Royal** *Cow's milk, semi-hard, from Thurgau in eastern Switzerland.*

Vacherin Mont d'or *Unpasteurized cow's milk, soft, made in the Jura in winter.*

GERMANY

Fairly mild summers and winters, and five different physiographic regions provide Germany with a small number of distinctive cheeses.

CHEESES OF ITALY

Numbered symbols indicate the main areas of production of Italian cheeses, which are described more fully in the A–Z listing on this page.

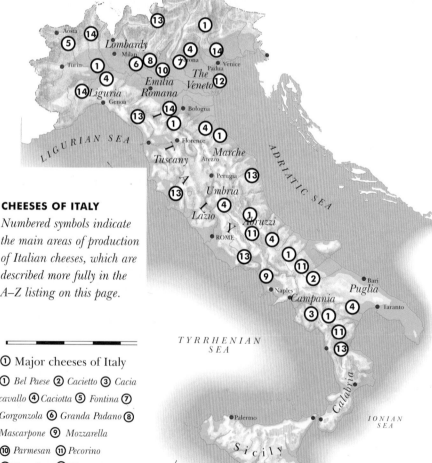

① Major cheeses of Italy

① *Bel Paese* ② *Cacietto* ③ *Cacia cavallo* ④ *Caciotta* ⑤ *Fontina* ⑦ *Gorgonzola* ⑥ *Granda Padano* ⑧ *Mascarpone* ⑨ *Mozzarella* ⑩ *Parmesan* ⑪ *Pecorino* ⑫ *Provolone* ⑬ *Ricotta* ⑭ *Taleggio*

Bavarian Blue *Cow's milk, semi-soft, from southern Germany.*

Bruder Basil *Cow's milk, smoked, from Bavaria.*

Edelpilz *Cow's milk, soft. Made all over Germany.*

Limberger *Cow's milk, soft. Made all over Germany.*

Tilsit *Cow's milk, semi-hard, with caraway seeds. Made all over Germany.*

SPAIN

Manchego is the most familiar cheese outside Spain. It goes particularly well with a sherry aperitif.

Cabrales *Goat, cow or ewe's milk, semi-hard, veined, from Asturias region.*

Mahon *Cow or ewe's milk, semi-hard from Minorca.*

Manchego *Ewe's milk, semi-hard, some matured. From Ciudad Real and La Mancha.*

THE NETHERLANDS

Edam and Gouda are the best known cheeses from this tiny country, rich in dairy produce. Edam, which is made from skimmed milk, is the lowest in fat of the semi hard cheeses. It has achieved worldwide popularity.

Edam *Skimmed cow's milk, semi-hard, coated in red wax. From the town of Edam, north of Amsterdam.*

Gouda *Cow's milk, semi-hard, some matured, from the southern Netherlands.*

UNITED KINGDOM

The British climate, with its considerable rainfall, ensures that there is ample pasturage for dairy herds. In recent years, there has been a revival of many traditional styles and production methods. Cheddar is still the most popular variety and, although it is made in all of the former colonies and is a major export, West Country farmhouse cheddar still sets the standard.

Benleigh Blue *Unpasteurized cow's milk, semi-hard, blue-veined, from Devon.*

Blue Shropshire *Cow's milk, hard, blue-veined.*

Blue Vinney or Dorset Blue *Skimmed cow's milk, hard, blue-veined.*

Caboc *Double cream, soft, rolled in oatmeal, from Scotland.*

Caerphilly *Cow's milk, semi-hard Originally from Wales.*

Cheddar *Cow's milk, hard, ages well, pasteurized has the most complex flavor. Originally from Somerset in the southwest.*

Cheshire *Cow's milk, semi-hard.*

Cotherstone *Unpasteurized Jersey milk, semi-hard from Yorkshire.*

Devon Garland *Unpasteurized Jersey cow's milk, semi-hard, with herbs.*

Double Gloucester *Cow's milk, semi-hard.*

Hawkestone *Goat's milk, hard.*

Lanark Blue *Unpasteurized ewe's milk, semi-hard, blue-veined, from Scotland.*

Lancashire *Cow's milk, hard.*

Orkney *Skimmed cow's milk, semi-hard.*

Sage Derby *Cow's milk, semi-hard, with sage.*

Single Gloucester *Cow's milk, semi-hard.*

Stilton *Pasteurized and unpasteurized cow's milk, semi-hard, blue-veined. Originally from Cambridgeshire, now made in Leicestershire.*

Wensleydale *Cow's milk, blue-veined (some unpasteurized) from Yorkshire.*

UNITED STATES OF AMERICA

Although more cheese is made in North America than anywhere else in the world, such bounty has not been matched by an equally adventurous spirit. The requirement that all domestic milk be pasteurized restricts the growth of many bactreia beneficial to cheese flavor and development. Nevertheless, there is a new enthusiasm for cheeses produced by small creameries, most of them located in the wine-producing states of California, Oregon, New York,

and Washington. The bulk of American production continues in Wisconsin, New York, Vermont, Oregon, and Illinois.

American *Dyed, cheddar-style processed cheese, famously produced by the Kraft Company of Illinois.*

Brick *Mild, cooked cow's milk with washed rind from Wisconsin.*

Cabot *Medium strength, cheddar-style from Wisconsin.*

Colby *Granular, deep-orange, mild, cheddar-style from Wisconsin.*

Coon *Deep-flavored, brown-rinded, cheddar-style from New York.*

Cornhusker *A cross between cheddar and jack-style. Originated in Nebraska.*

Cottage cheese *Fresh, moist cow's milk cheese, made from skimmed milk.*

Cream cheese *The most famous variety is Philadelphia, actually made in New York.*

Creole *Fresh Louisiana cow's milk. Very rich and creamy.*

Leiderkrantz *A mild variation of Limburger, with a pungent paste and washed rind, made in Ohio.*

Longhorn *Medium-flavored, cheddar-style from Wisconsin.*

Maytag *A tangy, blue-veined cow's milk, invented in Iowa in 1941.*

Monterey Jack *A moist, pressed cow's milk, originating from the Californian town of the same name in the 1840s.*

String cheese *Several string scombined to make white, rubbery cheese for cooking. Introduced by Armenian immigrants.*

Swiss cheese *Emmenthal-type cooked cow's milk, invented by a Swiss immigrant in the 1850s.*

Teleme Jack *A mild version of jack cheese. Used for cooking, and in Tex-Mex dishes.*

Tillamook *Strong, full-flavored cheddar-style rom Oregon.*

Vermont Cheddar *Light, sharp cheddars made by small creameries in the state.*

Trappist *Generally mild, made by monks of this order in Kentucky.*

EGG: A MEAL IN A SHELL

*I*n many religions around the world, the egg is a symbol of creation, encompassing within its perfect oval the miracle of new life. An almost perfect food, its uses for the cook are innumerable.

ABOVE

For many people, brown eggs look more like farm eggs than white ones. In fact they have exactly the same flavor, they are just laid by different hens.

Early humans must have stolen eggs to eat, but once fowl had been domesticated, eggs were seen as far too precious to be eaten casually. They were known to be a very nutritious food by early physicians, such as those of the Hippocratic school on the Greek island of Kos. But a fully grown chicken provides more nourishment for more people than a single egg: there is an old French proverb which says "who steals an egg will steal an ox." From the late Roman period, there are recipes extant for many egg dishes very much like the ones we use today. Cakes, a kind of omelette, egg custards, beaten egg sauces, and hardboiled eggs used as a garnish, all appear in the work of Apicius, who probably wrote his cookbook in the first century AD.

The rules of Lenten fasting were formulated at the Council of Aix in 837 and eggs, being an animal product, were prohibited foods during times of fasting. In most Christian countries, eggs play a prominent role in the Easter festivities which mark the end of Lent. In the eleventh century, the Christian Copts of Egypt are known to have distributed eggs at Easter, and the earliest mention of an Easter egg hunt was in 1490. Hardboiled eggs are also served after the *Seder*, the ritual meal of the Jewish Passover.

Most of the eggs eaten worldwide come from the hen, which is descended from a wild jungle bird first domesticated in India and Indonesia. Domestic fowl and eggs spread from east to west early in history—the British already had them when the Romans invaded. Columbus took them to the New World, although Native Americans already made good use of the wild turkey, duck, and other native birds. Many birds other than hens are now farmed, such as quail and even ostrich, and their eggs are eaten, but in nothing like the number of hen's eggs. Duck and goose eggs are very rich and considered a delicacy in Europe, and both gull's and pheasant's eggs are sold by game merchants. The late Jane Grigson, a British food writer, used to amuse her younger guests by frying quail's eggs in butter and serving them on tiny rounds of toast.

Egg consumption has declined in recent years, particularly in the richer nations, whose national diet has come under scrutiny for being over-rich in cholesterol. While it cannot be denied that the cholesterol content of eggs is relatively high, they are also rich in lecithin which breaks up fat into globules and enables the body to neutralize the cholesterol. Some nutritionists argue that the natural lecithin in eggs protects against the build up of blood cholesterol. The protein in eggs is an exceptionally well-proportioned balance of amino acids, one of the best in nature. They are also a good source of vitamin A, one of the few food sources of vitamin D, and are also rich in B vitamins and digestible minerals. As well as lecithin, eggs also contain considerable quantities of inositol and choline which are also involved in the metabolism of cholesterol. Stale eggs, while they do not taste as good as fresh ones, are almost as nutritious, although they lose vitamin B12 as they age. Half of the folic acid in eggs is lost in cooking, but eggs are seldom eaten raw except by invalids (or people with severe hangovers, for which they are thought to be an excellent cure, particularly with a dash of eye-opening Tabasco sauce).

ABOVE
A nephrite egg, set with diamonds and mounted in gold, by Peter Carl Fabergé in 1901.

EGG COOKING

The flavor of eggs is affected not only by their freshness but what the bird has eaten. Grain is thought to give the best taste, but if hens are fed high-protein-concentrated fish meal, which is cheaper than grain, the eggs will have a fishy taste. Free-range hens, which forage for their food, usually produce eggs with a complicated flavor and natural yellow yolks. Battery hens are given artificial colorings to replicate the vivid color of natural yolks. Some think fertilized eggs are slightly more nutritious, but many—for example, high-caste Indians, or orthodox Jews—will not eat them for religious reasons because they may contain blood.

Egg Language

A person who "has egg on his or her face" because they "put all their eggs in one basket," is someone who looks foolish because they have been silly enough to risk everything on one enterprise. This is something an "egghead" would never do. A person who tries to "teach a grandmother to suck eggs" is probably not a "good egg" but a "bad" one, presumptuous and lacking in respect for the older generation. Perhaps they should be "egged on" to show proper deference.

Chocolate Soufflé

SERVES 4

2 tablespoons/30 g butter
2 tablespoons/30 g all-purpose flour
¾ cup (6 fl oz/175 ml) milk
½ teaspoon 2½ ml vanilla extract
⅓ cup (1½ oz/10 g) dark chocolate, chopped or grated
3 eggs, separated
¼ cup (2 oz/50 g) sugar

Melt the butter in a heavy-bottomed pan. Mix in the flour and continue to cook, stirring continuously, until the butter absorbs the flour. Gradually add the milk, vanilla, and chocolate. Continue to cook, stirring constantly, until the chocolate has melted and the sauce has thickened.

Whisk the egg yolks with the sugar until they are light and frothy. Pour the egg yolk mixture into the chocolate sauce and stir thoroughly but gently. Whisk the egg whites until they are stiff but not dry. Gently fold into the chocolate mixture, starting with just one spoonful and gradually adding the remainder.

Grease a 2 pint/1 litre soufflé dish and sprinkle the base with sugar. Pour the mixture into the prepared dish. Make a deep cut around the mixture, approximately 1 in/2½ cm from the edge. Bake the soufflé until it is well risen and set. Sprinkle with sifted confectioners' sugar and serve at once.

Prolonged cooking of whole eggs tends to make them rather tough. The whites coagulate at a slightly lower temperature than the yolks, which is why eggs to be poached in acidulated water can be dipped in boiling water for a second to slightly set the whites. The white will not fly about in the liquid while the yolks remain soft. When the egg is beaten to mix the yolk and white together, coagulation occurs at an even higher temperature, and higher still when a liquid such as milk, or water and sugar are added. In custard-making, where there is a danger that the mixture will curdle, it is useful to know that coagulation can be delayed a little by raising the temperature slowly. Custards must be cooked with great care, concentration, and constant stirring, so that they will not set solid. Rubbery hard-boiled eggs can be avoided by heating the egg slowly, either by putting it into cold water, bringing it to the boil, and then allowing the egg to remain in the hot water off the heat, or by plunging the egg into boiling water, then letting it sit to cook gently.

The art of making a fine omelette is not the same as common scrambled egg. Gertrude Stein wrote, in her *Autobiography of Alice B. Toklas,* of an incident involving her cook and the painter Matisse. On being informed that Matisse was staying to lunch, the cook responded that she would prepare scrambled eggs instead of an omelette. Even though it took the same number of eggs and the same amount of butter, she knew Matisse would appreciate the difference and note the subtle insult.

Hannah Glasse first published her cookbook in 1747, but it was still being reprinted in the next century. One of her oddest recipes is "To make an Egg as big as Twenty. . . They are used for grand Sallads." Egg yolks are boiled into a ball in a bladder and then the whites boiled in another large bladder surrounding the center "yolk" to form one large egg. She also gives directions for "an Excellent Sack-Posset;" 15 eggs, sugar, and Canary wine are cooked in a chafing dish over the coals, and then milk, boiled and flavored with nutmeg, is held high and poured over the eggs and wine mixture, stirred and served hot. These possets, or caudles, had been very popular for several centuries before Mrs. Glasse compiled her book. They are substantial drinks, which must have been very cheering on a cold, damp day in a house which was not much warmer inside than out.

OILS
& VINEGARS

Sweet oils and sour wine have featured in Western cuisine since ancient times. Pressed from seeds, fruits, and nuts, "sweet"—non-rancid— oils are used for their flavor and for their tenderizing and lubricating properties in sautés, marinades, and a host of dressings and sauces.

Vinegar, originally a by-product of wine-making, is made from diverse bases such as rice and barley, apples, and grapes. The results are equally varied: from rich and musty balsamic vinegar to delicately acid rice vinegars.

OILS–FOR HEALTH & FLAVOR

*O*ils are the vegetable alternative to butter and animal fats. They comprise a wide, and sometimes dauntingly unfamiliar, family of culinary ingredients and cooking mediums.

Research seems to prove that sesame oil is the most ancient of all the oils. Once, there were other oils which distinguished historic cuisines: radish and flax oils among the ancient Egyptians; almond oil for Hittite banquets, rocket seed oil in medieval Europe. Today, reminders of older regional tastes can be seen in the poppy seed oil of northern France, and the roasted perilla oil, made from a pea-flower vine, in the cuisines of China and Japan.

Oils have many uses. Some can be used for sautéing and deep-frying, some can be emulsified in salad dressings and sauces, some can be used as marinades or as basting agents, one or two excel at all of these. All vegetable oils are derived from either plant seeds, such as corn (maize) seed, cottonseed, grapeseed, groundnut, rapeseed, safflower seed, sesame seed, soya bean, and sunflower seed, or from fruit. The latter group includes avocado oil, olive oil, palm oil, and all the nut oils.

ABOVE

The sunflower is the source of one of the world's most versatile oils. When the plant is black and withered, the seeds are ripe for harvest.

OILS FOR HEALTH

While all oils share the same calorific value, approximately 120 k/cal per tablespoon/15 ml, the majority of seed oils are higher in polyunsaturates. These polyunsaturated fatty acids (PUFA) are thought to benefit the maintenance of low cholesterol in the diet, and thus a healthy heart. The

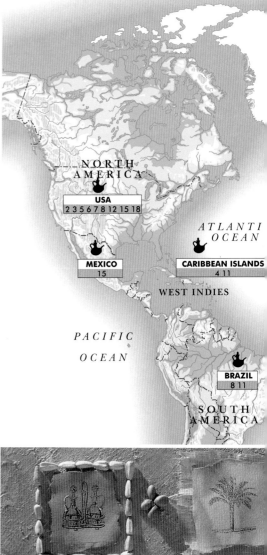

oils highest in PUFAs and lowest in saturated fats are, in order of preference: safflower, sunflower, soya, cottonseed, and corn oils, but only the first two fulfill the double criteria of being widely available in the West and excellent general-use products. Recent research, however, is now pushing the monounsaturated oils—principally olive oil— back into the limelight as the best all-round choice. The healthy properties of the "Mediterranean diet," rich in olive oil, are increasingly appreciated.

OILS FOR FLAVOR

Certainly the oil used will often decide the character of a dish. The rich, robust flavors of Asian sesame oil need to be used frugally and with assertive ingredients. The pale color and light taste of sunflower oil makes it the perfect vehicle for other flavors, whether in a herby mayonnaise or bringing out the freshness of a perfectly sautéed fish. A fine extra virgin olive oil may be so delicious that, with a dash of salt and grind of fresh pepper, it is all that is needed to make a plate of tomato slices memorable.

The Olive: Christian Symbol

The ancient pagan associations of the olive with peace and fertility survived into monotheistic cultures. When Noah's dove returned to the ark bearing an olive branch, it symbolized Yahweh's restoration of peace and tranquillity after the Flood. At the Baptism of Christ, the Holy Spirit appeared in the form of a dove bearing an olive branch. Depictions of the Annunciation of the Virgin usually show the Angel Gabriel holding either a lily or an olive sprig, reinforcing Christ's title "Prince of Peace."

OIL PRODUCTION
This map shows the wide variety of oils produced all over the world.

Major oils and major producers

BRAZIL
8 *(groundnut oil)*
11 *(palm oil)*
BRITISH ISLES
3 *(canola & colza oils)*
CARIBBEAN ISLANDS
4 *(coconut oil)*
11 *(palm oil)*
CHINA
8 *(groundnut oil)*
15 *(safflower oil)*
16 *(sesame oil)*
17 *(soya oil)*
EGYPT
6 *(cottonseed oil)*
15 *(safflower oil)*
ETHIOPIA
6 *(cottonseed oil)*
FRANCE
3 *(canola & colza oils)*
7 *(grapeseed oil)*
9 *(hazelnut oil)*
10 *(mustard oil)*
13 *(poppy seed oil)*
14 *(pumpkin seed oil)*
18 *(sunflower oil)*
19 *(walnut oil)*
INDIA
3 *(canola & colza oils)*
4 *(coconut oil)*
6 *(cottonseed oil)*
8 *(groundnut oil)*
10 *(mustard oil)*
16 *(sesame oil)*
ISRAEL
15 *(safflower oil)*
ITALY
1 *(almond oil)*
JAPAN

17 *(soya oil)*
LEBANON
13 *(poppy seed oil)*
16 *(sesame oil)*
MEXICO
15 *(safflower oil)*
MOROCCO
6 *(cottonseed oil)*
NIGERIA
11 *(palm oil)*
SENEGAL
8 *(groundnut oil)*
SOUTHEAST ASIA
4 *(coconut oil)*
16 *(sesame oil)*
17 *(soya oil)*
SPAIN
3 *(canola & colza oils)*
18 *(sunflower oil)*
SYRIA
16 *(sesame oil)*
U.S.A. (GENERAL)
3 *(canola & colza oils)*
7 *(grapeseed oil)*
15 *(safflower oil)*
U.S.A. (CALIFORNIA)
2 *(avocado oil)*
12 *(pistachio oil)*
U.S.A. (MIDWEST)
5 *(corn oil)*
U.S.A. (SOUTHERN STATES)
6 *(cottonseed oil)*
8 *(groundnut oil)*
U.S.A. (WEST)
18 *(sunflower oil)*
WEST AFRICA
4 *(coconut oil)*
11 *(palm oil)*

THE OTHER OILS

Olive oil has been the traditional Western alternative to solid fats, but there is now a variety of choice available to the modern cook. Some of these oils are general-purpose cooking mediums, but others have limited or specialized uses.

ALMOND OIL
Produced mainly in Italy from either sweet or treated bitter almonds. Used almost exclusively in confectionery.

AVOCADO OIL
Second to olive oil in monosaturated oils (65%), but with a higher saturated fat profile (20%), this is a recently popular cooking oil, produced in California.

CANOLA OR COLZA OIL
Treated but cold-pressed rapeseed oil, a cheap staple of Eastern European and Indian cooking. High in polyunsaturated fats (75%) it is often the basis of inexpensive vegetable oils.

COCONUT OR COPRA OIL
Among the most saturated of vegetable fats, it is widely used as a frying oil in Southeast Asia, the West Indies, and parts of India and Africa.

CORN OIL
A refined oil, extracted from maize germ, which can be heated to 340°F (170°C), and is thus useful for deep-frying. It can be filtered and kept for reuse.

COTTONSEED OIL
Popular for its cheapness, lack of flavor, and all-purpose usefulness. It is approximately 50% polyunsaturated, with the remaining fatty acids equally divided between mono- and saturated.

GRAPESEED OIL
The refined oil is high in polyunsaturates (particularly in linoleic acid, or Vitamin F), and is used in marinating.

GROUNDNUT (PEANUT) OIL
Probably the world's most widespread cooking oil. It can be heated to 425°F (218°C), is invaluable for deep-frying and stir-frying. Its lack of flavor makes it useful in salad dressings and in cold sauces. It is 50% monosaturated and 30% polyunsaturated.

HAZELNUT OIL
Often sold under its French name, *huile de noisette*, this is a gourmet cold-pressed product. Do not heat or keep longer than six months. A product of southwest France, it is used as a dressing for salads.

MUSTARD OIL
This has always been an important cooking oil in India. It lends subtle flavor to curried foods and to Indian pickles such as lime and mango.

PALM OIL
One of the staple oils of African, Caribbean, and Brazilian cooking, expressed from the fruit of *Elais guineensis*. High in saturated (40%) and monosaturated (40%) fats, and used in the production of margarine.

PISTACHIO OIL
Cold-pressed Californian oil is of limited, though richly-flavored use in cold meat and fish salads. Do not heat.

POPPY SEED OIL
The cold-pressed oil is occasionally used in the Levant and eastern France.

PUMPKIN SEED OIL
This gourmet oil is high in polyunsaturates. Produced commercially in France (*huile de potiron*), it is used in salad dressings.

RAPESEED
See Canola/Colza oil

SAFFLOWER OIL
Has the highest level of polyunsaturated fats (75%) of any oil and is also rich in Vitamin E. Expressed from the seeds of the thistle-like *Carthamus tinctorius* (Mexican saffron) grown in the Middle East, China, and North America. It is used in cooking, and in salad dressings and mayonnaise.

SESAME OIL
Used throughout India, the Middle East, South, and Southeast Asia. Colorless sesame oil has virtually no flavor; strong-flavored black sesame oil is particularly popular in India; dark sesame oil (oriental style) is extracted from toasted seeds. It is used in marinades, salad, and vegetable dressings, and cold noodle dishes. Do not heat.

SOYA OIL
This is one of the most common vegetable oils in use worldwide. It can be used for cooking and salads, and is reasonably high in polyunsaturates (55%). It cannot be reused after heating.

SUNFLOWER OIL
Extracted from the seeds of the native North American sunflower (Helianthus annuus), this is now widely grown in the warmer regions of Europe. High in polyunsaturates (65%), and very low in saturated fats (only 5%), it is an admirable all-round oil with an unobtrusive taste.

VEGETABLE OIL
A generic name for commercially-bottled mixtures of oils, usually with a cottonseed or rapeseed base. These oils have almost no flavor and are used primarily for deep-frying.

WALNUT OIL
A cold-pressed product of southwestern France, much valued as a dressing for salads. Do not heat; store in a glass bottle in a dark place; use within six months.

OLIVE OIL

It is assumed that some time between five and six thousand years ago, one of the eastern Mediterranean civilizations found that, given careful pruning and a site which conformed to its requirements (hot summers, but winters chill enough to set the fruit), the scrubby olive bush literally blossomed.

Civilizations with farming skills were needed to encourage and refine the habits of the tree, and were rewarded with wealth and prosperity. The Phoenicians probably brought the tree to Massilia (Provence), where it prospered; the Greeks felled their native forests and built an entire export industry on olive oil in the sixth century BC; the Romans became such connoisseurs of the fruit they could identify the provenance of olives and their oil, blindfolded, at banquets.

The tree benefited the local economy in other ways. From first, and later, pressings came oils for other uses: for perfumes and unguents, for bathing and funeral rituals, for lamp fuel (used from ancient times and into the twentieth century in some parts of Europe and Asia), and lastly, for soaps. The olives themselves were served as snacks and appetizers, and used in cooking. The dried pulp still makes a potent fertilizer, while the wood has always been prized, and sculpted into everything from fertility statues to salad bowls and serving platters.

Today, production of olive oil is particularly associated with four countries: Italy, France, Spain, and Greece. Italy and Spain produce the bulk of refined olive oils and blended virgin oils used for general cooking. At the other end of the spectrum are single-estate extra-virgin Tuscan oils and those from the Baux region of Provence.

ABOVE
A Cypriot olive vendor and her wares. Black olives like these also yield unctuous oil.

THE MEDITERRANEAN OIL
Originally produced by the classical civilizations of Greece and Rome, olive oil is still a Mediterranean commodity, and— along with Spain and France—Greece and Italy still dominate the olive oil industry today.

Olive oil production

VINEGAR: SOUR TREASURE

The origins of the name, vinegar, are a key both to its venerable history and its European roots. Vin acer *in Latin,* vyn egre *in Norman,* vin aigre *in French, this sour wine has been a widespread cooking ingredient and condiment for many centuries.*

The Greeks kept bowls of vinegar (known as *axybaphon*) on the table; bread was dipped into it and sometimes it was sprinkled liberally over food. The Romans did the same, but also diluted the sour wine with water to serve as a fortifying beverage. As their legions passed through Germany, France, and Britain, so the taste for vinegar followed, and lingered after their departure.

Changes in taste were forced by local availability and historical accident. In Britain and parts of Germany, wine was a luxury; by early medieval times "alegar" (ale, and later, beer vinegar) was the common man's alternative. In Byzantium, the triumph of Islam eventually spelled the demise of vinegar culture, since the Prophet forbade the drinking of wine and other fermented liquors. But in wine-rich France, vinegar-making developed into a craft, particularly in Orléans, an important wine-port on the Loire. The Vinegar Merchants' Corporation was established there in 1394; in time, its rules became the guidelines for the industry.

TYPES AND USES OF VINEGARS

Wine vinegars These can be made from white, red, or (less frequently) rosé wine, usually French, Italian, Spanish, or American. The best is aged for a lengthy period in oak casks. White is the most versatile wine vinegar, and can be used for sauces (Béarnaise, Hollandaise), and with fish, poultry, and white meats. Red vinegar is preferred for certain red meat sauces and dressings for green salads. Spanish sherry vinegar (*vinaigre de Xerxes*), from Jerez, has a characteristic tang; it is best used in cooked dishes and in warm salads. Balsamic vinegar, a variation of true wine vinegar, is used in cooking or salads.

How Wine Vinegar is Made

The very basis of a good vinegar is a good wine; if the wine is unpalatable, then the resultant vinegar will carry this legacy. The traditional process, pioneered in Orléans, introduces wine into oak casks, which contain a proportion of old vinegar and the vinegar yeasts from a previous fermentation (the *souche*). In time, and under the right conditions (in the dark, in a climate between 68–86°F/20–30°C, and allowing contact with air), the action of a fungus, *Mycoderma aceti*, will begin to form a light gray veil. With the passage of days it grows into a thick, sticky skin which converts the alcohol in the wine into acetic acid. When the process is complete, the vinegar can be drawn off, filtered, and aged longer in other casks, if desired. In practice, professional producers keep the casks constantly on the go, removing some vinegar and adding new wine. The operation is dependent on a large rota of casks at different stages of fermentation, and demands expert judgment as to the finesse and readiness of the product, and the recording skills of a statistician.

Cider vinegar Pale gold in color, this is perhaps the most adaptable vinegar and can be substituted in many situations in which wine vinegar is called for (although not for classic sauces like Béarnaise). It is also appreciated in its own right for its delicate, applelike flavor. It is particularly well-paired with fish and poultry. If necessary, cider vinegar makes an acceptable stand-in for rice vinegar in oriental dishes.

Malt vinegar The descendant of alegar, malt vinegar is made from a quasibeer, fermented for the purpose. Its bacterial acedation is assisted by the addition of beech shavings, and its color improved by the addition of caramel coloring. The formation of the vinegar, and the subsequent ageing, takes a matter of weeks or months,

LEFT
Vinegar has always enjoyed acclaim both as a prophylactic and a curative. This picture is from a German health manual of the Renaissance.

ABOVE
The medieval church at Modena, the home of balsamic vinegar. It is made from fresh grape must (juice), which has not yet fermented into alcohol.

Herb Vinegar

Vinegar flavored with dill makes excellent salad dressing and mayonnaise, and is delicious over warm lentil and rice salads. Basil vinegar is wonderful in dressings for tomato and mozzarella salads, in cold pasta salads, and drizzled over hot pasta, tossed with fresh tomato sauce. Thyme and rosemary vinegars are especially good with meat and fish dishes.

MAKES ABOUT 4¼ CUPS (1¾ PINTS/1 LITRE)

1 large bunch fresh dill, rosemary, basil, or thyme, tender (nonwoody) shoots only
4¼ cups (1¾ pints/1 litre) cider vinegar
An extra large bunch of the chosen herb
3 tablespoons crushed dill seeds, if using frozen dill
2 garlic cloves, halved

Wash and pat dry the dill, rosemary, or other herb. Loosely fill a 4¼ cup (1¾ pint/1 litre) pickling jar with a glass lid. Bruise the stems and leaves with a wooden mallet and loosely pack the jar. Pour the vinegar over them, cover the jar, and let it stand in a dark place for 2 days. Uncover, stir the mixture, then push the herb as far as possible down into the jar, so there is a layer of vinegar above it. Cover again and leave in a cool, dark place for 2 weeks.

Strain the vinegar through a cheesecloth-lined strainer and reserve; discard the herb. Wash, pat dry, and bruise the second bunch of your chosen herb. Pack the same jar loosely with it; add the dill seeds (if using) and garlic. Pour over the strained vinegar; cover and let stand in a cool, dark place for 2 days. Uncover, stir, then push the herb, seeds, and garlic into the jar; stand in a cool, dark place for another 2 weeks.

Strain off the vinegar as before and pour into clean, hot bottles with tight-fitting, nonmetallic tops. The vinegar will keep in a cool, dark place indefinitely.

rather than the years required for good wine vinegar. Malt vinegar is the traditional accompaniment to British fish and chips, and is also used in the preparation of chutneys and pickles, but its overpowering flavor does not recommend it for use in salads or sauces.

Rice vinegar: Made from rice wine, the most commonly available is colorless, though it can also appear in red and black varieties. It is mildly flavored (the Japanese version, *yumabukusu*, is somewhat stronger) and is usually used in soups, sweet-and-sour dishes, and with certain fish and rice recipes.

Distilled and spirit vinegars: These are usually made from malt or grain alcohol, and are distinguished by a complete lack of color and high acidity. Because of their preservative qualities, they are used primarily for pickling vegetables (particularly onions), and for certain recipes in which marinating strength but not flavor is required.

LEFT
Tarragon vinegar, seen here on the right of the photograph, is a classic herb vinegar. It is used in salads and with fish.

ABOVE
Malt vinegar, is a traditional British condiment. It is a popular accompaniment to fish and chips, and is widely used in pickles and chutneys.

SUGAR, HONEY, & OTHER SWEETENERS

Honey is perhaps the oldest sweetner. It was traditionally regarded with an almost mystical reverence, and it is still ascribed with restorative and palliative powers. Crystalline cane or beet sugar cannot compete with that reputation, but

its convenience has allowed it to supplant honey as the everyday sweetener. In the past 60 years, sugar substitutes have been developed which deliver sweetness without its accompanying calories.

SWEETS FROM FABLED LANDS

*S*weetheart, honey, honeypie, honey bun, sugar, sugarplum—these perennial endearments are born of an ancient affection for sweetness. Despite the dangers of addiction, no society in history has ever banned sweet flavors or found it possible to exist without them.

THE PERENNIAL SWEET TOOTH

From earliest times, humans have sought out sweet things to eat, braving the stings of guardian bees to raid their golden horde, a quest immortalized in early cave paintings from Spain and Turkey. The first written allusion to honey-gathering and honey bees was in an Egyptian papyrus of 5000 BC, and there are several references in the somewhat later books of the Old Testament. Although of differing genus and species, honey bees flourished worldwide, so honey was a widely known delight. In about the seventh century BC in the Middle East, wild bees were encouraged to take up residence in especially constructed hives, and beekeeping became a major rural pursuit.

RIGHT

This painting, Venus with Cupid the Honey Thief *(detail), by Lucas Cranach the Elder (1472–1553) celebrates the golden nectar as the food of love.*

Potent Leftovers— From Sugar to Rum

Rum was simply the unwanted byproduct of sugar-making which, when left undisturbed, began to bubble. When Spanish colonists found "sugar wine" palatable, it soon became profitable. The Dutch and English planters took up the manufacture, and by 1657 it was being made in New England from imported Barbadian molasses.

By 1688, rum was standard issue in the British Royal Navy and Army (it was thought to be an antidote to scurvy), and a "tot" was also distributed to merchant seamen. It was shipped by Caribbean distilleries to Britain, both as a payment for goods delivered to the islands, and as prepayment for slaves from the African coast to work the plantations.

At about the same time, the peoples of ancient Bengal had hit upon the idea of crushing the canes that grew in the Ganges plains to extract the sweet syrup they contained. These canes, cultivated by both the Chinese and Indians for at least the previous 500 years, were chewed as an aphrodisiac and sweetmeat. Once a crude refining technique had been established, the new white, granular "spice" was named "Indian salt" until the Renaissance, when its wider cultivation rendered the name inappropriate.

SUGAR SHIPS

Sugar cane was grown around the southern Mediterranean in the thirteenth century. It was transported to the Middle East, Central Asia, and northern Europe by galleons, in desert regions by camel caravans.

■ Main sugar-producing areas

▬ Major sugar trade routes

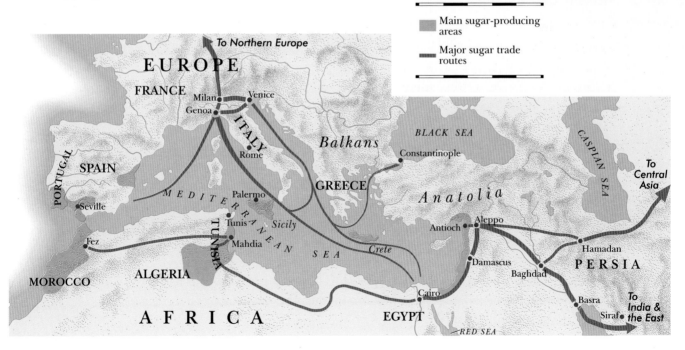

Metheglin

This is Cornish mead, a descendant of the honey drinks associated with the Celts and Druidic festivals It was considered the drink of immortality and of the gods; dead Irish kings were immersed in it and copious amounts drunk in fertility rites.

4 lb/1.75 kg honey
2½ quarts (4 pints/2.4 litres) water
100 hops
⅔ cup (5 fl oz/150 ml) brandy
A mixture of herbs taken from sweetbriar, thyme,
   rosemary, lavender, heather, or borage

Bring 2½ quarts (4 pints/2.4 litres) water to a boil with the herbs, then cool completely. Strain, reserving the water and discarding the herbs. Add the honey to the water, bring to a boil and continue at a low boil for one hour. Skim well, then add the hops. Boil for 30 minutes longer, then let stand for 24 hours. Strain the liquid into bottles or a cask, adding some of the brandy to each bottle. Stopper the bottles or cask tightly; keep at least one year before drinking.

Other natural products were used as sweeteners during historical times, and many remain in use today. They include cooked dates and figs, whose rich fruit sugars lift both savory dishes and desserts in North Africa and the Middle East, palm sugar, and cloyingly sweet maple syrup and sugar. In regions and social groups restricted by economic forces, byproducts of sugar-making have been used as cheaper alternatives to refined crystals, while modern, commercially available alternatives and artificial substitutes have taken their place on supermarket shelves and in the food industry.

None of these has managed to usurp sugar from the prime position it assumed during the period of colonial exploitation. Sugar, like salt before it, became a "white gold"—as necessary to pleasure, if not to survival. But its social and economic legacy was far more ambiguous; the disturbing reverberations are with us still.

ABOVE
The remains of sugar mills, such as this one on Nevis, dot many islands of the West Indies, mute witness to a brutal regime of repression and death. But the plantation houses were oases of culture and comfort.

THE AMBROSIAL COMB: HONEY

U*ntil the end of the Middle Ages, honey was the undisputed queen of sweet additives. It was also one of the earliest condiments, added at table even to savory dishes.*

Originally gathered from the wild, then farmed, no cooked fruit could match honey's fulfilling sweetness. It did not take those living close to the land long to realize that the flowers on which the bees fed determined the character of the honey. In classical times, both the "Hymettus" honey of Greece, with its perfume of thyme, sage, and marjoram, and that of Narbonne, in France, with its accents of rosemary, were shipped across the Mediterranean to grace the tables of gourmets in Rome.

ABOVE

Woven, plaited hives such as this were among the earliest housing for farmed bees. Reputed to be the invention of Caucasian tribesmen, it spread to the Celts and others. Cork and wood were also used.

RIGHT

The companions of this early French housewife and bee-keeper include a bear, arch-detector of hives, and some oversized bees. But honey was really harvested when the bees were away from the hive.

FOOD OF GODS AND MEN

Honey has always had an aura of exclusivity and epicurean excess. According to legend, it was the food on which Zeus was weaned and was a gift of Bacchus, together with wine. In other cultures, notably those of ancient India and the Mayan civilization of Mexico, it also ranked as a divine nourishment. The Celts, Scandinavians, Germans, and Slavs brought it down to a more mundane level by using it to make mead, which they drank to the point of inebriation in pagan festivals and celebrations held in special "mead halls."

199

HONEYS FOR EVERY TASTE

The best honeys usually specify the flower from which the nectar was obtained, for this is what gives honey distinctive flavors. The map shows which honeys are produced where. The numbers on the map are identified in the key below, and there are honey descriptions beneath that.

EUROPE-WIDE 3 (clover), **11** (rape or colza), **13** (woodland flower); **BRITISH ISLES 2** (borage), **5** (heather), **6** (herb flower – mint), **9** (meadow and wildflower), **12** (raspberry); **FRANCE 1** (acacia), **4** (French lavender), **5** (heather), **6** (herb flower –rosemary & thyme), **8** (lime blossom), **9** (meadow & wildflower); **GERMANY 8** (lime blossom); **GREECE 7** (hymettus); **Hungary 1** (acacia), **ITALY 6** (herb flower – sweet basil); **ROMANIA 6** (herb flower – mint); **Spain 6** (herb flower – rosemary & thyme), **10** (orange blossom)

1 Acacia Light yellow, clear, thin, and very sweet. **2 Borage** A very light and clear honey with a subtle flavor; generally expensive. **3 Clover** One of the most popular honeys in both Europe, Canada and the USA. It is thick and can be pale or light amber. **4 French lavender** Honey from the lavender on the slopes of Mount Ventoux in Provence is among the world's most coveted and expensive. **5 Heather** A strong-tasting, dark, slightly bitter honey which can come from ling or bell heathers or a mixture of the two. **6 Hymettus** This highly perfumed honey has the taste of mountain herbs, particularly thyme. **7 Herb flower** Honeys made from mixed herbs, or single herb types, such as the rosemary and thyme honeys of Spain and Provence, the sweet basil honey of Italy, or mint of Romania and England. **8 Lime blossom** A popular honey in Europe, derived from the nectar of linden tree blossoms. It has a distinctive, full flavor. **9 Meadow and wildflower** These comprise nectars such as clover, trefoil, bramble, and gorse. They are generally light, clear honeys with a delicate flavor. **10 Orange blossom** From Mexico, Spain, and South Africa, this is a smooth, pale honey. **11 Rape or colza** Pale, smooth honey, very sweet. Inexpensive and often used in cooking. **12 Raspberry** A light, opaque honey with exquisite overtones. **13 Woodland flower** These honeys can be mixed – including horse chestnut, sycamore and hawthorn – or single-species.

Among the Egyptians, Chinese, and Indians, honey's power was called upon in rituals of rebirth and purification. It was also used to fight the horrors of decay, as when the Cretans and Babylonians embalmed their dead in it—an extravagant extension of honey's acknowledged success as a preservative for meat and fruit, one of its earliest uses.

But honey also became essential to everyday life. It was a major cooking ingredient among ancient peoples; the Egyptians, Greeks, and Romans relied on it to baste and stuff meat, fowl, and grape leaves. The Romans used it in one of their most fabled dishes, potted dormouse (a subspecies of the edible dormouse, *Glis glis*, subsequently became extinct through the popularity of the recipe).

SCANDINAVIA

RUSSIAN
FEDERATION

3 11 13

GERMANY
3 8 11 13

3 11 13

UKRAINE

11 13

HUNGARY
1 3 11 13

ROMANIA
3 6 11 13

BLACK SEA

BALKANS

3 11 13

ITALY
3 6 11 13

TURKEY

GREECE
3 7 11 13

Greek Siphnopita

This Greek Easter speciality is found throughout
the islands.

SERVES 6 TO 8

2 scant cups (8 oz/250 g) all purpose flour
Salt to taste
2 sticks (8 oz/250 g) butter, softened
2½ cups (1 lb/450 g) curd cheese
⅓ cup (4 oz/115 g) honey
4 large eggs
2¼ teaspoons ground cinnamon

In a bowl, combine the flour and
salt. Work in the butter with
your fingers, adding about 3
tablespoons water to make the
dough malleable. Form into a soft
ball and chill for 30 minutes.
   Preheat the oven to
350°F/180°C/Gas mark 4. Line a 10-inch/25 cm
springform pan with the dough, using your hand
to smooth it into the pan and up the sides. Bake
blind for 10 minutes, or until golden. Leave to
cool on a wire rack.
   Turn the heat up to 375°F/190°C/Gas mark 5.
In a large bowl, beat the cheese with the honey.
Stir in the eggs, one by one, beating well after
each addition, then stir in 2 teaspoons cinnamon.
Pour the filling into the cooled crust and bake for
30 to 35 minutes, until the filling is just firm and
the top golden. Sprinkle the pie with the
remaining cinnamon. Serve at room
temperature or slightly chilled.

They were also responsible for a still-vibrant, European tradition of baked
honey-and-spice cakes. By medieval times, Europeans and the peoples of the
Middle East used honey in every course from soup to fruit and nuts, glazed
with honey to become sweetmeats. If it was not actually incorporated into the
cooking process, it would often be added liberally to food at the table.

FAREWELL MY HONEY

The ascent of sugar spelled the demise of honey as a cooking essential,
although it still retains its elevated position as a condiment, particularly at
breakfast and teatime ("honey still for tea?"). The equally sweet, but virtually
tasteless, sugar was far more adaptable in combination with other assertive
flavors, such as the coffee and tea which were to become so popular, and its
crystalized state made it more versatile.

REFINED SWEETNESS

There are several theories for the origins of sugar cane (Saccharum officinarum). Certainly, there is nowhere in the world where the giant grass is found in its wild form.

ABOVE

In the streets of Ho Chi Minh City, an elderly couple strip sugar cane to sell, either to be used in cooking or chewed au naturel *as a sweet. Cane for sugar is put through a crusher before boiling.*

Sugar cane cultivation, which began in India, passed eastward to China and westward to Persia. From here, knowledge of how to crystalize its secret nectar—"the reed that gives honey without bees"—passed on to Egyptian and Phoenician traders, and then to the Greeks and Romans. Up to and including the time of the Crusades, it was an Arab-traded and Arab-cultivated spice, which could not compete with homegrown honey in terms of price and accessibility. It was sold only by apothecaries, mainly as a medicinal aid "bestowing heat and energy." But the Crusaders managed to pack some shoots in their saddlebags, and the Knights Templer and Hospitaler took over cane cultivation in Cyprus. By the fifteenth century, the Venetians, who dominated both Mediterranean trade and the island of Cyprus, had added sugar to their exports, and Egypt had become another supplier. By the sixteenth century, sugar was among the most fashionable "spices," taking the place of honey in everything from meat pies and rice dishes to comfits and sweetmeats. The Renaissance sugar barons soon amassed huge fortunes as their galleons plied the sea routes to British and Hanseatic ports, evading extortionate overland duties and tolls.

A NEW WORLD FOR SUGAR

The dependence on sea power and competition for lucrative sea routes led to the discovery and exploitation of new sources, and eventual markets, for many products, none more so than sugar. The first experiments in growing sugar in far-flung territories began in Portugal's Cape Verde Islands, off the west coast of Africa. But it was when the entrepreneurial Portuguese and Spanish turned their eyes westward that a new industry was born. The notorious growing conditions for cane—moist rich terrain, abundant rain but no frost, a drying heat wafted through the fields by gentle winds—were met by the volcanic soil, fairly constant ambient temperatures, predictable rains, and trade winds of

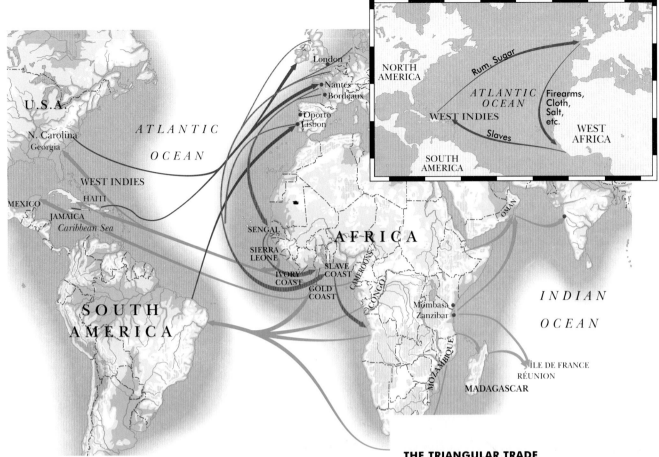

Cuba, Hispaniola, and Brazil. The Dutch began planting in the East and West Indies, the British in Barbados, and the French in Martinique. Refineries proliferated in the islands themselves and across the Atlantic at the receiving ports. Meanwhile, the demand for sweetening agents grew, particularly for white sugar. The fashion for coffee, chocolate, and tea in the eighteenth century meant that consumption of cane sugar trebled.

CANE IS BEET
The discovery that sugar of comparable quality could be extracted from a relative of the turnip, which subsequently became known as the sugar beet (*Beta vulgaris*), struck a heavy blow to the throne of "King Cane." In 1868, Claus Spreckels of San Francisco patented a process which refined cane sugar in eight hours rather than three weeks. A cheaper source and cheaper technology forced sugar prices down—boon to consumers.

Today, more than half the world's sugar is processed from sugar beet, but much of it is used in commercial production and industry. The general public still prefers to buy "pure cane sugar" over the counter—whether from Hawaii, Mauritius, or the East Indies.

THE TRIANGULAR TRADE
European exports were bartered for African slaves, who were transported to the Americas and, in turn, exchanged for sugar and tobacco.

———— Export of European goods

———— Slave route

———— Export of tobacco and sugar

The Origins of Evil

In 1506, when the Spaniards arrived with their first plants on the islands of Hispaniola and Cuba, they needed a workforce to tend the sugar crop. They turned to Portuguese slave traders, already importing African slave labor into Brazil, and the Dutch, British, and French followed suit. Iniquitous slave traffic became an important international commerce until final abolition in Spain's colonies in 1879. The Caribbean never recovered from the decline of the sugar industry.

DESSERTS OF EUROPE

Europe presents a selection of delicious regional dessert specialities. As well as national dishes, certain European towns have also become associated with specific desserts. The dishes are described in the numbered keybox (below).

🍮 Dessert dishes

🏺 Towns associated with particular desserts

Austria 🍮 *Apfelstrudel:* Apple and raisin roll in flaky pastry. 🍮 *Linzertorte (Linz):* Raspberry tart with lattice pastry top. 🍮 *Sacher Torte (Vienna):* Low, round, glazed chocolate cake with raspberry filling under chocolate glaze. **Belgium** 🍮 *Waffle:* A light batter cake cooked on a special griddle, giving an incised puffed design. **Denmark** 🍮 *Rodgrod:* "Red" pudding made of raspberries, redcurrants etc., thickened with cornstarch. **Egypt** 🍮 *Umali:* Corn pudding in syrup. **England** 🍮 *Eccles cake (Eccles):* Small currant pastries. 🍮 *Plum pudding:* Dome-shaped steamed suet pudding containing dried and candied fruit. 🍮 *Steamed toffee (brown sugar, butter and milk) and ginger pudding.* 🍮 *Summer pudding:* Sliced, white bread lining a pudding basin with a filling of strawberries, raspberries, blackcurrants etc. and fruit coulis. 🍮 *Syllabub:* Lemon-flavoured whipped pudding, served in a glass. **Finland** 🍮 *Queens cake:* A speciality made with cream and fresh fruit.

France 🍮 *Charlotte Russe:* Dessert consisting of a custard fruit filling surrounded by lady fingers. 🍮 *Clafoutis (Auvergne & Perigord):* Baked batter poured over fruit. 🍮 *Crème Brulée:* Caramelized sugar crust over vanilla baked custard. 🍮 *Crêpes (Brittany):* Pancakes with sweet fruit fillings or lemon and sugar. 🍮 *Ile flottante/oeufs à la neige:* Two meringue in custard desserts. 🍮 *Nougat (Montelimar):* made with egg whites, suga, honey and nuts.

🍮 *Paris Brest (Paris):* Split, ring-shaped pastry, stuffed with cream and topped with almonds. **Germany** 🍮 *Pfeffernusse (Bavaria):* Dark, sugar-dusted honey biscuits flavored with anise and other spices. **Greece** 🍮 *Baklava:* Walnut flaky pastries in honey syrup. 🍮 *Galaktoboureko:* Vanilla custard wrapped in filo pastry. **Holland** 🍮 *Waffle.* 🍮 *Spekkak:* Indonesian/Dutch layered spice cake. **Hungary** 🍮 *Dobostorte:* A rich, many-layered mocha cake. 🍮 *Palatschinken:* Sweet pancakes with jam, chocolate or nut filling. **Italy** 🍮 *Cannoli (Sicily):* Pastry horns stuffed with sweetened ricotta. 🍮 *Crostada di ricotta (Rome):* Cheesecake. 🍮 *Panforte (Sienna):* Large, flat, round, compacted fruit and nut cake. 🍮 *Veronese cake (Verona).* 🍮 *Zabaglione:* Whipped egg yolks and Marsala. **Morocco** 🍮 *Gazelle horns:* Crescent-shaped

pastries. 🍮 *Sellou:* Ramadan-breaking honey and flour dessert. **Poland** 🍮 *Piernik:* Spice and honey cake, dusted with icing sugar. **Russia** 🍮 *Blintzes:* Russian Jewish cheese-filled pastries, fried in batter. 🍮 *Kulich:* Sweet yeast bread with preserved fruit and nuts inside. 🍮 *Pashka:* Tall, cylindrical Easter cake with glaze dripping down sides. **Scotland** 🍮 *Dundee cake (Dundee):* Dark, heavy Scottish fruitcake. 🍮 *Shortbread:* A rich butter cookie. **Spain** 🍮 *Turron:* Almond nougat from Spain. **Switzerland** 🍮 *Sazlburger nockerl:* Baked sugar and egg meringue soufflé. **Turkey** 🍮 *Baklava.*

CANADA

UNITED STATES
OF
AMERICA

ROCKY MOUNTAINS

GREAT PLAINS

California

Texas

MEXICO

GULF OF MEXICO

Lake Superior

Lake Michigan

Lake Huron

Lake Erie

Ohio

Mississippi

Pennsylvania

APPALACHIANS

Southern States

Florida

New England

BOSTON

NEW YORK

BALTIMORE

CHARLESTON

KEY WEST

LOS ANGELES

ATLANTIC
OCEAN

SOUTH
AMERICA

DESSERTS OF U.S.A.

A cornucopia of regional dessert specialities for the sweet-toothed. Many of these favorite desserts have now become popular world-wide.

④ Dessert dishes

⑲ Towns associated with particular desserts

MEXICO ① *Bunuelo* ② *Crème caramel flan* ③ *Sopaipillas* **U.S.A.** ④ *Cobbler* **BALTIMORE** ⑤ *Strawberry shortcake* **BOSTON** ⑥ *Boston cream pie* ⑦ *Hot fudge sundae* **CALIFORNIA** ⑧ *Banana split* **CHARLESTON** ⑨ *Lady Baltimore cake* **KEY WEST** ⑩ *Key lime pie* **LOS ANGELES** ⑪ *Hot fudge sundae* **MIDWEST** ⑫ *Brownie* **NEW ENGLAND** ⑬ *Apple pie* ⑭ *Indian pudding* **NEW YORK CITY** ⑮ *Baked Alaska* ⑯ *Cheesecake* **NORTH CAROLINA** ⑰ *Chess pie* **PENNSYLVANIA** ⑱ *Angel food cake* **SOUTH** ⑲ *Ambrosia* **TEXAS** ③ *Sopaipillas* **VIRGINIA** ⑰ *Chess pie*

OTHER SWEETENERS

There are still regions and situations where sugar did not become all-conquering. Whether for reasons of climate, import costs, or diet there are cuisines that savor alternative sweeteners.

Recipes from the New England of the Pilgrims, and even later, make much reference to maple syrup. The natives of tropical Africa, India, and parts of southeast Asia boil down the juice of palm shoots to make palm sugar. These are just two examples of alternatives to cane or beet sugars. In addition, contemporary preoccupations with slimness and health, as well as commercial imperatives for easily assimilated sweeteners, have stimulated the production of new alternatives to sugar.

MAPLE SYRUP AND SUGAR

Once a much valued seasonal alternative to honey for the Native Americans living around the Great Lakes, Lake Champlain, and the St. Lawrence Valley, maple syrup has become an expensive and increasingly rare condiment for those who demand nothing but the best on their pancakes.

The technique of boiling down the "sweet water" tapped from a 40-year-old sugar maple tree (*Acer saccharum*)—also known as the "hard" or "rock" maple —was introduced to the British colonists by their generous neighbors. It became a substitute for expensive, and later highly taxed, imported Barbadian sugar, and a competitor to molasses. During, and after, the American Revolution, both maple syrup and its crystalized sugar became patriotic sweeteners, used in everything from baked beans, cured ham, glazed vegetables, bread, pastries, and candy to beer and wine; plans were even devised for using it to make the early republic self-sufficient in sugar. Later, it became a weapon in the fight against slavery in the West Indian colonies. Canning enabled the syrup to reach a wider market, and effectively spelled the decline of maple sugar, whose current use is almost wholly restricted to decorative candies.

Today, the major syrup-producers are Canada, and the states of New York and Vermont—the latter is considered the source of prime syrup. The sugaring season is toward the end of winter, when nights are still cold but the burgeoning spring causes the sap to run under the bark. Sugaring time in Vermont was traditionally a time for community gatherings and, once upon a time, sleigh rides to the sugar house, where the newly-boiled syrup was served up like a new wine.

A spile (like a spigot) is inserted to drain the almost tasteless juice into a bucket. This is then boiled down over a fire to produce the thick, incredibly sweet syrup, graded from A (light and fine-flavored) to C (dark and better for cooking). Its expense is explained by the time needed for the tree to mature, by the labor-intensive character of the work, and by the fact that 34l of sap (just under the output of an average tree) are required to make a mere 4l of syrup. Though there are numerous cheaper imitation "pancake syrups," there is nothing to match the real thing.

MOLASSES

When the sugar cane is crushed and the juice extracted, it is concentrated by rapid boiling. The resulting syrup is subjected to centrifugal action, separating the solid crystals of raw sugar from their liquid residue (the molasses), a process that may be repeated several times. Generally speaking, the darker the molasses, the less sweet it is. Like maple syrup, there are different grades, depending on how early in the centrifugal separation the

Cheat Sweets

Ordinary white sugars can be replaced by naturally extracted sugars or commercially produced sweeteners:

Aspartame An artificial sweetener (trade name Nutra-Sweet) created in 1965 to sweeten without adding calories. It is 200 times more cloying than sugar.

Dextrose Also called grape or corn sugar, a clue to its sources. A commercially constructed sugar used to thicken and sweeten pastries, candies, and soft drinks.

Glucose Every living thing contains this organic compound. However, the glucose syrup used for jam-making, confectionery, and canning is an industrial creation made by the hydrolysis of potato starch.

Invert sugars One additive is a blend of dextrose and fructose used as a sweetener in confectionery, soft drinks, and prepared foods. The other variety, a compound of glucose and fructose (called "total invert sugar"), is used in pastries to prolong shelf-life.

Saccharin 350 times sweeter than sugar, this (almost) no-calorie substitute accounts for about 70 percent of artificial sweeteners used in the U.S.A.

Sorbitol An artificial sweetener which also thickens; used in diet soft drinks and confectionery.

Broiled Indian Maple Salmon

This is an adaptation of the planked salmon prepared by the Algonquin and other east coast Native American tribes when Atlantic salmon were plentiful. By the turn of the twentieth century, however, the Atlantic salmon had been virtually fished out of existence.

SERVES 6

6 salmon fillets, each 6 oz/175 g
8 tablespoons maple syrup
3 tablespoons peeled and grated gingerroot
2 garlic cloves, minced
1½ teaspoons crushed dried chilies
Salt and freshly ground pepper to taste

Place the salmon, skin-side down, on an aluminum-lined grill rack. Preheat the broiler. (Alternatively, place on a fish rack over ash-gray hot coals.)

In a small heavy saucepan, combine the maple syrup, ginger, garlic, chilies, seasoning, and ¾ cup (6 oz/175 g) water. Bring to a simmer, but *do not boil*, and reduce the sauce by about half. Cool. Place the salmon 4 inches/10 cm under the heated broiler and broil for about 4 minutes. Baste the fish with the sauce and continue broiling for 6 to 7 minutes longer. Serve immediately.

RIGHT
The thick, pale treacle known as "Golden Syrup" has been a staple of British cooking since the turn of the century. The dead lion with bees ensuing from its innards recalls the creation myth of honey-making bees – and thus of sweet delights.

molasses is bottled. If the resulting residue is then bleached, it is referred to as "sulfured molasses;" most purists prefer unsulfured. Unlike refined sugar, which has no nutritional value, molasses contains notable quantities of iron and potassium, as well as some calcium, thiamine, and phosphorus.

Molasses was the most popular sugar substitute in eighteenth- and early nineteenth-century America (much was shipped there from the West Indies to make rum). After sugar became more affordable in the 1880s, it became an affectionately maintained relic of the "olde time" American kitchen, now costing twice the price of refined white sugar.

TREACLE

True treacle, as known from Victorian times, is a pale, refined molasses, which is markedly sweeter and less "burnt" tasting than its parent molasses. Where molasses is used in American recipes, treacle can sometimes be substituted in Britain, but less frequently the reverse.

CORN SYRUP

This thick, glucose syrup is derived from heating cornstarch and water under pressure, using hydrochloric or sulfuric acid as a catalyst. Its most common use is as a thickener and sweetener for candy and snacks, as an extender mixed with more expensive honey or maple syrup, and as the base filling for that most typical of southern desserts, pecan pie.

TEA, COFFEE, & CHOCOLATE

Originally from the East, tea is enjoyed around the world. In China it is drunk with meals; in Japan it merits its own highly stylized ceremony; in Britain and Ireland it starts the day and provides an afternoon break. Breakfast

is unthinkable in many Western countries without coffee and office life centers on the coffee machine. Chocolate was a gift from the New World. It was considered a savory spice until the addition of sugar showed its possibilities as a beverage and sweetmeat.

$\mathcal{T}$EA: THE GLOBAL DRINK

*M*ore tea is consumed around the world than any other beverage except plain water. Tea originally came from China, the most populous nation on earth, where it is still the national drink.

A century before the birth of Christ, tea was described in Chinese texts as an elixir that prolonged life. Tea is still being promoted as a healthy drink. Recent research has suggested that, because it contains antioxidants called polyphenols, drinking five cups of tea a day provides the same quantity of these beneficial substances as two servings of vegetables. Green tea contains more antioxidants than black, but both are said to help prevent free-radical damage, and are claimed to be an effective prophylactic against heart disease, stroke, cancer, and many viruses. The only caveat is that it should not be drunk with meals as the tannin tea contains can interfere with the body's absorption of iron.

Perhaps this infusion of leaves in hot water became, over the centuries, a universal habit in many countries because of a continuing belief in its life-enhancing properties. Wherever the offer of a cup of tea is the first duty of a host or shopkeeper anxious to make a sale, it is still prepared according to precise local custom. The kind of tea and what is put into it, whether it is milk, sugar, or lemon, varies considerably from country to country. Even in England, where the ubiquitous tea bag, haphazardly dunked into a mug has almost completely taken over from the elegant rituals of an earlier age, brand loyalty is awesomely fierce. Many English people, traveling away from home, feel quite deprived if their favorite tea bags are not available.

THE TEA TRADE

The first nation to import tea from China was its near neighbor across the Sea of Japan. It was first used medicinally, later it was almost exclusively used in Buddhist monasteries, where tea was prepared and drunk as an aid to meditation. Eventually, tea drinking became an everyday activity for the Japanese, taken for granted and consumed with relish but without reverence.

LEFT

A tea party in Russia, painted in 1851. There is no samovar on the table, indicating that this is an "English-style" party.

Russia has a long border with China and tea is known to have arrived in Russia by caravan in 1618. Tea became extremely popular among all classes, and the samovar may prove to be a more enduring emblem of that vast land than either the imperial double-headed eagle or the hammer and sickle. In Russia, as in the Middle East, tea is drunk out of small glasses. In North Africa, green tea is brewed with fresh mint and sugar and is drunk from glasses throughout the day. In the East, Europe, and the Americas, tea-drinkers prefer porcelain cups or mugs.

The Chinese still use loose tea and brew it both in the cup and in teapots. The Chinese have a fine appreciation of the subtle differences between different varieties of tea and have a great many to choose from. Some are used for special purposes, such as the strong tea from Fukien province which is drunk in very tiny cups before dinner. Lighter teas, such as those with jasmine, rose, or other flowers, are served after dinner to aid digestion. In general, the Chinese prefer their tea much weaker than the robust cup most people in the West prefer.

The major world tea-producers are China, India, Sri Lanka, Kenya, Indonesia, Japan, Georgia, and Azerbaijan. Almost a third comes from India, where tea plantations were started up by the British in the 1830s. Tea bushes are kept clipped for easier harvesting, which is still done by hand, but this pruning also stimulates the growth of "flushes" of tender young shoots and the new leaves which command a higher price. The flavor of tea grown slowly in the cooler air of altitudes between 3,000 to 7,000 feet is regarded as the finest. In addition to local growing conditions which affect flavor, and processing after the tea is picked, quality is also graded by the size of the leaves.

The three basic categories of tea are black, which is fermented; those called "oolong," which are semifermented; and unfermented tea, which is referred to

RIGHT

The Mad Hatter's tea party in Alice in Wonderland *shows a typical English setting for tea on a sunny summer afternoon with an iced cake and scones.*

The Boston Tea Party

On the night of December 16, 1773, a group of patriots crudely disguised as Native Americans climbed aboard three ships anchored in Boston Harbor. In a protest against the tax on tea, imposed by the English parliament to salvage the ailing fortunes of the British East India Company, the "Indians" seized 342 chests of tea worth £9,000 and dumped them overboard. The British government closed Boston Harbor to commerce until compensation for the ruined tea was paid by the city. Further restrictive laws curtailed the Americans' rights of self-government. Their response was to hold the First Continental Congress, the first serious move toward independence.

RIGHT

*Tea is still picked by
hand, usually by
women, as is shown
here on a tea
plantation in India.*

Afternoon Tea

On September 25, 1660, Samuel Pepys noted in his diary that he had drunk his first "Cupp of Tee (a china drink) of which I never had drank before," courtesy of an East India merchant. Tea, imported from China via Holland since 1658, was initially expensive—£2 a pound. Tea imports from Malaya brought the price down to £1 a pound by the end of the century.

London's first tea garden opened in 1732, in Vauxhall, south of the Thames, where the middle classes and the newly rich could stroll about showing off their fine clothes and jewels. But tea did not become the drink of choice for all classes of British society until the tea plantations of India and Ceylon were producing a less expensive product in the nineteenth century.

Not all that long ago, at the top end of the English social scale, making tea involved the host or hostess mixing different varieties of loose tea to their own special recipe. These were scooped with a special silver caddy spoon from beautiful locked tea caddies, and different blends might be made for different times of day. This care is now displayed by ever-diminishing numbers of connoisseurs.

The pot must be warmed first with boiling water, even if tea bags are used. The water for making tea must always be freshly boiled, and many people now use filtered or bottled water instead of water straight from the faucet. The usual quantities of loose tea are one teaspoon for each person and one for the pot. The English like their Indian tea far stronger than any other nation and almost always serve it with milk. They use more tea to start with and let it steep, or brew, longer. Lemon is sometimes taken with China tea, which is never drunk with milk.

as green. Black tea is fermented by bruising, wilting, and drying the leaves, then rolling them, which exposes more surfaces to the air. As their juices oxidize, they turn reddish brown. The tea is then blown with hot air which kills off the active enzymes. The smoky China teas, such as Lapsang souchong are wood-smoked, which gives them their distinctive tarry taste. To make green teas, the freshly picked leaves are dried immediately so the action of their enzymes is stopped and oxidation is prevented.

Other classifications relate to the size of the leaf. The best tea comes from the top two leaves and the bud. Orange pekoe, for example, denotes a fairly large leaf; when it includes the bud as well, it is known as flowery orange pekoe, while leaves called simply pekoe are smaller and less choice. Many leaves are broken during processing. The largest are classified as broken orange pekoe, followed in descending order by broken pekoe, pekoe, fannings (used in tea bags), and finally, dust. Black teas, especially those from India and Sri Lanka, have a deeper color and stronger flavor. Those from Darjeeling have an aromatic flavor, reminiscent of peaches, and are left to steep longer than green teas to enhance the flavor.

Green teas are classified by age and style. In China and Japan, tea leaves are not usually harvested every week but only four times a year. The "first picking," or "first crop," are very delicate and are the most prized; successive pickings are deemed to be of lesser quality. Gunpowder, for example, consists of young or slightly more mature leaves rolled into small pellets, while "young hyson" refers

to leaves which are slightly twisted or rolled. *Yin hao* means silver tip, from tender shoots picked in the spring.

Indian teas are usually known by where they are grown: Assam, and Darjeeling near the Himalayas in northern India; Ceylon (Sri Lanka), or Kenya. Most teas are skillfully blended commercially for consistency of taste, but many specialist tea merchants also offer a selection of teas from single plantations. These have the discreet variations in flavor appreciated by gourmets as no two are ever quite the same, and are more expensive than blended teas. The famous tea department of Fortnum & Mason, in London, for example, lists an Assam Sankar described as "the finest second flush from the Sankar tea estate—a whole leaf grade giving a mellow liquor and malty character."

TEA TIME

This map shows the original areas of tea cultivation, and the spread of tea-drinking. In seventeenth-century Europe tea was an expensive commodity until the British and Dutch introduced tea cultivation to their Asian and African colonies.

Original tea-growing areas

Tea-growing intro-duced by British and Dutch colonists

Spread of tea-drinking

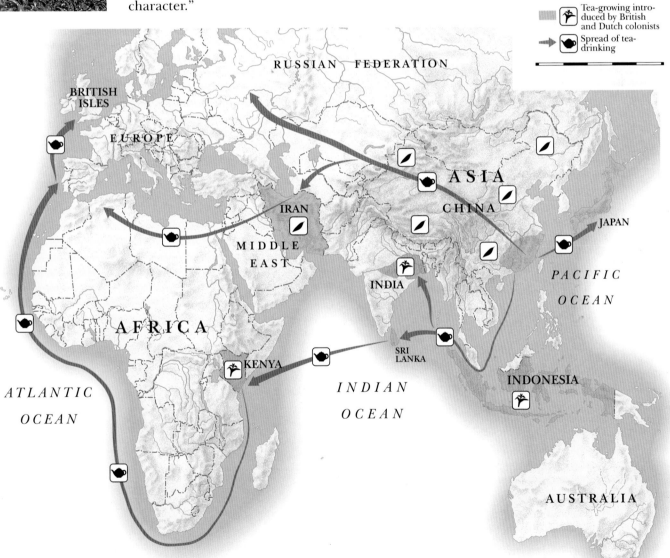

AN A - Z OF TEAS

Indian and other black teas

ASSAM
Strong, gives a rich full cup.

DARJEELING
Called the champagne of tea; light and delicate.

CEYLON
Smooth, but full of flavor, slightly delicate. Often blended with tea from India for popular blends.

KENYA
Rich color and strength, good value, and often used in blends.

Fruit

Earl Grey

Assam

China

EARL GREY
Scented with oil of bergamot, extracted from the peel of a small bitter orangelike citrus fruit. Named after the second Earl Grey, who gave his personal formula to his grocer who was a partner in the Robert Jackson company. Jackson's of Piccadilly, in London, have a legitimate claim to make the original Earl Grey tea but any tea scented with bergamot is called Earl Grey.

GUNPOWDER
Green, the leaf is rolled into tiny balls. It is pale in color, with a sharp, distinctive taste. Used in North Africa to make mint tea. (The Koran forbids fermented drinks.)

JASMINE
Green tea mixed with jasmine flowers; very pale and delicate.

KEEMUN
Black tea from Keemun in the Huangshan mountains south of the Yangtse; scented and delicate in flavor.

LAPSANG SOUCHONG
A large leaf from Fukien province which is smoked to give it a tarry taste so strong it must be stored away from other teas.

OOLONG
Lightly fermented, with a flowery flavor.

ROSE CONGOU
Leaf, mixed with red rose petals; very aromatic.

RUSSIAN CARAVAN
Black tea from Georgia and Azerbaijan with a distinctive, robust flavor.

JAPAN
Japanese tea is always green. *Sencha* is one of the highest quality; the leaves look like dark green needles and the brew is fresh and green.

Herb and fruit teas
A wide variety of "teas" are made from dried herbs or fruit. These are often sold for their health-giving properties and make a refreshing drink either on their own or sweetened with sugar or honey.

Italian China Tea or Coffee Granita

SERVES 6

If you make the granita in advance and freeze it, transfer it to a plastic container. Return to the freezer until required. Stir firmly before serving.

½ cup (3½ oz/100 g) sugar

1 cup (8 fl oz/225 ml) China tea made in the cup with 1 tablespoon loose tea, such as Lapsang Souchong, Rose Pouchong, Earl Grey, or Jasmine, strained, or very strong expresso coffee

Whipped cream for serving (optional)

Combine the sugar and 1 cup (8 fl oz/225 ml) water and bring the mixture to a boil, stirring until the sugar dissolves; set it aside to cool. When it is cool, stir in the tea. Pour the mixture into a metal tray or bowl and put it in the freezer. After 30 minutes, scrape down the sides of the container and stir with a fork, combining the solids with the liquid. Repeat every 30 minutes until the granita is a firm, flaky mush. It is now ready to serve. Top each serving with a spoonful of whipped cream.

COFFEE & CHOCOLATE

ABOVE
19th-century painted metal cask used to transport beans from Columbia and Central American countries.

BELOW
An English coffee-house painted in 1668; the customers are all men.

*T*he coffee bean and the cacao nib are both seeds of fleshy fruits. Coffee probably came from Ethiopia originally and was well known in the Middle East when cacao was discovered by the Spaniards in Latin America in the early sixteenth century.

Coffee's macho image is long associated with politics and intrigue in the Middle East, where men, not women, sat around drinking endless cups of coffee, hatching plots, and having subversive conversations. It was introduced to the French court of Louis XIV in 1669 by the sultan's ambassador, where it acquired a much more sophisticated cachet. It became extremely fashionable, a promotional exercise that paid off as the sultan controlled the agents who imported it through the port of Marseilles.

When the Ottomans were defeated by the king of Poland in Vienna in 1683, the Turkish army left behind a vast quantity of coffee beans. Franz Kolschitsky, who had been a prisoner of war employed in making coffee for his captors, opened a coffeehouse in Vienna, decorated in an opulent oriental style.

Within a few years, Kolschitsky had a chain of them all across central Europe. In England, however, coffeehouses were places where the customers were more likely to be doing business than discussing politics. The marine insurers who met in the late-seventeenth-century coffeehouse of Edward Lloyd formed a company which they

LEFT

The coffee beans in this botanical drawing of around 1800 are shown in various stages of maturity.

Dublin Coffee James Joyce

The Princess de Rohan gave this recipe to Alice B. Toklas for her first cookbook published in 1954. She described it as "excellent for after-dinner conversation." To make a French version use a brandy-based liqueur, such as B&B instead of Irish Whiskey.

SERVES 1

1 teaspoon sugar
Strong black coffee
2 jiggers Irish whiskey in a balloon wine glass
1 jigger heavy cream

Stir the sugar into the coffee, then pour it into the whiskey. Stir, and, as the liquid revolves, slowly pour in the cream, using a circular motion; let the cream float on top of the coffee but do not stir it again.

NORTH AMERICA

ATLANTIC OCEAN

HAWAII

CUBA

PUERTO RICO

JAMAICA

GUATEMALA

NICARAGUA

COSTA RICA

PACIFIC OCEAN

COLOMBIA

SOUTH AMERICA

BRAZIL

Latin America and Africa now produce most of the world's coffee and the U.S.A. is the largest importer. Caffeine is the most widely used stimulant in the world (the kola nut also contains caffeine). Coffee is often referred to by the name of the country it comes from or that country's most important port. Santos, for example, is Brazil's main port. It was founded in 1543 and by the middle of the nineteenth century was a leading coffee port, handling slaves who were imported to work on both sugar and coffee plantations. Other Latin American coffees come from Colombia, Costa Rica, Nicaragua, and Guatemala. Blue Mountain, said to be one of the best in the world, comes from Jamaica. Kona is grown on the islands of Hawaii.

The Kenya Peaberry is a small bean, and the coffee grown near Kilimanjaro is said to be softer in flavor than ordinary Kenya. From the Far East come coffees from New Guinea and Java; when the beans are matured, some are called Old Brown Java or Old Indonesian. India produces Monsoon Malabar and Mysore. The coffee called mocha usually comes from Ethiopia.

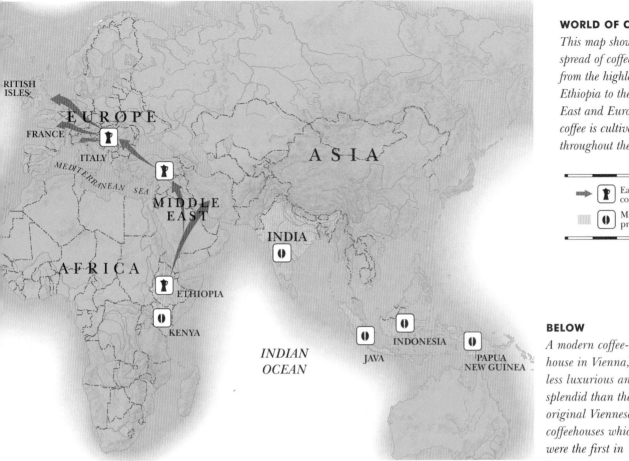

WORLD OF COFFEE

This map shows the early spread of coffee-drinking, from the highlands of Ethiopia to the Middle East and Europe. Today, coffee is cultivated throughout the tropics.

Early spread of coffee drinking

Major coffee-producing areas

BELOW

A modern coffee-house in Vienna, far less luxurious and splendid than the original Viennese coffeehouses which were the first in Europe.

There are two main types, arabica or robusta, and the best are said to be grown on volcanic soil 3,000 to 6,000 feet (914 to 1,828 meters) above sea level. The ripe coffee berries are picked by hand; robusta berries stay on the tree after ripening, but the arabica fall to the ground when ripe and are likely to spoil—frequent inspection makes them more expensive.

The way the beans are then treated affects the flavor. Some are washed and then pulped to remove the flesh of the berries, others are dried before the pulp is removed. The beans are then roasted, and the degree of roasting also influences the flavor. Once the beans are roasted, they begin to lose flavor, and flavor loss is hastened even more if they are ground. Many people prefer to grind their own coffee and try to obtain it as freshly roasted as possible. In the Middle East, people often roast their own coffee but it requires considerable skill. Even though the smell of roasting coffee must be one of the most beguiling in the world, most coffee drinkers leave the roasting to experts.

CHOCOLATE: FOOD OF THE GODS

Chocolate has a much more feminine character than coffee, perhaps because when it was first brought to Spain it was often prepared by nuns and drunk by upper-class Spanish ladies. Its botanical name (*Theobroma cacao*) refers to the Olmec, Maya, and Aztec reverence for it as a food of the gods, and any chocolate addict will confirm that it is indeed a divine food. Like coffee it contains caffeine and another stimulating alkaloid, theobromine. The Spaniards were told in Mexico that the drink made from cacao was an aphrodisiac and this no doubt helped ensure its success in Europe, even though cacao on its own is very bitter. Once sugar and another New World flavoring, vanilla, were added (the Aztecs used many flavorings for cacao, including chili, cinnamon, and other spices), the drink now called chocolate, from the Aztec *chocolatl*, became immensely popular.

The first chocolate house opened in London in 1657 but chocolate, like tea, was highly taxed and not as easy to smuggle, and it was far too expensive for ordinary consumers. It was not until eating chocolate was invented in 1876 in Switzerland, by mixing cocoa powder, cocoa butter, and sugar, that the seductive chocolate flavor became widely available. The Swiss still eat more

LEFT
Jean-Etienne Liotard drew this elegant young woman serving a hot chocolate drink in 1744 when it was the height of fashion.

ABOVE
Pretty tins such as this help sell the product.

BELOW
Packaging from San Francisco's famous Ghirardelli Chocolate Company.

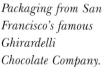

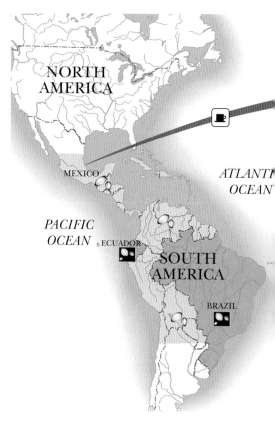

chocolate than anyone else; statistically everyone in Switzerland eats more than 20 pounds/9kg a year.

Cocoa is now grown in wet tropical lowlands in southeast Asia, South America, and West Africa. Three main varieties of cocoa are used in chocolate-making. The first is the criollo, which has the best aroma and taste but produces fewer pods. The forastero is hardier with a greater yield but lacks the superior flavor. Much easier to produce, it accounts for more than 85 percent of the world crop, and is grown in Brazil and the Ivory Coast. The hybrid trinitario is a cross between the two, and breeders are always trying to come up with even better hybrids.

As a general guide, quality chocolate has a high percentage of cacao solids, but more does not exclusively mean better. At the very top end of the market, the process of manufacture is extremely complicated. It begins with the quality of fermentation and how the beans have been dried. The aroma of sun dried beans is best because when gasoline or coal is used as fuel for the artificial drying process it taints the beans. Individual batches of beans grown differently require specific roasting to suit each one.

Additional refinements are flavoring with natural ingredients, and just the right amount of grinding and

The Chocolate-Making Process

The large pods which contain 20 to 30 seeds (or beans) are picked ripe and then left for a day to dry. They are then cut open, and the seeds with the fleshy pulp still around them are removed. The juice is drained off, and the seeds left to ferment, which enables them to be freed from the pulp and also makes them slightly less bitter. The most crucial stage in this process is germination; without it the beans do not taste of chocolate.

They must be left for several days after germination for the flavor to develop. The beans must now be roasted and their thin outer shell removed. The inner kernels (or nibs) are then ground into cocoa paste which can be pressed to remove the fatty cocoa butter. Most chocolate consists of a mixture of cocoa solids with the addition of cocoa butter, sugar, and flavorings, such as vanilla for semisweet chocolate, and milk for milk chocolate.

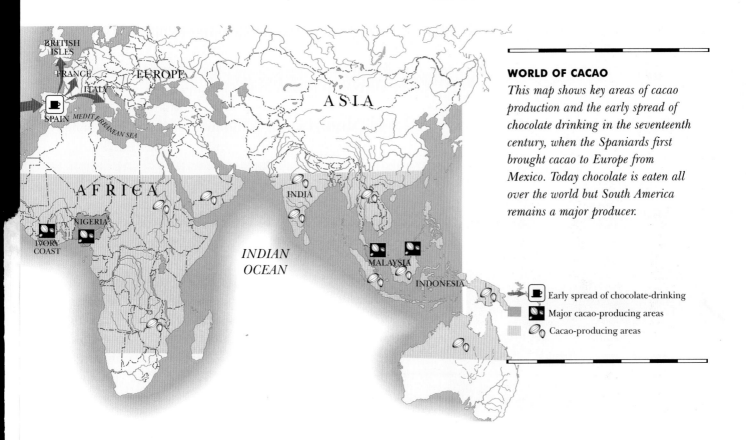

WORLD OF CACAO
This map shows key areas of cacao production and the early spread of chocolate drinking in the seventeenth century, when the Spaniards first brought cacao to Europe from Mexico. Today chocolate is eaten all over the world but South America remains a major producer.

Early spread of chocolate-drinking

Major cacao-producing areas

Cacao-producing areas

RIGHT

Before the Swiss invented a way of making chocolate into bars like these, chocolate was most often used to make a hot drink as the Aztecs did in Mexico before the Spanish conquest.

French Chambery Truffles

SERVES 4 TO 6

4 oz/115 g fine bittersweet chocolate
2 tablespoons (1 oz/25 g) butter, diced
1 tablespoon confectioners' sugar
2 medium egg yolks
2 teaspoons dark rum, brandy, or kirsch
Unsweetened cocoa powder for coating

Slowly melt the chocolate in a bowl over boiling water. Stir in the butter followed by the sugar, stirring until smooth. Take off the heat and stir in the egg yolks, one at a time, until well mixed in. Add the spirit and stir thoroughly. Leave the mixture in a cool place, but not the refrigerator, for 12 hours. Form the mixture into small balls with your hands. Roll each one in cocoa powder. Leave in a cool place until required.

conching, the elusive process, not fully understood, which gives chocolate its final character, balance, and smoothness. (The machine invented by Rudolph Lindt in Switzerland in 1879 was called the conche because it is shaped like a shell. It rolls and rocks the chocolate liqueur, the mixture of cocoa solids and cocoa butter.) The longer this is done the better the final result will be. It can be six to 12 hours or as long as 100. All this finesse is expensive, and chocolates produced in this careful way are called *grand cru*, a term borrowed from the wine trade. The range of flavors created at this level is remarkable; one blend might be 70 percent trinitario beans from South America made into dark chocolate with a strong, long lasting flavor; another might comprise 66 percent trinitario, but grown in the Caribbean, with a flavor described as fruity, woody, with a hint of fresh tobacco; another made with 64 percent criollo beans grown near the Indian Ocean can be flowery with a sweet almond aftertaste. Tasting chocolate of this quality is the ultimate, most intense chocolate experience.

One of the most popular flavors in the world, it is extraordinary to think that it all started with three chests of little brown beans shipped to Spain in the sixteenth century. Today more than two millions tons of cocoa are produced worldwide every year.

INDEX

CREDITS

Key: a above, b below, r right, l left

AA Photo Library 22a, 59a, 113ar
Abbie Enock 198r
Ace Photo Agency 45br, 85, 166a, 173a, 209
AKG London 54b, 68bl, 80a, 88b, 89a, 102bl, 115ar, 162ar, 163b, 185, 209b, 211r, 216a
Axiom Photographic Agency 22b, 25bl, 66bl, 80b, 112ar, 196bl
Christie's Images 15br, 28al, 197a
Douglas Dickens Picture Library 142bl, 210
ET Archive 8al, 9ar, 14al, 14bl, 16ar, 28b, 33ar, 44al, 61bl, 67a, 87, 94a, 97, 100al, 103br, 114al 130a, 149b, 176b, 193a, 199b, 176b, 193a, 199b, 215
French Picture Library 8bl, 138b
Harry Smith 42bl, 91, 106bl, 107ar, 108b, 110ar, 120b, 144bl, 145ar, 195a
Ann Hughes-Gilbey 72br, 79b, 112bl, 178, 180
Ghirardelli 218b
Giulia Hetherington 193br
The Image Bank 24b, 34br, 169b, 188
Image Select 29br, 207a
International Stock Exchange Photo Library 71br, Jon Arnold 32l
Julian Cotton Photo Library 18bl, 48l, 64b, 65ar, 75a, 86, 122br, 160, 174, 217
Medimage 17ar
Northwind 49a, 118bl, 129b, 131br, 134b, 148al, 161
The Robert Opie Collection 23bl, 40bl, 103a, 108al, 116bl, 128l, 194, 210
Panos Pictures 32al, 44bl, 121, 143br
Pictor International 30b, 38ar, 50a, 58a, 70b, 134a, 140b, 141b
Tony Stone Images 46ar, 69, 71, 72bl, 81, 87r, 100bl, 107b, 111bl, 132b, 150a, 150b, 154b, 206r
Travel Ink Photo Library 152b, 155, 157, 168a, 187, 195b, 202b
Tropix 173 (J. Schmid)
Visual Arts Library 78ar, 117ar, 136ar, 167b, 175a, 192, 211a
Peter Wilson 64ar, 73b, 76bl, 83, 98, 99b

All other photographs are the copyright of Quarto Publishing.

We would also like to thank the following who kindly lent us items for photography:

Divertimenti
139 Fulham Road
London SW3

David Mellor
4 Sloane Square
London SW1W

Pages
121 Shaftesbury Avenue
London WC2H